My Shadow Is My Skin

My Shadow Is My Skin

VOICES FROM THE IRANIAN DIASPORA

Edited by Katherine Whitney and Leila Emery

University of Texas Press ⏀ Austin

"The Name on My Coffee Cup," by Saïd Sayrafiezadeh, was originally published in the *New Yorker*'s Culture Desk blog on March 20, 2015.

Requests for permission to reproduce material from this work should be sent to:
     Permissions
     University of Texas Press
     P.O. Box 7819
     Austin, TX 78713-7819
     utpress.utexas.edu/rp-form

♾ The paper used in this book meets the minimum requirements of ANSI/NISO Z39.48-1992 (R1997) (Permanence of Paper).

Library of Congress Cataloging-in-Publication Data

Names: Whitney, Katherine, editor. | Emery, Leila, editor.
Title: My shadow is my skin : voices from the Iranian diaspora / edited by
     Katherine Whitney and Leila Emery.
Description: First edition. | Austin : University of Texas Press, 2020.
Identifiers: LCCN 2019026476
     ISBN 978-1-4773-2027-3 (cloth)
     ISBN 978-1-4773-2035-8 (library ebook)
     ISBN 978-1-4773-2036-5 (nonlibrary ebook)
Subjects: LCSH: Iranians—United States. | Iranian Americans—Ethnic identity. |
     Iranian Americans—Social conditions. | Iranian diaspora.
Classification: LCC E184.I5 M9 2020 | DDC 305.891/55073—dc23
LC record available at https://lccn.loc.gov/2019026476

doi:10.7560/320273

To my father, who inspired my love of literature,
and to my husband, the inspiration for this book.
—K.W.

For my parents, who always believed I could,
and for J, my moon and stars.
—L.E.

Contents

Foreword

What we hold dear is often the most difficult to reveal. Storytelling of the most intimate and personal nature is often what we most need to truly see ourselves, feel our vulnerability, and understand our own fragile humanity as well as our connection to others. Iranians and their descendants in the United States, as first- and second-generation Iranian-Americans, have had to contend with many impediments to sharing their personal stories. Iranians come from a culture filled with silences. Not only has the revelation of the self not historically been encouraged in Iranian letters, it has, in fact, been frowned upon. Until recently, when men dominated Iran's literary scene, women's voices and experiences were rather limited. As women have migrated out of Iran and reinvented themselves and refashioned the literary landscapes of their adopted nations, they have become more free to tell and write their stories; their voices are most certainly more audible. But omissions and indirectness by Iranian writers have also had a great deal to do with the long traditions of censorship and self-censorship that have dogged these writers for more than a century. Iranians come from a history of mistrust of those in power, and writers and intellectuals, who were often the ones to voice criticism, were subjected to a powerful state censorial apparatus that has also generated effective forms of self-censorship.

Silence is frequently a by-product of carrying the burdens and traumas of the past and of a nation's history. But for writers in the Iranian diaspora, many of the challenges of speaking freely, telling their stories, and revealing themselves have shifted and lifted. These writers have begun to loosen their tongues, expressing what is natural to them in the context of their new identities, in new languages and locations. They are rewriting themselves as individuals and artists who are governed by very different aesthetics and cultural experiences. Many of these writers are far less fearful about confronting cultural and familial taboos, and, as a result, they feel free to tell stories that have been hidden or hushed by secrecy, shame, and trauma. Many of these writers don't see themselves as exclusively Iranian or American but more so as living and writing in the "in-between," a liminal space that one could argue has not left Iranians since they arrived here, and one that overshadows even those born in the United States. As a result, narratives by writers of the Iranian diaspora articulate so much more than one culture and one history. They are composites—versions of Iranian diaspora experience reflected in the dramatic stories that have shaped twentieth- and twenty-first-century Iran. They are stories that speak to immigration, hyphenation, displacement, alienation, and longing, and to revisiting and revising lives made and informed by history and its ruptures.

My Shadow Is My Skin reflects the idea that without our stories, we are nothing. For Iranians of any generation, stories, myths, and poems—and the ways that their language reveals and conceals—are everything. And for Iranians in the diaspora, holding on to the tangible threads that connect us to a past, a country, and a culture that is both a trace and a marker of that history is an urgent endeavor. By challenging in our writing some of what we can now afford to question—the myths and presumptions we have about being American or about our Iranianness—we also share and tell stories that reinvigorate our connection to heritage and experience. *My Shadow Is My Skin* is a welcome addition to the many beautiful and poignant novels, memoirs, and poetry collections that have been published over the past two decades by a flourishing literary community that has much to tell and a great need to share with others. We have among us in the Iranian diaspora many accomplished novelists, memoirists, poets, and playwrights, but we still need the stories that live inside us, the ones that traveled with and through the acts of migration and movement to new locations and into new languages and storytelling modes. These are stories that are passed on by the deliberate telling of one generation to the next, as well as discovered and illuminated through the omissions and silences; they document and preserve personal losses, triumphs, and pain, and they also, sometimes humorously, get at the core of something we are still trying to identify both collectively and personally. *Are we Iranian? Are we American? Are we both?*

Stories often provide the most effective answer for difficult questions—not in a singular narrative, but in the collective and dissonant orchestral noise that we should not ignore or silence. There is not just one story, nor one kind of story. There are, indeed, many. These nonfiction stories offer another dimension of that multitude of stories that we crave and that are needed to counter the flat and tired images that have circulated in the media about Iran and Iranians for the past four decades.

It has been a great pleasure and an honor to watch and, in small measure, to assist these editors in their quest to build upon the growing corpus of Iranian-diaspora literature in the United States. Twenty years ago, I took on the role of coeditor of the very first collection of diasporic writing, *A World Between: Poems, Short Stories, and Essays by Iranian-Americans*, with both excitement and trepidation. I have marveled at the many wonderful writers who have emerged since; they continue to introduce and portray powerful characters and images of Iran and its diasporic culture in a multitude of genres and voices that now shape and influence American literature. This collection is just as important. Katherine and Leila have taken on the role of introducing yet more new voices as well as reintroducing some already-known writers in *My Shadow Is My Skin*. Every anthology editor sets out on a journey to offer something more, something new, and something essential, and they do so with a fundamental sense of urgency and love.

It is important that *My Shadow Is My Skin* is being published at a time when Iranian Americans are *yet again* living in the shadow of a renewed vilification of Iran. Americans need human stories to counter the escalating rhetoric and hostility that have dominated in Washington, DC, and that threaten to separate families and choke the Iranian people through such overtly hostile acts as the Muslim ban, the reimposition of sanctions, and the abandonment of the Iran nuclear deal. We need these writers to represent themselves and their own stories and the stories of their families, whose lives have been marked by forty years of turbulent history. We need so much more than the drumbeat of war, we need more than the rhetoric of powerful men bent on drowning out stories of real people's beauty, conviction, suffering, and loss, and we need to tell so much more than a national or nationalistic narrative. We need these stories and these authors more than ever. We need them like we need oxygen.

Persis Karim
Berkeley, 2019

Introduction

In the four decades since the Iranian Revolution in 1979, Iranian-Americans have made sense of their lives and reconciled their sense of belonging and not belonging through writing, first though poetry and memoir in the immediacy of migration and exile, and later in a developing and rich explosion of fiction. In the past decade, we have seen a blossoming of nonfiction writing that reflects complex voices and modern sensibilities and that reveals a broader range of stories and remembrances than ever before.

Literature traveled with those who left Iran after the revolution, in their suitcases, in their memories, and in the lifeblood that they passed on to their American-born children. So it is no surprise that Iranians in the diaspora have consistently gravitated toward the arts—and toward writing in particular—as a way to grapple with their experiences of immigration and alienation. Those who left—and in some cases fled—Iran have existed in the shadow of political and historical events that have loomed large over the past forty years. They hold inside them memories of growing up and living in Iran, traumatic recollections of war and political upheaval, and experiences of confronting discrimination and alienation in a new land. Those born in the United States also carry some of those traumas and memories as they carve out their own distinctive Iranian identities. But alongside these challenges, Iranian-Americans also carry stories of starting successful lives in a new country, learning different ways to express their Iranian-ness, and developing meaningful new connections to their heritage. The literary expressions that have emerged from these experiences are both unexpected and nuanced.

This collection before you, *My Shadow Is My Skin*, was prompted by our meeting in the spring of 2015 at a writing workshop titled

"Exploring Iranian Identity" in Berkeley, California. The workshop, directed by the novelist Anita Amirrezvani and the poet Persis Karim, offered participants—all of whom had some connection to Iran—an opportunity to work on intimate, identity-focused material. The participants wrote powerful narratives that they had not shared or even explored previously: stories about religion, sexuality, family secrets, war, racism, and episodes of deep pain and oppression by society and even by their own families. As participants ourselves, we were struck by the poignancy and immediacy of the narratives shared by our fellow writers. Our own workshop experiences compelled us to believe that even more personal and familial stories lay hidden, unexplored and in need of excavation. In that spirit, we embarked on a journey to bring together these types of nonfiction narratives.

Although the two of us—Leila, the daughter of an Iranian mother and an American father, and Katherine, the wife of an Iranian immigrant and mother of two half-Iranian children—might not seem like obvious candidates to edit a collection of writing from the Iranian diaspora, we came to realize that we were in fact ideal representatives of the diaspora's most recent iterations and thus well equipped for this endeavor. We represent facets of the larger, modern Iranian diaspora, beyond the first wave of immigration to the United States. We are both part of the diaspora and outsiders within it. Each of us experiences the Iranian diaspora and its accompanying "practices" in different ways and in ways that are distinct from those of our parents, our significant others, and our extended families.

Over the last four decades, assimilation, intermarriage, and new waves of migration have diversified the Iranian diaspora in the United States. Diaspora communities now include not just adults who immigrated from Iran after the 1979 revolution but also Iranians who immigrated as children and grew up in the United States, as well as younger generations born here. These diverse experiences have prompted more heterogeneous perspectives on what it means to be Iranian or Iranian-American—and even what constitutes an "Iranian diaspora"—in the twenty-first century. The narratives in this collection, and indeed many of the authors themselves, feel both Iranian *and* American. Others feel not quite either. As contributor Roger Sedarat describes it, "The hyphen between East and West has led me toward some illusive unity, even while keeping me separated, as a kind of minus sign."

This collection takes its name from a phrase in contributor Cyrus Copeland's essay "Shadow Nation." *My Shadow Is My Skin* reflects the notion that many of the authors in this anthology find themselves living in the shadow of their past histories or under the shadow of their families' expectations. Some of the authors describe living in the shadows, not wanting to reveal their Iranian heritage, or coming out of the shadows to live a more authentic life. For others, this shadow is fully integrated into who they are—it is part of their physical body. They wear the shadow of Iranianness like a skin. Many of these authors also write about the color of their skin being what keeps them in the shadows, their otherness excluding them from being fully accepted by other Americans and sometimes even by fellow Iranians. As Neda Maghbouleh writes in her essential work *The Limits of Whiteness: Iranian Americans and the Everyday Politics of Race*, "Iranians have been pitched across a white/non-white American color line for over a century." Indeed, particularly for the younger, American-born writers in this collection, their identities have been shaped—and continue to be shaped—by the complex social entanglements of racialization in the United States.

These nuanced personal stories are acts of witnessing, typically overlooked or obscured by the steady stream of negative headlines about Iranians and Iran. Particularly at this time in history, we need people to emerge from the shadows and reveal their truth. Thus, in curating this literary collection, we aim to move the canon of Iranian-diaspora writing to another level, beyond the kinds of antagonistic, superficial portrayals perpetuated by the news media, to feature real people, real stories, and real experiences of Iranians and the greater Iranian diaspora in the twenty-first century.

Previous anthologies—such as *Tremors: New Fiction by Iranian American Writers*; *Let Me Tell You Where I've Been: New Writing by Women of the Iranian Diaspora*; *A World Between: Poems, Short*

Stories, and Essays by Iranian-Americans; *My Sister, Guard Your Veil;
My Brother, Guard Your Eyes*; and *Love and Pomegranates: Artists and
Wayfarers on Iran*—gave attention to the growing corpus of the Iranian literary diaspora. In *My Shadow Is My Skin*, we turn to the tradition of nonfiction to claim and craft personal narratives that haven't
yet been shared. This collection also embraces contemporary voices
that are bravely expressing themselves in new ways. To that end, we
have sought to elevate feminist and queer voices and to include writers whose experiences reflect intersectional perspectives.

As we assembled and edited *My Shadow Is My Skin*, we were
aware of the looming fortieth anniversary of the Iranian Revolution
and the significance it holds for so many in the Iranian diaspora.
However, we wanted the writing in this collection to move beyond
that singular historical event and its immediate fallout to show how
the diaspora has evolved, modernized, and operated in a variety of
contexts and moments. Today, Iranians in the diaspora are living
under the shadow of President Donald Trump's Muslim ban, height-
ened bellicosity toward Iran, increased sanctions, and the looming
prospect of military conflict between Iran and the United States.
This atmosphere amplifies the need for Iranian-Americans to share
more nuanced, three-dimensional perspectives on their heritage. *My
Shadow Is My Skin* is emerging at an essential moment for Iranian
Americans, giving them agency in representing themselves in all their
complexity.

This collection brings together thirty-two authors, both established and emerging, whose writing captures diverse perspectives and
complex attitudes toward Iran and America. The authors include
recent immigrants alongside those who came to the United States
immediately after 1979. Their narratives span the period from the
1979 revolution to the current era of Trump. Roughly half of the
authors were born in Iran and emigrated to the United States. The
other half were born here to Iranian or Iranian and American parents,
or married into Iranian families. A third of the contributors are bicul-
tural, having one Iranian parent and one parent from another culture.

We intentionally combine original essays with works that have been published previously to present a broad and inclusive view of the diaspora in the twenty-first century. Some authors speak from the perspective of later adulthood, looking back on events in their earlier lives, sharing stories of immigration or describing the challenges of making a new life in America. Others are younger writers with distinctly modern points of view who are contending with their more politicized identities. These personal narratives of immigration, sexuality, marginalization, marriage, religion, and identity offer an antidote to the recurring—and once again more vehement—stereotypes and reductive representations of Iran and the people who have a connection to it. In a time of "fake news" and vitriol aimed at both immigrants and the Middle East, *My Shadow Is My Skin* pulls back the curtain on a community that rarely gets to tell its own stories or write its own history.

While we have organized the essays in this collection into thematic categories, the narratives themselves defy simple categorization. They are wide ranging in their scope and touch on multiple themes that reflect the challenges of finding a comfortable identity within the greater Iranian diaspora.

The first section of the book, "Light/Shadow," explores secrets kept and told, stories of shame turned to pride, and accounts of people emerging from the shadows to claim their true identities. Cyrus Copeland describes his Iranian identity as a shadow that he's proud of: "For the past forty years I have taken my shadow—my Iranian heritage—and inverted it. My shadow is my skin. I advertise it." Jasmin Darznik exposes her Iranian mother's inability to tolerate her daughter's desire to be more like the American girls she grew up with in Northern California. "There are things you shouldn't say," she recalls her mother telling her, "not even to yourself."

The second section, "Coding/Decoding," focuses on attempts to navigate the complicated fault lines between being both Iranian and American and feeling a lack of belonging to either culture. The authors in this section negotiate the communication and miscommunication that are part and parcel of living a hyphenated life. Raha Namy translates the languages of love and sex across the cultural divide, where English is preferable in bed because the Persian equivalent is "vulgar, unacceptable, unladylike." In recalling an elementary school presentation on Iran from which her classmates and their parents were conspicuously missing, Amy Malek describes the ways in which Iranians "are always negotiating [their] belonging in multicultural America" whether they realize it or not. Roxanne Varzi, born in Iran to an American mother and an Iranian father, questions whether she is in fact an immigrant and wonders how to explain President Trump's Muslim ban to her eight-year-old son.

The final section, "Memory/Longing," examines what is missing in a bifurcated life. Farnaz Fatemi, having returned to Iran as an adult, writes lyrically of an Iran both familiar and unfamiliar, a country she urges Americans to see—one that, she admits, "owns" her. Darius Atefat-Peckham discovers more about his Iranian heritage—and the mother he lost when he was a young child—through learning Farsi as a teenager. In "The Iranians of Mercer Island," Siamak Vossoughi writes about a group of Iranians living in the United States whose nightly singing evokes a melancholy that is ever present in the psyches of an older generation of immigrants and a longing for a country that in some ways no longer exists—a country that is both known and unknowable to him as a young boy.

In bringing these diverse stories together, we ask where have we of the Iranian diaspora been, where are we now, and where are we headed? We hope to broaden the discussion around these questions at a time when such conversations are critically needed. We hope that the readers of *My Shadow Is My Skin* discover, in this tapestry of stories, the intricate ways in which the Iranian diaspora has evolved over time and, indeed, continues to evolve. And we hope that through these deeply personal narratives, readers of all backgrounds may see pieces of themselves reflected back at them.

My Shadow Is My Skin

LIGHT/SHADOW

The Summer I Disappeared

Jasmin Darznik

The year I turned eighteen and lost my virginity, my mother made me disappear.

It started when she shook me awake early one morning and told me to pack up some clothes. I didn't know where we were going, or why we were going anywhere at all. It was August and I should have been starting college at UC Berkeley soon, but instead, I was suddenly driving south toward Los Angeles with my mother. This was 1991. *Worthless, shameful, disgusting*—the words she'd been screaming at me had bled into one another, a constant litany—but that day she was quiet, her eyes fixed on the road ahead.

The morning was still thick with fog when we set out from Northern California. An hour into the drive, it was blazing hot, the hills had gone from green to yellow, and she still hadn't said a word. The air conditioner in the car was broken, so we drove with all the windows rolled down, which only filled the car with gusts of heat and dirt from the highway. My mother was a terrible driver even under normal circumstances, but that day, she kept swerving and once she sent us careening onto the shoulder and toward a lettuce field, only to yank the wheel back at the last minute. At one point, it occurred to me that she was going to kill me, and maybe herself too.

I only felt myself breathe when we stopped for gas. I took my time in the store, staring at the rows of chips and candy, picking up one package only to put it down and pick up another. I didn't really want to buy anything, but being in public made me feel safe. Back in the car she peeled open a package of donuts. She was wearing raspberry-red lipstick, and I watched the lipstick stain the donut each time she took a bite. Her hair was scraped back off her face and her roots were showing. As a young woman she'd often been compared to Elizabeth Taylor. She was forty when we came to America, fleeing the revolution in Iran, and now she was fifty-three. Until recently, she'd been managing a motel she and my father owned and cleaning rooms, working fifteen-hour shifts. "America made me old and ugly," she always said. It also made me what she told me I had become: *kesafat*. Dirty, disgusting.

In all the years that came before, when I was nine and then thirteen and then sixteen, my mother had told me that if I lost my virginity, my life would be over. I never heard her say anything more true. I turned my face toward the window, where California rushed by along the freeway, where everything I knew was flickering past me, where I recognized nothing and I was nothing.

I was five years old when my family came to America. Mine was one of the few Iranian Muslim families in Marin County, California, and also one of the few immigrant families in Tiburon, the small town where we settled. My parents owned a twenty-room motel off Highway 101, where they took turns sitting at the manager's desk. We lived in an exquisitely decorated home that we couldn't really afford and that we would eventually lose. My mother drove a secondhand silver Mercedes, though she told everyone we'd bought it new. My father, an alcoholic, was gone for months at a time; this was another of our secrets. He'd been an engineer in Iran, and immigration hit him hard, knocking him into drinking and depression. It was my mother, really, who raised me.

She was devout, but she didn't wear a veil. What was most Iranian and Islamic about us was how she raised me. I wasn't allowed to go to parties or to have a boyfriend. I couldn't shave my legs or pluck my eyebrows; like sex, these were things you only did when you got married. My best friend growing up was American, a Catholic girl with parents nearly as strict as my own, but the year I turned twelve I was suddenly forbidden from sleeping over at her house anymore. My mother never exactly said why, but I knew it had to do with the fact that my friend had an older brother. "Men only want one thing," she told me, and that, apparently, included my friend's fourteen-year-old brother. At school, I spent a lot of time reading in the library or down by the creek behind the building. At home, I sat cross-legged on my bed and spent hours writing in my journal. I never locked the door because I wasn't allowed to. "Daughters shouldn't keep secrets from their mothers," my mother always said, but I did, or tried to. I wrote about everything in my journal—how much I hated her, where I'd go if I ever figured out a way to leave home, all the things I could never tell anyone.

I wasn't allowed to have a job, but my mother encouraged me to take classes at the local community college on top of my regular high school classes. That's where, in the spring of my senior year, I met my first boyfriend. I saw him infrequently and only in secret, so he wasn't really my boyfriend, but that's what I called him in my journal. He offered the kindness and attentiveness I craved. He didn't push me to have sex; I decided it. I thought I would be transformed by sex, or at least be more like American girls. Mostly, though, I wanted to rid myself of my virginity, and that's what I eventually did: I just got rid of it.

A few weeks afterward, I came home from school and found my journal splayed open on my bed. She'd hit me before, but not like she did that day. She locked the door behind her and her face was strangely calm. Her silence always frightened me more than her screams. She walked toward me until she was so close I felt her breath on my cheek. "*Kesafat*," she finally said. "You're *kesafat*." Dirty, disgusting. "Do you understand?" I did. She slapped me so hard it stung. I drew up my hands, but even though I stood a foot taller, she was far stronger. I slipped away in my head. It made her furious. She hit me again and again, and eventually the trance broke. By the time she stopped, her face was flushed from exertion.

"There are things you shouldn't say," she said, "not even to yourself."

In Persian the word for "virgin," *dokhtar*, is the same word for "girl" and also for "daughter." To lose your virginity is to lose your girlhood and also your place in your family. I wasn't my mother's daughter anymore, but this only made her tighten her grip on me. By then, we'd lost our house and sold the motel. For the first time in years, my mother was home all the time, except that home was now a small apartment at the edge of town. I was now forbidden from seeing my friends. I was forbidden from driving. I was forbidden from using the phone. It was lonely and terrifying to be cut off from everything and everyone in my life. My mother called my school and said I was sick. I wasn't allowed to leave my room. Then, just as suddenly, I went back to school, except that now, my mother drove me there and back each day. In June, I graduated from high school. I stayed home, and I read and read and read. I thought I'd be starting college soon. Berkeley was just across the bay and I'd have to live at home, but everything in me was poised to begin that life, to be just another college girl. Then one morning in August, my mother drove me away.

What I couldn't know back then was that once, my mother herself was made to disappear. Before she was formally promised to her first husband, she was taken to a room in a part of Tehran she had never been to before, and when she got there she was told to undress and lie on a table. She was twelve years old. No one had told her what to expect, and so when a woman entered the room and spread her legs open she began to cry. A hand clamped over her mouth. She was sure she was about to die. The exam took just a few minutes, and when it was over her mother—my grandmother—was told that she'd passed, that she was a virgin and therefore could be married.

On her wedding night, her husband of five hours shoved her onto the ground and raped her. Even when she became pregnant, he didn't stop raping and beating her. She thought, many times, of killing herself, and once she nearly did.

Not every Iranian woman's story went like this back then, but my mother's did. What was truly unusual about her story, however, was that she got out. Her father interceded on her behalf, and she was able to divorce her first husband. But there was a catch: she had to give up her child and she had to pretend she'd never been married. To many, a divorcée wasn't much better than a prostitute; having lost her virginity, she'd lost her value. The whole family was sworn to secrecy about her marriage and divorce. Her father moved her to a new school, clear across town, and enrolled her under a made-up name. She tossed away her single, cherished tube of lipstick, and she began wearing her hair in pigtails again. The plan worked in that many years later, she did what few divorcées did: she remarried, this time as a woman in her twenties and to a foreigner.

Eventually, she became a midwife, one of the few professions open to women of her generation. Mostly this involved delivering babies, but it also involved conducting virginity tests, hundreds of them. One day she would tell me that she always felt sorry for the girls who'd lost their virginity before marriage. They could lose everything if they were found out, she'd say, and they very often did. They could be disowned, beaten, even killed. These were the days before "embroidery," surgical reconstruction of the hymen that restored a girl's virginity, or at least the virginity of girls with both means and sympathetic families. My mother told me that if she thought a girl was in trouble with her parents, she'd just sign the certificate anyway. "But what happened to her when she didn't bleed on her wedding night?" I asked her, and she had no answer, or none that she could give.

My mother drove me south until the sunset cracked red over the horizon, and then she stopped. The motel where we stayed was in a small town outside Los Angeles called Calabasas, and it looked just like any one of the hundred roadside motels we had passed that day. Our room, which faced the highway, had a king-sized bed and an eerie, antiseptic feel.

The first night in that room I waited until my mother fell asleep, then I hugged my knees and cried. The air conditioner hummed all night, drowned out only by the roar of cars and trucks outside. I cried quietly because I didn't want to wake her. I didn't want her to know how frightened I was, and how broken.

We stayed in the motel for twenty-six days. My memories of that time would always stay fragmented and blurry, but I clearly remember standing by the window and watching my mother smoke and pace the parking lot. Within a few days, she stopped screaming and hitting me. Instead, she cried. If we went back home, she was sure I'd eventually contrive some way of seeing my boyfriend, and that other Iranians would find out. In our small community, a family's honor was bound up with its daughters' virtue, and years of living in America had, if anything, only hardened those binds. The prospect of exposure was so awful it kept us in Calabasas, day after day. Some nights we sat in silence through one sitcom after another and then we fell asleep, backs to each other. Faint as my memories are, my body has always remembered those nights, their deadness.

"I won't let you throw your life away with this man," she told me one night as we lay in the dark. "I won't let you shame us like this."

We never went back home. I applied to UCLA, praying I'd get in and that my mother would let me go. A male cousin was already at school there, and when I was accepted for the winter term, he was charged with keeping an eye on me. This meant that I could only go out at night if he'd be there too. Otherwise I had to be home by sunset, no exceptions.

By then, my mother had arranged for all our things to be packed and shipped to Southern California. She rented a house for us a few miles from campus. For a while we lived off the money from the sale of the motel, though eventually, my mother started a small business selling secondhand clothes. My father, now sixty-five and sober, slumped into retirement. My mother cut off all contact with her old friends and ordered me to do the same. She kept a distance from other Iranians in LA, and her one friend was a German woman she saw only occasionally. I never heard her tell anyone the reason why we'd moved to Los Angeles, but if she did, I imagine she said it was because that's where I'd been accepted to college. Relatives got the same story. If they ever suspected something else, they never said anything—silences like these are frequent and unremarkable in my family.

Nearly all the other Iranian girls at college also lived at home. I suspected they had their own secrets, but like me, they seemed skilled at hiding them, especially from one another. We were good students, studying to be lawyers, dentists, engineers, and doctors, but most of all, we were good girls, or seemed to be. My mother never told me not to tell anyone what happened—why I didn't go to Berkeley, why we suddenly moved to Los Angeles the summer I graduated from high school. She didn't have to. For the next several years, until I won a fellowship to graduate school and moved clear across the country, I pretended to be the daughter my mother wanted me to be, the good daughter, the star student, the virgin. I played the part well because it was the part I was raised to play and because I knew now what it would cost not to play it.

The thing that saved me was the thing that got me in trouble in the first place: words. Before I graduated from college, I took a literature class, where I read Maxine Hong Kingston's *Woman Warrior*. When I came to the line about not knowing what part of a parent's immigrant past is craziness and what part is culture, I felt my whole body tense with recognition, then gratitude.

Eventually, I wrote my own book about my mother. I pushed her again and again, insisting that the only story worth telling was the whole story, but I was unable to bring the same honesty to bear on the stories I told about myself. I included only the barest outline of what happened when I lost my virginity. The twenty-six days in Calabasas didn't show up at all, not in that book or in anything I wrote afterward. For years I worried that to tell this story would be to have Americans say, "Of course that happened. That's how those people are." So few Muslim women's voices are heard, and I told myself that to write about abuse in Iran and in the past was one thing, but to write about it here and now, when Muslims in America are too often pitied or demonized, was another. But I wonder how much of my silence is American, not Iranian, in its origins. My shame about sexuality springs from my Iranian background, but it merges so thoroughly with American silences about abuse that in the end, it's hard to tell where one ends and the other begins.

I tell myself now, as I could not have told myself then, that my mother did her best. She raised me with an iron will and her own hard-won sense of what it took to survive as a woman in this world.

I've forgiven her, though even now, twenty-five years later, anger will sometimes flare up in me, and I'll have to tell myself that she did what she did out of love and fear and because she'd left her country, but she hadn't left her past and she never would.

In my story, as in her story, there is no before and after, no clear beginning or resolution. Part of me will always be the eighteen-year-old girl who was taken away from all she knew, just as part of my mother will always be the twelve-year-old girl who was taken away from what she knew. But there's also this: I don't want to be silent anymore. I don't want to pretend that what happened didn't hurt me. I don't want to keep secrets anymore, especially not from myself. I look back at that eighteen-year-old girl who spent twenty-six days in a motel in Calabasas, and I know it can take a long time to tell a story, if you ever tell it at all. But I tell what happened to me because, after all these years, I finally want to say that it is mine to tell.

Sacrifices

Iraj Isaac Rahmim

Shortly after my new girlfriend, Debbie, took me to meet her parents, I sat locked in their apartment with her stepfather, Jack, holding a knife to my neck. We were in the living room, Jack with his leather-handled army knife and I, staring at each other and listening to my girlfriend and her mother, now locked out, fist-banging on the door. They sounded scared: "Jack, please don't hurt him."

Debbie and I had met only a month earlier. She had answered my ad for a roommate, "open-minded M or F," moved in within a week, and we fought and then had sex the very first night. She never moved to her own bedroom.

She was average looking in most respects, with straight blonde hair down to the shoulder blades and a bit of a baby face, with red apple cheeks, very light blue eyes, and an easy and generous smile. She was neither too thin nor fat, neither tall nor short. Now, many years later, I for the most part picture her sunk comfortably into an old overstuffed sofa, smoking and drinking a glass of red wine just poured from a screw-cap jug, and looking at her raised bare feet. "I have perfect feet," she would say. That was important to her. She was twenty-nine; I was eighteen.

I had come from Iran to the United States two years earlier, first to Oklahoma, which I had not liked, and then, a few weeks later, to San Diego. The "open-minded" in my ad, at least to me, meant don't hate me because of where I am from. She wondered out loud what I was looking for, and I set her mind at ease. This was 1980. It was the time of first-prize pigs in county fairs named Ayatollah, of "Camel Jockey Go Home" slogans, and of "No Dogs or Iranians Allowed" signs in restaurants. This was also the year that President Jimmy Carter, in part to prop up his flaccid presidency during the hostage crisis, ordered all Iranians to be "registered," which included fingerprinting and prison-style photographs, and so somewhere there is a file with a photograph of me staring blankly into the camera, holding a board bearing my last and first names and an INS registration number. That number became my naturalization number when, over a decade later, I took US citizenship.

Early during my stay in San Diego, I was often mistaken for a Mexican. An Iranian friend, the only other in a high school of 1,600, mentioned that they hate Iranians here.

"We'll just tell them we're Mexican, then," I replied enthusiastically.

"They hate them even more," he said.

Years later I heard that a relative was claiming to be from Switzerland. That would be safe, for sure, but for the accent and the looks.

Around the same time, postrevolutionary chaos in Iran cut off funds to students abroad, and so young men and women from good homes, beloved and protected by doting parents, often overpampered, were left stranded. We went out and got jobs, and moved to smaller apartments in poorer neighborhoods, and found roommates. We learned that the only work available to smart and only partly educated doctors and lawyers and engineers is fairly menial: attending gas stations and newspaper stands, delivering pizza, selling ice cream, and, if you were lucky, grading homework at college. I did most of these, with mixed results. The hourly minimum wage was $2.95 then, and that, minus taxes, was what you got. Although delivering pizza had tips, the income was offset by the need to have your own car and insurance and pay for gas. Selling ice cream was particularly disastrous for me as my assigned route consisted primarily of housing projects for the Vietnamese boat people, who were poorer than most poor. They would send their sweet-faced and smiling three- or four-year-olds, running happily, smacking their lips, almost tasting the ice cream they would choose, holding out only a penny or at most a nickel. That was all they could afford. Sometimes I gave them the ice cream; sometimes I did not.

Some students managed by turning this into a game. I remember a competition to see who had the lowest monthly food bill. Thirty dollars was the answer, the winners being two women who every day cooked a variety of subtle stews and elegant rice dishes, filling their house with aromas of bright spices and wonderfully fresh basil and tarragon and parsley.

Some did not manage. A friend returned home when his money ran out, was dispatched to the front—the war with Iraq had started—sent me one or two passionate patriotic letters, and then no more. Another dealt drugs and disappeared. To our inquiries, his family replied that he had moved to another state to study aerospace engineering.

Many plowed ahead, navigating through this unanticipated and unwelcome phase of insecurity in limbo. We knew that it was all temporary, which made this, like most student poverty, different from real poverty. The student is passing through a stage, whether or not planned, while the real poor are held by the poverty, almost owned by it, having no faith that it will pass, imagining no plans to work through it. The real poor often give in to despair and passively accept their status. In a sense, being poor as a student is not being poor at all; it is simply getting an education.

Back home in Tehran, my mother sacrificed animals and fed the poor. I did not know much about poverty as a child. I knew that there were poor people; I had seen many. I knew that they were less fortunate than we were and that we should help them.

Many times, after an illness or some danger or even a long trip, the rabbi and his assistant arrived at our house, a sheep in tow with a rope around its neck as leash. They prayed and sharpened a large knife, they held the sheep and gave it water to drink, and then they quickly ran the knife across its throat. Blood spouted. The sheep screamed and fell, and convulsed and kicked air, and blood circled the drain in the yard. They rubbed the bloody knife across my forehead, or my sister's, and read from the Torah.

A few years ago, when my uncle died, being by his side, I held his still warm hand until cold, and then his forehead until it too was yellow and void of blood, and then his shoulders and chest, chased by the wave of death from extremities inward, covering his body with a sheet only after the warmth and color of life had fully retreated.

The sheep, in contrast, were skinned warm. Their blood applied to my forehead, even with the steely knife, felt a comfortable temperature. They were then cut into portions, some for the rabbi and his assistant as payment for services, some for us and our friends and relatives, and the rest in small plastic bags for the poor.

All parts of the sheep were used. The bones, with some meat and fat attached and marrow inside, were good for soups and stews. The head and hooves were delicacies for breakfast. The skin for leather. We would go and distribute them in the *mahalleh*, the Jewish ghetto by the old well. I remember some bags with only tail fat in them. My mother said, "The poor love fat." This sounded miserly and mean-spirited to my ears but was a matter-of-fact statement with neither malice nor condescension, and I imagine that she instinctively knew what took me years to understand: that for those who do not have, all nourishment—even fat—is blessing, that perhaps there is the grace of nature in loving fat.

In danger, my mother called out to the prophets instinctively, "*Ya Abram Isagh o Yaaghoob*," and vowed "a sheep." I have, to shock my American friends, joked about the terror and guilt we lived under, knowing that any accident or illness, say, a broken leg due to a misstep, or even a cold, could result in the death of an innocent animal. In fact, my sister and I were very much pained and horrified by the spectacle. Once, my sister disappeared on the same day that our car had been stolen, and my mother vowed, one at a time, two sacrifices. My sister was found; she had fallen asleep behind a bed. The car was not. One sheep only.

In Tehran, beggars knocked on our door daily. They were an army of the broken. Men and women and children, they were missing an eye or limbs, a leg, an arm, fingers. They wore the colorful, loose-fitting garb of the provinces, often mended and perhaps handed down. Sometimes the women had blue-green tattoos on their cheeks and foreheads. They spoke with thick, beautiful Kurdish or Turkish or Gilaki accents. Mostly, when the door opened, the words streamed, sing-songy and drawn out: "*Khanem jaan* please please help I am hungry I am thirsty I have no sleep I am a stranger I have no one My husband beats me My wife died and left me with these orphans Make me a sacrifice to your son For the sake of your boy May Allah save him for you A sacrifice for his head." Some did not talk; they stretched out a hand and stood bent, with their heads down, or just looked at you. My mother usually would give them some coins or call out to the maid: "Bring some food for this lady." If it was in the morning, you could hear the clack-clack of the garbage man pushing his cart down to the corner. "Bring the trash also," my mother would add.

An old, respected relative once said that the poor, the beggars who knock on our doors, are actually not poor at all. "They are rich. You always hear lots of coins jingling in their pockets."

I remember, the skeptical experimentalist that I was, running to my room, putting a jacket on, and filling its pocket with all the coins I could find. And then counting, and counting again, several times, to see how rich you could be if all you owned was coins in a pocket. Perhaps my relative's mind was hard at work, as mine was to be some years later, justifying our own good fortune.

Once, we took up a collection in my elementary school to bring orphans over for lunch on Mother's Day. "Five *tomans* for each orphan. We will all have *chelo* kebab for lunch." I brought ten *tomans* from home. Two orphans. I would be kind to them. We would sit and eat and talk, and perhaps even play in the yard on jungle gyms or kick soccer balls. I remember the disappointment when only a handful of orphans were brought in for the entire school. They came in a bus, and they sat apart from us, at a long table with the teachers and the principal, quiet and polite, eating slowly. We looked on with envy.

Another time, we went on a field trip to the southern portion of Tehran. Our principal, on the bus with us, looking at the crowded, dusty streets with potholes and mud and people wearing threadbare clothes and shoes, said, "This is where the real people live, my children." There was a very famous nightclub, right in the middle of all that scarcity, with glittering signs and fancy posters. My mother was not happy when I mentioned this. "Why do they put something like that in the south of town? People all dressed up every night with expensive cars. The poor will see them and want."

In San Diego in 1980, out of money, I went to college full time, got a job, moved to a cheaper neighborhood, and was frugal with expenses. It was time for a roommate, and there was Debbie. It turned out that she was looking for an open-minded roommate as well; her five-year-old son would move in with us shortly.

On the first night, we fought over towels. She did not like my towels, which I had brought from back home. "Too frilly," she said as she moved them aside unceremoniously and put hers up instead. The ensuing fight was loud and hurtful. To this day, when in a flight of fancy I envision a new relationship, the idea of a woman's unfamiliar towels next to mine disgusts me, more so than the thought of any other intimacy.

The fight moved to my bedroom, I do not recall how, with both of us lying on my very large bed and my hand on her arm, caressing it and contemplating asking her to move out. Instead, I moved over and kissed her, undid the belt on her bathrobe, and pulled it open. It was a short, brown towel robe with white edges going all around it. It was thin and a bit tattered, and the brown contrasted well with her very white thighs and belly. She had nice, small breasts. I pulled her panties off. The sex was hurried, and then we slept.

I am not sure why she slept with me. As for myself, I was far from home and alone, and I was eighteen.

The women I tried dating before meeting Debbie were all older as well. There was the twenty-eight-year-old Japanese pianist I met when we both took the TOEFL exam and made the mistake of taking to my high school football game. "This is a high school game," she said, barely audible over the screams of the bouncing cheerleaders. I never heard from her again. There was Linda, the twenty-five-year-old married waitress in a pizza place where I worked, who asked if

I could "keep a secret" before kissing me while we parked one night in front of a delivery. And then the college senior, Olga, blonde and with a beautiful reddish tan, who was smart enough to soon discover that I was just a lonely and insecure teenage boy.

Debbie and I lived together with her son for over a year, and we stayed friends for many years more, even as we both moved into and out of other relationships. Perhaps in me she saw potential, both emotional and economic. I do not know. It is possible that her standards in a lover were not particularly high either. She had never met her father, and J.D., her son, barely knew his. Though she was married before living with me, and would marry again, she had not married J.D.'s father. Perhaps she was determined to provide him with a father of some sort, and I would do.

She worked as a waitress at the local Bob's Big Boy diner. Over the years, she had many jobs. She sold cigarettes to gas stations and convenience stores. She was a shop clerk, a secretary, an attendant at an X-rated movie theater, and for a short while a long-haul truck driver. But she always came back to waitressing in local diners, as though these were home. (Her mother had been a waitress for most of Debbie's childhood years.) I remember feeling so sorry for her when she came back every day at the end of her shift, wearing a clownish brown country maiden uniform, her face flushed and shiny from the heat and sweaty and oily to the touch, her blonde hair pulled up, by then somewhat fuzzy and disheveled. She would take off her bulky and ugly white waitress shoes and be embarrassed about the smell. "My feet hurt so bad," she would complain. She did not have a car. Sometimes I gave her a ride. Sometimes she walked.

She had taken a few college courses in the past and always talked about going back for a degree. She would sit at the kitchen table and fret about which local junior college to attend once she got the money together. "Grossmont is really close and pretty. I have friends who go there," she would say, "but Mesa has both communication and accounting." Those were her interests. I do not remember what degree she wanted, or what job she would have. She did take some classes, but never got anywhere. She would start with enthusiasm, buying notebooks and books and pencils and new school clothes, and then drop out, talking of child care and tuition costs and work, or just being tired.

Her friends, by and large, disapproved of our relationship, some unhappy with our age difference, most with my nationality. The exception was Dennis, the gay Christian minister with a PhD in computer science, an outsider himself, who became my piano teacher for a while and introduced me to marijuana. On the other hand, there were all her other friends. One day we went to a couple's house. The husband was a retired army captain, and his wife I cannot remember too well; they were close friends of Debbie's. We stood for a few minutes in the living room near the door. They did not greet me, nor shake my hand, nor talk to or even look at me. On the way to the car, Debbie apologized.

"My friends think I'm a traitor for being with you."

"Then why did you bring me here?" I yelled.

That period left scars. Minor indignities, accumulated, still play tricks on my mind. Was that security car following us around the yacht club parking lot because of what I look like or because I was only driving an old Honda? Were the teenagers in the clothing store giggling, looking at me, because of where I am from? What was that secretive smile between my girlfriend and the salesperson about?

I remember one day many years later, standing by a seaside restaurant near Cape May in New Jersey, engrossed in the handwritten menu on a whiteboard, reading carefully, imagining the taste and texture of each item. It was late autumn, with cool, salt spray–like air and the very noisy sound of seagulls, which were flying all around. My then girlfriend, who had been standing about ten feet away, walked over and, with uncharacteristic warmth, put her hand through my arm and said, "Let's go." A distance away, by the wooden rails on the boardwalk, she asked if I had not heard the teenager screaming. I had not. She could hardly believe it. "He was taunting you, a few feet away, calling you 'Habib' again and again and laughing, and then he ran away, maybe to get some friends."

Another time, when I was a graduate student, I was walking

down the street in New York, sporting an unkempt beard and looking shabby, with torn jeans, an old black US Army jacket with metal chain clips instead of buttons, and a shrunken made-in-Pakistan T-shirt full of holes and spots. A young woman walked toward me, deep in thought. Suddenly she looked up, ten or fifteen feet away, made an exact ninety-degree move across the street, went past me, and then returned to her original path. I remember the innocent flash of fury at the moment, as though I would have been justified, right then and there, to turn and follow her, to walk fast behind her, to make her afraid, to attack her in a dark corner. In retrospect, I cannot be sure what she reacted to. I remember thinking later that I had glimpsed that day the life of a young black man.

We visited Debbie's mom, Emily, and her husband, Jack, about a month after Debbie moved in with me. There were blocks of cheap-looking beige stucco apartment complexes in their neighborhood, each building with parking spots in front with years of motor oil streaks, a couple of small palm trees by the narrow entrance, partially rusted grids on the first-floor windows, and a cracked eight-by-ten pool. They had names such as the Beverly Hills or the Oceanview, as if to hide the reality that this was right behind the red light district and certainly far from either the Pacific Ocean or Beverly Hills.

Their complex was on an inclined dead end, backing into a dusty, treeless hill strewn with pebbles and debris. The dark walkway and stairs leading to their small one-bedroom were narrow, and you had to be careful not to get scratched by the sharp edges of the communal mailbox or the bulletin board riddled with pins that held up for-sale-this-and-that flyers with cut-out phone numbers along the bottom, one on top of the other.

The apartment looked small, the furniture was worn and ugly, and there was a musty smell with a fog of smoke in the air. The shaggy yellow wall-to-wall carpet had dark traffic streaks from the living room to the bathroom, and there was yellow Formica and dark-brown wood veneer everywhere. It all reminded me of any other hundred-dollar-or-two apartment I had seen.

Emily looked old beyond her years, which even the baby face

reminding me of Debbie could not hide. She opened the door wearing a long, unsexy see-through night robe, holding a glass of wine in one hand and a cigarette on a five-inch stick in the other, like a bad imitation of a fifties actress. She laughed heartily and gave me a hug and a big kiss on the cheek. She stood a bit unstably. This was not her first glass of wine.

Jack was leaning comfortably in his pea-green stuffed chair. A filterless cigarette dangled on his lower lip, seemingly glued to it by his saliva. Empty cans of Milwaukee's Best sat on the end table beside him. He got up with a quick jerk, and he had stature. He was perhaps 6'3" or 6'4", with a gray ponytail and a sparse, unkempt red-and-gray beard that partially covered his sun-scarred face. He looked to be about fifty and had dark circles around his small, sunken eyes. He had no shirt on, and his white and hairless body was covered with tattoos of skulls and snakes and eyes. The tattoos on his hard belly, which nevertheless hung somewhat over his belt, looked stretched and a bit larger and lighter.

He was friendly, and we talked and drank, and Emily was lovely, motherly and flirtatious, doting and drunk, all at the same time. I do not know how the discussion turned to my background, and with my naïve answer, "Iran," Emily shifted in her chair. Jack leaned forward and frowned.

"So what are you doing in San Diego?"

"Well, I go to college. I'm studying to be an engineer."

Emily forced out a laugh. "Wow, you can make a lot of money with that, no? You gonna stay here and work?"

Jack was looking down. There was a tear in his easy chair with cotton and bits of colored thread and rubber pushing out. He got up suddenly, grabbed Debbie and Emily by the wrists, and, with their eyes wide, dragged them the few steps it took to get to the front door, shoved them out, and locked it. I do not think the meaning of Jack's actions penetrated my mind at that instant; I sat without reacting, and at any rate, there were rules of proper decorum to meeting people for the first time, especially "in-laws," from which I would not deviate. Jack turned slowly and came back, bent down with a groan by the end table, with it squeezing his naked belly, felt for a moment under it, and pulled out the knife. I had not seen it before. I also noticed a diagonal scar on his lower back, long and wide. He sat beside me and put the blade on my throat. The blade was curved, and it felt cold and smooth. The banging on the door was loud. Emily begged Jack for my safety.

"Do you know what happens when a man's throat is cut?" He smiled and pulled toward me.

From close by, I noticed some brown bits of tobacco lodged in the crannies of his crooked teeth. I smiled back. He had a hammer tattooed on one forearm and a wrench on the other, both dark blue, each perhaps three inches long. He put his free hand, the one with the hammer tattoo, on my arm. His fingers were rough, like coarse-grade sandpaper. His nails were bitten off irregularly, and what was left was black and dirty underneath.

I had just taken a course in human biology, and I *did* know the answer. With the blade pressed against my skin, I found myself describing the trachea, its function in moving fresh air from the mouth and the nose to the lungs and high-carbon-dioxide air back out. I also talked about the possibility of cutting key arteries, which carry blood to and from the brain, whose incision would result in bleeding and death.

With the knife at my neck, a certain tunnel-vision clarity of mind had taken over. The kind you have when another car comes toward you on a two-lane highway with the high beams on and you unknowingly focus on a dark and relatively limited feature of the road, the side bumps or the center line, perhaps, so as to not get blinded. Perhaps Jack's holding the knife, in addition to being a threat, was also unwittingly protective, focusing my mind on the task at hand, slicing it into smaller, more manageable pieces.

Years later, when I told this story to others, they said I was brave. Not so. There was no bravery, since there was no fear. The knife had performed, without any interference by me, a kind of surgery, peeling away fear and insecurity and self-doubt. It was like when I first came to the United States. For me it was not Coming to America, the

Land of the Free, but a flight, a taxi, a hotel, a driver's license, used car, apartment, gas, electricity, telephone. A deconstruction, a fortunate deconstruction that made the complex simple, cut the whole into portions.

That night Jack watched me, as I talked, with a progressively less pronounced smile. He looked puzzled.

"I think this is all poppycock," he said with his voice lowered.

"Yes, it is," I smiled and nodded. I did not know what the word *poppycock* meant and what he was referring to but, having been awakened to the moment, had no wish to be disagreeable.

He took a drag from his cigarette, dropping a length of ash onto the couch beside me, got up and put the knife back under the end table, and sank back into his easy chair. The dark circles under his eyes appeared larger than before. The ash sat there perched on the edge, in one piece.

I looked around at the mostly bare walls. There was a badly framed painting of a window opened out to the sea from the beach, with white-capped surf, and seagulls and clouds in the blue sky, inviting one out to feel the cool, fresh wind on the face. There was also a shadow box, on the opposite wall, holding two purple-ribboned medals and a small, bronze Vietnam Veterans of America banner, all posted on a velvety back. Perhaps I was to be an outlet for years of defeat and resentment, an explanation, or maybe a scapegoat—as he himself had been and was still—cleansing him, cleansing them, bearing all sins and guilt into the wilderness. But I did not cooperate. Perhaps he had felt a momentary superiority to me, and it was gone.

We sat like that, silently, for a couple of minutes. The banging and pleading outside continued, but not as loudly, and then I got up and let the women in.

Not long after, Jack was killed in a bar fight, or perhaps from a heart attack while sleeping. To be honest, I cannot remember which, but I recall telling people years later that it was a bar stabbing. Regardless, I feel that he deserved better than to die in his sleep, and we will call it a bar fight.

Emily asked Debbie and me to go over and take whatever of his we wanted. His things were in two piles in the living room, his clothes and hats and shoes on one side and his tools and cups and dishes and army gear and knickknacks on the other. There wasn't much there at all. The piles, with items irregularly loaded one on top of the other, reminded me of the heaps of dry brushwood we used to burn in the streets and jump over in celebration of an old Zoroastrian holiday at the end of the winter season. We sang about decline and renewal. "My yellow flesh to you; your redness of life to me."

Searching through the piles, I found the leather-handled knife. When I touched its blade, it was still smooth and cold, and also comforting now. It felt pleasant against the skin. I also took his down army sleeping bag since it was in good condition and would be useful to me. It was green and very long and was shaped like a tight sarcophagus. There were multiple instruction labels on the edges and inside; in time I memorized these. You would get in and zip it up from the inside, all the way to the chin. If you did this perfectly, only your eyebrows, eyes, nose, cheeks, mouth, and chin would be visible. Thinking about it now, in that sense, it was not unlike a woman's proper Islamic hijab. Inside was warm and tight and soft, and you felt protected. The zipper was smooth and quiet. To open it up in a hurry, you just had to bring your arms up to chest level and jerk them apart, and you were free. I imagine it would have been a very useful feature in the jungles of Vietnam.

After Debbie and I broke up, we kept in touch for some years as we moved into new relationships. She married a couple of times, and divorced, and moved in and out of her mother's home. Her son, J.D., usually lived with her, and occasionally with Emily or his father in Canada. In a good year, when Debbie had a job, she and J.D. would live in a two-bedroom apartment, and when things got tight, they would move a few doors down and squeeze into a one-bedroom. I would go and have dinner with them, or take her out to dinner, or take J.D. out to the park, and sometimes Debbie and I would have sex. It was rarely satisfying, but it was familiar. I remember the overpowering need to get out after being with them for an hour or two, to leave her and her family far behind, to cover their voices and sights and smells with other ones, newer ones. I remember thinking that even the smells in a hopeless house are different, or at least magnified. Dogs smell more doglike, and must mustier, and smoke lingers on longer, as though you need money to cleanse the air, to move the air.

We lost contact after I moved to New York for my doctoral studies at Columbia University. I tried to find her a couple of times, but not too hard. Visiting with her was visiting the underbelly of my adopted country, or perhaps it was a reminder of years past, trying to recapture the good and make sense of the bad. It never works anyway.

I still have the green sleeping bag and that knife, even though I have bought and used newer and better ones since. Now, decades later, I live with another woman in the fashionable part of town. Behind our home, by our two-car garage, where we keep our matching BMWs, his and hers, there is a shed. The green sleeping bag and the knife sit there along with other residue, all boxed and neatly labeled and stacked in rows.

Shadow Nation

Cyrus M. Copeland

For decades now, I've been trying to come to terms with my shadow.

That's not some fancy spy terminology or ironic way of throwing shade. I'm being sincere. Carl Jung says the "shadow" is that part of our personality we reject out of fear, or ignorance or shame. I'm Iranian-American. For the past forty years, I have taken my shadow—my Iranian heritage—and inverted it. My shadow is my skin. I advertise it. "Hey, it's your favorite Iranian" is how I often answer the phone—or occasionally, "Hey, it's your favorite Islamic terrorist." An invitation to my party might read, "Get bombed with your favorite Iranian." And if you were my paramour and threatened to leave, I'd take you hostage. Were you to laugh at me, as most do, I'd advise you never to laugh at an Iranian! Do you want another international incident?

As a self-appointed goodwill ambassador of a rogue nation, I figure Jung was onto something. He says the way to heal ourselves is by integrating our shadow. "To do this, we are obliged to struggle with evil, confront the shadow, to integrate the devil."

These days, it doesn't get any more devilish than the Great Satan and the Axis of Evil. Decades after a revolution that foisted Islamic fundamentalism on an unready world, we castigate and condemn Iran for its apparent fundamentalism, its sexism and suppression of women and gays, its stubborn refusal to listen to logic or play by the rules, and its grab for nuclear power—not recognizing that these aren't exactly issues we have put to bed in America. If we all have a shadow, Iran is America's. It represents everything we fear and have not yet reconciled within our own country.

To wit: in 1979, a few days before he was taken hostage at the US Embassy in Tehran, Chargé d'Affaires Bruce Laingen penned a strategy memo on how to negotiate with the new Iranian regime—starting with a few cultural observations. "Perhaps the single dominant aspect of the Persian psyche is an overriding egoism," he wrote. "Its antecedents lie in the long Iranian history of instability and insecurity which put a premium on self-preservation. The practical effect of it is an almost total Persian preoccupation with self and leaves little room for understanding points of view other than one's own."

Overriding egoism? Preoccupation with self? These are the exact same accusations the world now hurls at the United States. In fact, Iran and the United States are two of the most ethnocentric countries on the face of this earth—both perceiving the world through their own unique lens. Later in the memo, Laingen criticizes Iranians for their lack of trust, and if you think about it, you begin to understand why they don't trust Americans. Imagine you're an Iranian. Look to your left. There's Afghanistan, occupied by the United States. To your right, American-occupied Iraq, in ruins. Looking to history, a 1953 coup led by the CIA to destabilize Iran's government. Would you trust us?

Let's not forget that when Iran *did* try and engage with America over the nuclear issue more than a decade ago, they were told by the Bush administration, "We don't negotiate with evil." Does anyone outside of superhero movies actually speak like this? These days both Washington and Hollywood love casting Iran as The Bad Guy. Movies and TV shows are full of Iranian spies, terrorists, and angry mullahs. We project our shadow onto our enemies, onto screens big and small.

But unlike, say, North Korea, another "Axis of Evil" country whose one-note foreign policy never changes, Iran and America are countries that respond to each other. For over forty years, we have fought over nukes, hostages, drones, downed civilian airliners, computer sabotage, espionage. But we have never stopped engaging. It's like that weird dynamic siblings have—it might be dysfunctional, but it is a relationship. Which means that we can do what parties to a relationship do: argue bitterly, equivocate, judge, defend, and finally make up—just as we did with Britain, Germany, and Japan. It's no accident that our closest allies were once our bitter enemies.

More than two decades after being held hostage for 444 days, Laingen wrote,

> The United States and Iran must talk. Not with the mutually negative public rhetoric that for the twenty-seven years since the 1979 hostage crisis has eroded the trust needed for any diplomatic exchange . . . but frontally and frankly as responsible powers with shared interests in a critically important part of the world. The absence of dialogue has made no sense on any count—strategic, human, historic, political, cultural.

Or psychological. If Iran is America's shadow, it holds the key to our evolution through the buttons it pushes in us. So what kind of country do we want to be? One that extends an olive branch or levels a gun? For me, being Iranian-American is like being a child of international divorce. For forty years, I've watched my mother- and fatherlands demonize and duke it out with one another. But let me tell you what all children of divorce know: we never stop hoping our parents will get back together.

Two Minutes to Midnight

Daniel Rafinejad

Author's note: This is an actual email correspondence between a former student and me, printed with permission. Some names and identifying details have been changed.

> For conservatives, the nation is conceptualized (implicitly and unconsciously) as a Strict Father family, and, for liberals, as a Nurturant Parent family.
>
> George Lakoff, *Moral Politics: How Liberals and Conservatives Think*

April 1, 2018

Hi Danny,

Hope this email finds you well! This is so incredibly random, but I was a student of yours ten years ago at the summer intensive Persian class at UCLA. I hope you remember me! I was the half-Iranian/half-Filipino kid? You were an amazing teacher, and I could really speak Farsi after that summer. Now, all these years later, I'd like to continue with lessons. I'd love to be able to speak to my dad's family in Iran. Would you be able to recommend anyone in LA?

I have another question, also totally random, and I hope you don't mind me asking. On the last day of class, when you were saying your goodbyes, you mentioned that it had been a difficult summer for you and that you'd been struggling. I remember you said you were on antidepressants. I've been struggling a lot this year too. It sounds so stupid, but I feel like it all has to do with the election. What's happening in this country is making me so stressed out and depressed, but I'm addicted to the news and to social media. I feel hopeless, like nothing's going to change, but I can't stop myself from reading everything about Donald Trump. I'm finding I'm drinking more than usual and that the smallest thing will set off my rage. How are you dealing with this last crazy year? Do you think antidepressants would help me? You seemed so wise and so together that summer, even though you were going through a hard time. I thought I'd ask for your advice. If you don't have the time, or you don't want to answer, no worries at all.

Thanks so much,
Linus in Los Angeles

April 3, 2018

Dear Linus,

Of course I remember you! Thank you for your kind words. Let me start by saying that you are feeling hurt and angry because you're a compassionate, thoughtful person—the opposite of "stupid." I'm sorry you're having a rough time. I could give you anodyne advice, like "Limit social media engagement to fifteen minutes a day," or "Join more marches and protests," or "Immerse yourself in Persian," but I don't think that's what you're asking me for. Whatever I said in that classroom ten years ago struck you as honest and maybe a bit courageous, so I'm going to try to reply with honesty and courage. I apologize in advance if any of this comes across as condescending. Without worksheets and vocab quizzes, I don't have the authority I have in the classroom.

Right now, at this moment in the Time of Trump—April 2018—my mother and father are seventy-two and seventy-four, and they live in Northern California. They are generous, jovial, weird, fucked-up people. I love them, and not just out of filial duty. I respect my mother for her artist's eye and for the poetic way she speaks. I respect my father for his industry and for his sense of adventure. They are as blind to race as any two people I've ever met. I'm in awe of how, as immigrants in this country, they've succeeded, even flourished, during very uneasy times.

For years, however, I *hated* them. I hated them because they didn't protect me, and I hated them because they were too scared and too weak to accept me.

An adult man, not in my family, sexually molested me from the time I was nine until about six months after I turned thirteen. He was in his fifties, and he smelled of pepper, Colton aftershave, and Carefree sugarless bubble gum. He made me jerk him off; he made me suck him off; he penetrated me with objects and with his body. If I resisted, and I seldom did, he would humiliate and strike me.

Like most victims of abuse, I told no one about it, but I changed dramatically. You can see it in my school pictures. First grade, second grade: a tousled but happy kid, not so different from any other, a precocious glint in the eyes. Third, fourth, and fifth grades: I don't just look sad or hollow, Linus, I look *deformed*. My face and my body are twisted in aged, criminal anguish.

How could my parents not see that? How could they not notice my sudden change in habits? That I stopped bathing? That I stopped eating? That I threw myself off the roof of my father's Jeep to break my arm for a *second* time? That I began to exhibit other weird behavioral problems, night terrors and rages and panic attacks, to say nothing of the cuts and bruises and blood stains? Wasn't it their job to see these things, to make the right conclusions, to protect me?

I didn't tell them about it until I was eighteen, and they didn't believe me. We didn't speak about it again until I was thirty-six, and then they did believe me.

The summer I turned twenty-one, I told my parents I was gay. My mother promptly called me an animal, told me I would die of AIDS, and wrote me in a birthday card that as a gift *to her*, I should promise I wouldn't open my heart to a man "for many, many years."

In a very air-conditioned Starbucks in Mountain View, California, that same summer, my father informed me that I had two options: enter into a sexless marriage with a woman or live with him and my mother until they died. And/or take up bowling. He actually offered *bowling* as an alternative to loving another human, Linus.

Because of their otherwise open-minded, Berkeley-in-the-sixties attitudes, I was stunned by their homophobia. But it was just that: fear. There were no openly gay people in the Iranian community of the Bay Area, and my parents didn't socialize with non-Iranians. The only gay person my mother knew was her hairdresser, who died of AIDS. Parents want to see themselves reflected in their children, and when mine didn't see themselves, they pinned their biggest fears— disease and death for my mother, ostracism for my father—on something that seemed as natural to me as my smile.

So I didn't listen to them.

I fell in love with a man, a fellow grad student at UCLA. Four years later, he developed pancreatic cancer and succumbed to it very shortly thereafter. I was twenty-nine; he was thirty-six. My parents never met him. They didn't even know he existed until he got sick, when we needed money for his treatment.

A month before he died, my parents visited. As my mother and I pulled up to the little pink house my boyfriend and I shared, I told her how excited he was to meet her.

She refused to get out of the car.

"I can't," she said. "I can't go in."

She waited in the parked car while I went into the house and did whatever I needed to do, which was probably what most caretakers do, just sit quietly. I then drove her back to her hotel.

Why am I telling you these sad, personal stories? What do they have to do with the president?

We see our president as a parent, and our country as a family: this is our "homeland," founded by "fathers" we're supposed to respect and love. Such thinking isn't unique to the United States, of course, but we're additionally taught that we live in the *greatest*, richest, most powerful country on earth, headed by "the leader of the free world," and that is unique.

Like our parents, our presidents can seem the most familiar and the most elusive figures in our lives. Our mothers and fathers, whether or not they're any good at it, guide us through childhood, life's most vulnerable time, when we aren't capable of seeing them as anything less than godheads. We comprehend neither their intentions nor their reactions. As our parents do when we're children, the president seems everywhere—in our living rooms, on our computers, at our kitchen tables—and we're never quite sure how much power he has or how far he'll go with it.

As a kid, I'd fantasize I was part of a highly classified government experiment. Even then, I saw, or wanted to see, the state as a safe, familial extension: the government was testing how much a little boy could endure when bad, crazy parents tried to raise him. (That was also why I had been given to despicable Iranians.) If I lost my mother at the mall, or if she was late picking me up after school, I'd comfort myself with the thought that nice NASA scientists in white coats would soon come marching in (carrying an ice cream cake) and congratulate me for bravely suffering those horrible people. Then they'd introduce me to my "real" mother and father.

When I was a teenager, I'd think about getting a gun, shooting my parents in their sleep, and then killing myself.

Since Trump's election, I've thought how fabulous it would be if a good Supreme Court justice (or NASA scientist, for that matter) called for an immediate referendum on the president. I've wondered why it's taken so long for a madman, some despondent follower of his, to try to assassinate him. I know a referendum is impossible, and, of course, I don't want Trump to die. Nor do I want my parents or me or anyone to die, but you can see how my thinking as an adult about Trump resembles my thinking as a child about the two people who ruled over my small world.

How can he not see the damage he's causing? Isn't it his job to be unselfish and observant? To care for us, his people? To get out of his own head and, out of love for his "family," face the diseases in the room?

My mother and father failed me with Trumpian magnitude, and though I tried to be an expat from my family, I couldn't, and I can't. I believe in them. I believe in us. There's a hard part of me, in the black deep of my heart, that will never forgive them and will always be angry, but there's another part, rising and mutating, that loves them, that's proud of them, that cares for them. Even though they'll never be who I'd like them to be.

You care for this country, Linus. Like me, you're not ready to leave, even though there's never been a perfect president. Nor has there ever been a time when America was great, to its people or to the rest of the world.

Now, of course I'm not asking you to honor Trump. We *must* fight. He's a priapismic orange abscess squirting pus on institutions that till now seemed elastic enough to become *more* inclusive with each generation. He's a disgrace. What I'm trying to say is that I understand why his presidency feels so damn personal. Everyone's projecting, and on all sides. Trump was right when he said, "I could stand in the middle of Fifth Avenue and shoot somebody and I wouldn't lose voters." His "base" loves him like he's Captain von Trapp. Children of dangerously abusive parents still cry and reach for Mommy and Daddy when Child Protective Services intervenes. I can tell you all these rough stories about my own parents, but if you were to turn and say to me, "Wow, your mom's a bitch, Danny," I'd reply with something like, "Hey now, OK, watch it, she's not *that* bad; she's never groused about my wearing ladies' perfume."

The president changes at least every eight years, while we're stuck with our parents for life. This administration feels permanent now that the *Bulletin of the Atomic Scientists* has moved the Doomsday Clock to two minutes to midnight, but we have to believe in the resiliency of American democracy.

The good news is that we're no longer children. We have our autonomy and our voices.

The other good news is that the United States is enormous, while our immediate families are tiny. We're alone only if we choose to believe we are. My family is just three people; I have no siblings, no extended family to speak of. My—our—country, however, is the third most populous on earth, an entire swath of continent and more.

On the morning of 9/11, I was in San Francisco teaching English to a group of Persian-speaking Afghan refugees. I broke the news of the attacks to the class, but I was still hoping it was all a *War of the Worlds*–like hoax done with special effects. Suddenly, the big boss of the center I worked at, a stocky, middle-aged man whom I'd met just once before, burst into the classroom and announced that classes were canceled for the rest of the day. Then, in front of this room full of strangers, he sat on my desk and broke down in sobs. I had no idea what to do.

I put a hand on his shoulder. His body burned through his chambray shirt.

"I'm so sad for us," he said.

For *us*. The word clanged across the classroom and across my heart, as I looked at the students looking down, embarrassed, at their workbooks or watching, with polite alarm and curiosity, this big white man weep into his palms. I knew he didn't mean "us" as in "all of humanity." He meant "us Americans." Not them, those Afghan students who'd fled the Taliban and whose country, within weeks, would be bombed in retaliation. Whether or not this man, whose name I don't remember, intended to include the likes of you and me is immaterial, Linus; we are part of that "us."

In your email to me, you reintroduced yourself as the half-Iranian/half-Filipino guy, not as the guy with the father born in Iran and the mother born in the Philippines. Maybe you weren't born in the United States, but I remember you as an American college student who spoke American English . . . in America. You referred to the United States as I do: as "this" country. We have to stop doing that, Linus. We have a right to this country. It is ours. This is *our* fucked-up family.

Make a list, on a piece of paper, of all the things you love about the USA: history, culture, politics, people, sports, places. Any and all of it. I'm serious. I did it, and it helped. High atop my list, for example, is the English language. I *love* English. America gave me English. I love its arcane orthography ("bough," "rough," "through," "cough," "though"), and I love the way it scans (how "the little red house" sounds better than "the red little house").

I love American literature, especially the literature of the South. I find the South exotic on the one hand and on the other hand, a lot like Iran, with its pride and loss and terrible pain. A black Alabaman woman sitting next to me on a flight from Rome to New York said, "You must come to Birmingham! You should have gone there before Rome!" I was stunned. Rome has the Colosseum; Birmingham has . . . a jail? But thinking about that moment now, I'm moved by her love for that red state. How many times have I told people, "Go to Iran! I promise it's *nothing* like what you imagine!"

I love American pop culture, particularly from 1939 to 1976, from the release of *The Wizard of Oz* until the Bicentennial (also the year of my conception, when my mother's autobiography ends— more on that later). Everything from that period fascinates me: its movies, music, design, the portrayals of races and identities and sexes, as odious as many of them were.

I love Broadway and Motown and Laura Nyro and Madonna.

I love *Peanuts* cartoons.

I love Kellogg's/Post/General Mills breakfast cereals.

I love white tube socks. (Try handing out unworn tube socks to panhandlers. It's a small, nice thing to do, and they're always grateful to get them. No one thinks to give the homeless socks. You can hand out any kind of sock, of course, but white tube socks are cheapest.)

I like baseball, although I've never been to a baseball game, never even watched a baseball game, and all the baseball players I knew in high school were dicks. Still, it strikes me as uncommonly democratic, a team sport where each player gets his or her own moment.

I'll even say I love a few living, working politicians, including Congresswoman Rosa DeLauro from Connecticut (her style!) and Congressman Jerry Nadler from New York (or at least his office employees, who are very nice on the phone) and Senator Maxine Waters from California (brava!), and, as everyone should, Justice Ruth Bader Ginsburg.

I love New York City. I love Hawaii. I love many of the cities and towns of the Rust Belt, especially Detroit. I was touched by how vibrant a town Minneapolis is in spite of the brutal cold. I've been there only once, and for maybe forty minutes, but I *loved* the Dr. Pepper Museum and Mausoleum, or whatever it's called, in Waco, Texas.

The night of the presidential election, my Iranian-American friend texted me and wrote, "We're dead on both sides of the hyphen." I refuse to be dead, on either the Iranian or the American side, and you do too. Let's refuse by finding the things we love, and let's refuse—and now I'm going to get a little New Agey, Linus—by embracing radical responsibility and compassion and curiosity. Let's do that by listening and by telling our stories.

It's no accident that the #MeToo movement began during Trump's tenure or that actual children organized the March for Our Lives on March 24. Women and young people are threatened and angry that a chauvinist predator is the American paterfamilias. Their speaking out—telling the country their intimate, traumatic stories— is as daring as it is political. This culture often judges survivors of trauma as tainted and our stories as ugly or crude or manipulative.

But storytelling is a reach toward others. What I said on that last day of class felt like a hand stretched out to you. Similarly, I feel closer to you just by having read your brief, sweet, tentative email. You may still see me as an "amazing teacher," but I hope you now also see me as a scarred man whose agency was not taken from him at nine, when he was molested, nor at twenty-nine, when he thought he had lost everything, nor at thirty-nine, when Trump became president.

This country is losing its single story. That terrifies Trump's supporters, who have always owned it. I'm certain, however, that Trump's voters wouldn't feel so endangered if they knew their own pasts better. Personal narratives, whether glorious or ugly, cannot be taken from us.

You may know that South Carolina was the first state to secede from the Union in the Civil War. If the white people of South Carolina knew the stories of their ancestors—the names and details of their immigrant relatives, the names and details of those men and women who owned other humans and fought for the Confederacy, those families who witnessed the loss of their children to the war, to hunger, to disease—they wouldn't feel so threatened, for instance, by the possible removal of the obelisk in Aiken, South Carolina, honoring Confederate soldiers, on which a plaque is engraved, mockingly, "They gave their all in defense of Home, Honor, Liberty, and the Independence of their native land." Knowing their histories, they may realize that the Confederacy was an *enemy* of the United States; to honor those who "gave their all," therefore, is to honor traitors. Or they may at least allow that detestable plaque to be removed. (The obelisk can stay as a reminder of a heinous past.)

It's no accident either that heredity/lineage services like 23andMe and Ancestry.com are so popular now. We need personal histories that predate our births. We need "people" from whom we came. Around 2003 or 2004, before the Obama administration, I noticed that white hipster men in LA were starting to dress like turn-of-the-century barbers. There was a man in Silver Lake who sported a thick shop-broom mustache, always wore suspenders, and—no joke—rode around town on a penny-farthing bicycle. Then, two Septembers ago, on Governor's Island here in New York, I stumbled upon a group of a dozen or so young women and men (all white) having a picnic and pretending to be in the 1940s. Theirs was a smaller, later version of the famous annual summer Jazz Age Lawn Party, also held on Governor's Island. Everything about them was period: wardrobe, hair, makeup, even language. I overheard one man sincerely turn back to another and say, "Got any lettuce on ya, fella?" (*Lettuce* is 1940s slang for paper money. I had to look that up.)

Maybe the Silver Lake hipster was a bicycle repairman building his workshop's brand. Maybe those picnicking youngsters were doing some sort of performance art. Maybe it was even a political response to the Jazz Age party. Regardless, the fact that these white people were so sedulous in their commitment shows that they want to connect or engage with some white-dominated past and culture they can own.

I don't think those white kids have ever felt hyphenated. Nor do I think those kids are tiki torch–carrying racists. I think they looked around and noticed something lacking in their lives and, quite innocently, became nostalgic for an era in American history in which they could claim roots, whether it's the Ellis Island/Ragtime era or that of the Greatest Generation. I'm not even talking about biology, though that's what those DNA tests are all about. Most of my friends who were adopted, for example, have no interest in finding their birth parents. I mean a clear narrative that shows us whose struggles and sacrifices brought us to our lives here, in America, right now.

If you haven't, Linus, go get your personal history. Record the stories if necessary. Ask your Iranian grandfather, your Filipino aunt, your oldest cousin for their stories, and listen to them. And don't limit yourself to your family! Ask your friends and their parents and grandparents, *especially* your white friends' parents and grandparents. They've made your reality too.

My mother has written a two-volume autobiography called *Frog in My Throat*. The title is an attempted translation of the Persian word *boghz*, a word whose first meaning is "spite" or "grudge" but that in colloquial speech signifies an overflow of feelings: a lump in one's throat. (Some bad Persian-English dictionary must have translated that as "a frog in one's throat"; *boghz* has nothing to do with a scratchy voice.) Volume 1 is my mother's life in Iran, until the age of eighteen; volume 2 is ages eighteen through thirty-two, her age when I was born.

My mother wrote it in English with the help of a ghost writer. Because she didn't want readers' prejudices about Iran to color or dilute the sorrow that gave her such a lump in her throat, she set the story of young Sara (her) in a nameless land with characters that bear Anglo names. So Behjat al-Sadat, my grandmother, is Betty; Mohammad Ali, my grandfather, is Mike. Many of the names don't really fit the 1950s–1960s period of the first volume; she has friends with names like Caitlyn and Madison.

My mother grew up wealthy as landed gentry before the land reforms of the last shah's "White Revolution" in the mid-1960s eradicated the feudal system. The book gets stranger when Sara starts talking about "her villages" and "her peasants."

She even commissioned a friend to paint the cover, which is a portrait of my mother with—you guessed it—a green frog superimposed on her throat. The book is bonkers.

I excoriated my mother for writing this book, which she saw as a perfect fit for Oprah's Book Club. ("I'm making a vision board!" she announced.) I told her the book was physical proof of her narcissism, while the ridiculous names of the characters, her family, were proof of her self-hate. I told her how hurt I was that she thought her life suddenly stopped at my birth. I lambasted her for the cover, for the words that clearly weren't hers, for the self-pity and complaint on every page.

If you were to ask me what my biggest regret in life is, it's that I was so cruel to her about the book. I regret having said all those things, and I regret that I haven't apologized to her properly. She didn't see the book as self-aggrandizement; she saw it as something beautiful and generous. I no longer see plastic-bound copies of Volume 1 lying around the house, and she never talks about it. I think she's stopped working on it entirely.

I should have just convinced her to keep the setting and the names Iranian to honor her family and her "peasants." I should have realized the Anglicizing was an attempt, in her weirdly tilted way, to become part of the American story. She may not have been there since 1975, but she can't take her story out of Iran, just as you and I can't take ours out of America. And though she claims Iran is "no longer hers," I know she loves it. Her love of Iran—an effortless, organic love—is what pushed me to study Persian in the first place.

There's some self-help movement now that I know about only from Instagram: something about the bravery in vulnerability. Look it up if it interests you. It may be silly, but, again, I see it as a sign of the times.

Thank you for being vulnerable in your email to me, and thank you again for writing me. There is indeed a bonanza of self-help out there now, and I know you have loved ones with whom you can discuss how the world makes you ache. You chose to write to me, however, and I feel privileged.

Linus, please don't deform your body with alcohol or rage at the television or at bad drivers or bad baristas or bad anybody. Turn feeling into action. Be courageous.

Let's love more and listen more and share more, and let's endure. Not endure as in "to bear, to tolerate," but endure as in "to last, to continue, to gain worth." *Endure* is from the Latin root *durus*, hard, as in durable or dour. There's a way to be vulnerable and durable during dour times. Let's be that.

Sincerely yours,

Danny

P.S. You know the answer to your question about antidepressants: I can't tell you to go on them or not. I do recommend seeing a psychiatrist and talking to him/her about medication. I don't recommend listening to the advice of nonprofessionals. You don't need some well-meaning-but-misinformed Uncle Harry telling you that Prozac leads to suicide or that meds make you "feel happy for no reason" and rob you of authentic experience. Los Angeles County has one of the best mental health systems in the country. There are clinics with free counseling and psychiatric services. Seek them out if cost is an issue.

P.P.S. Limit social media engagement to fifteen minutes a day. Join more marches and protests. And please immerse yourself in Persian. I don't know any Persian tutors in LA right now, but I'll ask around and get back to you.

When We Were Lions

Mehdi Tavana Okasi

One night twenty years ago, sometime between two and three in the morning, I came out of a deep sleep to a song that has remained my anthem. But I couldn't have anticipated its enduring effect back then. I was unable to verbalize my attraction to the song, which I think is what happens at the beginning of any new wonder. This was sometime in September of 1997, and I was still living in the first and only house my family has ever mortgaged in this country. We'd been in that house in Marlborough, Massachusetts, for about a year. Before that, we'd lived a life of tenancy in a Section 8 apartment in Medford, a six-minute walk from the Johnnie's Foodmaster grocery store that marked the border into Malden, where we were forewarned not to venture.

I'd fallen asleep that night wearing my Walkman, tuned to KISS 108 FM; iPods hadn't yet been introduced onto the market. I remember the crescendo carrying me as if by canoe out of my deep sleep:

> . . . days go by I'm hypnotized
> I'm walking on a wire
> I close my eyes and fly out of my mind
> Into the fire.

It took me several days to discover the singer's identity, and until I did, I was a teenager obsessed. There was no Google in 1997, and taking to the internet in search of answers to every question wasn't yet common. Besides, my family didn't have internet; we owned a beautiful leather-bound *Encyclopedia Britannica*, which, like most things we've ever owned, was purchased on credit. So I listened to the radio obsessively until they played the song again and I could discover from the DJ the name of the song and the singer. It took maybe three days, and once I had Shawn Colvin's name, I took to the phone and finally, on a Sunday afternoon, after maybe my eighth call to the radio station, the DJ, exasperated and frankly somewhat dubious of my zeal, finally played "Sunny Came Home." I was prepared: a blank cassette tape in the deck, my fingers simultaneously poised over the Play and Record buttons. I wanted the world to share in my excitement, so, pre-Facebook, I took to literal walls, writing Shawn Colvin lyrics across classroom whiteboards at my high school.

Lately, I've been thinking about why, of all songs, it's "Sunny Came Home" that I continue to love. The song is about a woman who comes home one day, sits down in the kitchen, and opens a book and a box of tools. She's been thinking about her life. She's come to a major decision. "It's time for a few small repairs," she says. She gets her children and then strikes a match and sets fire to her house. The lyrics of the last verse go:

> Light the sky and hold on tight
> The world is burning down
> She's out there on her own and she's alright.

Colvin then pares down the chorus into three utterances, each progressively shorter than the one before, until she sorrowfully almost whisper-sings the very last word of the song: home.

The song tells my family's story. It evokes the ethos of my mother's experience as a political refugee fleeing Iran with two young children, arriving in America in 1987 with a hundred dollars and nowhere to call home. My mother, too, had sat in a kitchen one day and opened a book. The circumstances of her life had brought her to a moment of great decision. Iran was nearly seven years into a bloody war with Iraq, which was continuing its assault; her world was indeed burning down. The United States had cut all diplomatic ties with Iran and was secretly supplying weapons to Saddam Hussein, who continued to drop mustard gas and long-range missiles. Estimates place the total death count on both sides at well over a million souls. So one day she took a long shower, donned her chador, and sat down to seek *istikharah*, or counsel, with God. The decision that weighed on her forced my mother onto a wire: should she flee Iran with her two young children in hopes that America would give us refuge, or should she stay home and raise us in a country at war, not only with Iraq but also with itself?

My mother made several trips abroad after marrying my father. In Europe, she'd seen a life free from imposed religious ideology. But even when she was a child, my mother had pleaded with her father to send her abroad to study. Back then, the word *abroad* was an abstraction; only the rich ever went there, and my mother's family wasn't rich. But she grew up, became a teacher, married my father, had me, followed by my brother, and saw enough of the world to know that there was another way to live. The day the school at which she taught appointed students to monitor teachers' hijabs, even going so far as to have these students search their teachers' bags for contraband, my mother knew she had to leave.

Her family tried to frighten her into staying. If you're caught, my grandmother told her, how will we answer your children? What should we tell them became of you? My father told her that if she wanted to go, she'd have to find the way herself. He'd follow. And he did, about four years later, after an imprisonment of which he still won't speak, after losing our home in a real estate scheme that left my family homeless on two continents.

In that kitchen in Iran, like Sunny, my mother opened a book, the Quran, to an *ayah* (verse) that she later recalled as reading "You will be left neither hungry nor naked." This was in response to a single question that she begged of God: should she go? That verse sealed our fate. My mother gathered my brother and me, closed her eyes, and we flew. She'd packed her copy of the Quran; her tools were her jewelry, most of which she sold along the way to grease the palms of immigration officers and airport security guards and border police, and to pay the men who directed us out of Tehran and to Istanbul, then Belgrade, then Vienna, and finally, nearly a year later, to Boston.

Taking us from Iran as she did, political refugees without asylum, with no certainty of being granted entry by any country, my mother, in essence, burned down our house. If we'd been forced to return to Iran, it would have meant prison or much worse. During that difficult year of our crossing, when everything was uncertain, my mother couldn't think of return or home; like Sunny, she closed her eyes and pushed ahead into a future that burned daily with uncertainty. It kept her from sleep as we were shuttled between holding cells, makeshift dormitories, and airport waiting rooms, questioned by men who wielded power with guns and with pen and paper. And then there was the day in Vienna when my brother accidentally overturned a pot of boiling water on his arm, suffering major third-degree burns, and my mother, unable to speak German, panicking and desperate for help, burning as my brother burned, tried to get him to a hospital before it was too late.

Once we had our green cards, we returned to Iran for a visit after eight years gone. My mother was reunited with the family she'd left behind, but for my brother and me, it was as if we were meeting everyone for the first time. The years had washed away whatever intimacy we'd once felt. But our family gave our aloofness no space. My cousins and uncles and aunts flooded us, carrying us in their tide. I remember turning to search for my mother and seeing her outside Mehrabad Airport, at three in the morning, falling to her knees to kiss the ground.

My grandmother first regarded me as if I might be an apparition, a trick of the light, but once she had my face solidly in her hands, she praised Allah and refused to let my brother and me leave her side. In the end, my grandmother's warnings to my mother on the eve of our departure all those years ago had proven true. In America, my mother had received news that her favorite brother, the one who had become like a father to her after her own passed away, the brother who had supported her through college and in the years after, when she worked as a young teacher, had died suddenly of a heart attack. Because we didn't have our papers yet, my mother hadn't been able to return for his funeral. Her sorrow grew large in America. It made her hair fall out; she became diabetic.

When I first started working on my novel, I spent a great deal of time meditating on the narrative power of beginnings. In Farsi, children's stories always begin, "*Yekee bood, yekee nabood, gheraz Khodah, heechkas nabood . . . ,*" which roughly translates as, "One was, one wasn't. Besides God, no one was . . ." This, in contrast to the way American children's stories begin: "Once upon a time . . ." In the Iranian beginning, the self is ambiguous, and in the American version, the ambiguity lies in time. This tension continues to resonate with me because the stories we first hear mark us in ways that are never really lost.

As I listened to children's stories in Iran, the power of the beginning shifted my imagination inward, to the self, to my existence as the will of God. In America I read stories that began, "Once upon a time," and my gaze moved to the landscape, to the makeup of that world, to far-off places. This tension, between consciousness and time, between the self and the world, between the private and the public, is one that I've struggled with as I've come to understand the power of narrative and the place to begin a story. I am pulled between those forces: how to be, but also how to be in the world.

I tried to begin my novel by fictionalizing the scene of our reunion, but failed. The airport felt thin, our emotions, melodramatic. My family became caricatures of themselves. I was trapped in a well of my own making, private and dark and separate from the world. So I put the novel aside, but I kept returning to that night at Mehrabad Airport. When I received news of my grandmother's death, I remembered her face and how she'd looked at me as if I'd disappear. The airport felt fraught, at once tense and celebratory. Revolutionary Guards and police patrolled and the portraits of Khomeini and Khameini admonished us from above, reminding me how all our joys and sorrows were felt under that heavy gaze. It was a moment both private and incredibly public and yet I didn't know how to negotiate between the two in my fiction, so I avoided it altogether, and the pendulum of my writing swung in the other direction.

Saturday, June 20, 2009, around 6:30 p.m. The Amir Abad neighborhood of Tehran. A traffic jam. A woman is standing on North Kargar Street, shouting along with other protesters, "Where is my vote? Down with the dictator! Election—not selection!" A movement is underway across Tehran against the fraudulent reelection of Ahmadinejad: green bandanas, headscarves, ribbons, bracelets, face and body paint, makeshift flags of green cloth in the hands and on the bodies of Iranians who pour into the streets for presidential candidate Mousavi.

When the Islamic Republic banned journalists from covering the protests in 2009, a new phenomenon, the citizen journalist, took up the mandate to inform the world about what was happening on the streets of the capital. In the days before and after the election, Iranians took to social media to document the movement. Government officials hadn't anticipated this. And on this day, it's a camera phone that films Neda falling to the ground. At first it seems as though perhaps she's only fainted. "Don't be scared," a man is heard shouting. But then blood rushes from her mouth, her nose, and it rivers across her face. Her eyes are open. They're looking into the camera. She's looking at me, as if to say, "Look at what is happening." Blood pools into one eye, completely obscuring it. Amazingly, she dies with open eyes. She dies looking at us.

In the video that I watched on loop from my apartment in Lafayette, Indiana, where I'd just completed graduate school, a man runs to her and presses his hands against her chest wound in an attempt to slow the bleeding. A story circulates that Neda's last words were "I'm burning." But who knows whether this is true. In the video, a man is shouting, "Don't be scared, Neda," until the volume of blood makes him scream. She was twenty-six years old, three years my junior, at the time of her death.

A few weeks after, I returned to Boston for good and joined demonstrations in front of the Boston Public Library, shouting against Ahmadinejad's fraudulent reelection. In Paris, the photojournalist Reza Deghati printed placards of Neda's smiling face and shipped them to demonstrators around the world to hold before their faces. While the Iranian government had permanently silenced

Neda—whose name in Farsi means "voice"—her death inspired humanity to speak. Although she wasn't the only one to die during those many months of unrest in Iran (*Frontline's Tehran Bureau* estimates that 107 people were killed), Neda was the only one to capture the world's imagination.

On January 4th, 2011, shortly after 2:00 a.m., Boston police reported to 141 West Newton Street and found Ali-Reza Pahlavi—the youngest prince of the Pahlavi royal family, which was ousted by the Islamic Revolution in 1979—dead from a self-inflicted shotgun wound to the head. Ten years earlier, it had been his sister, Leila Pahlavi, whose body was discovered, hers in a London hotel room. An autopsy revealed that she'd ingested five times the lethal level of Seconal.

At a vigil for Ali-Reza, I stood among an idle group of some thirty Iranian-Americans on Boston Common, trying futilely to keep my candle lit against the biting wind. My mother was with me. We recognized a few other Iranians and made awkward conversation. Commuters rushed past us into Park Station; it was perhaps 6:30 at night and people were trying to get home and out of the cold. We waited for someone to speak, but no one did. At one point, someone attempted to start us all in a song of remembrance, but not everyone knew the words and our voices wouldn't come together in any meaningful way and so we all grew silent.

Ali-Reza Pahlavi was only thirteen years old when the revolution forced his family from Iran. At one time, my mother's generation must have looked at the young prince and imagined great fortunes for their own sons, for their country. And here they stood in the New England cold, unable to articulate the effect of his death, hoping for their collective presence to assign some meaning. We stood shivering until it began to snow and then abandoned our vigil.

That night sparked many questions that keep me returning to this notion of public stakes pressing on the private imagination. I wonder what it means for the cultural narrative of my generation that our dethroned prince and princess, two of the shah's four children, committed suicide. I am reminded of the inherent promise in "Once upon a time." Those words conjure castles and thrones and banquets, a narrative where the prince and princess prevail, always changed for the better. So what does it mean to live in a time when our once prince and princess have taken their own lives? What will become of any of our stories when this is how my generation's narrative begins? Where do we go from here and how do we tell this story?

Among my generation of Iranian-Americans—born there, raised here—I've discovered a sort of apathy at the deaths of our prince and princess. There are no professed royalists in the Iranian diaspora of Boston that I know of, and understandably so. The Pahlavi dynasty had its own brutal tactics. But despite this apathy, I suspect that many of us recognized in Ali-Reza's death a fear that we'd rather forget, or leave unacknowledged. While we don't know why Ali-Reza and Leila Pahlavi took their own lives, in our private imaginations we understand what it means to never find a home, to never be accepted completely because of our names. Perhaps Ali-Reza and Leila couldn't ever find their places in this world, given what their family had lost, how far from grace they'd fallen. Perhaps they too were caught between culture and politics, outraged by Iran's violations of its citizens' human rights that leave those of us in the diaspora tripping over our words, on the one hand to condemn and on the other to try and defend our people, to respect Iranian lives, because if we don't, then no one will.

I grew up with a desk-sized Iranian flag in my childhood bedroom. It was a prerevolution flag, of the Pahlavi Dynasty, depicting an image of a lion wielding a sword, framed by the sun. After my family was able to return for a visit, I brought back the new flag, of the Islamic Republic, and displayed that too, bringing both flags with me when I moved into my dorm room at college. To me, the prerevolution flag recalls the Iran of my parents and their parents and the stories of the great kings of Persepolis, the Zoroastrians from which Persians hail and for whom fire is sacred. It reminds me of a time when we were lions, proud of our history, bright-faced to the world, wielding our strength with honor and dignity.

The new and current Iranian flag signifies the Oneness of Allah, a highly stylized composite of Arabic phrases that look, to me, like a bunch of parentheses, one set enclosing upon another. I have a stake in this flag too, because it flies over the heads of much of my family who still live there. I don't have the luxury of forgetting them. Growing up in the United States, a sworn enemy of the country where I was born, I also know too well what it means to live on the fault lines of conflict, to live under a gaze of suspicion and distrust, to answer that inevitable question, "Where are you really from?," and recognize the immediate shift when I say "Iran."

In the HBO documentary by filmmaker Antony Thomas entitled *For Neda*, Iranian journalist Saeed Kamali Dehghan worked secretly to locate and film interviews with Neda's family for the first time. The Islamic Republic had banned Neda's family from speaking with journalists, and even prohibited a public funeral for fear that it would incite more demonstrations. In the documentary, Neda's mother shows us Neda's bedroom. The camera pans to her desk, into her closet. As her mother holds up an outfit that Neda had recently purchased but never worn, she breaks down; in that private space where Neda rested her head, the full weight of the government's atrocity is felt. I, too, lose my breath as I watch Neda's mother clinging to her dead daughter's dress, never worn. I think about what Neda must have imagined the day she purchased it. What occasion was she saving it for?

Neda's mother tells us about her daughter's obsession with Googoosh as the camera pans to Neda's desk and music collection. Googoosh, arguably Iran's most famous singer and actress, was Neda's favorite, and she'd been taking singing lessons so she could sing her idol's songs. Googoosh herself lived through a long period of political unrest in Iran and was imprisoned in Evin on four different occasions, until she was finally able to leave the country in 2000. In the documentary, Thomas interviews Googoosh about Neda. "It's wonderful that my music resonated so well with Neda," Googoosh says, "but her voice is more powerful than mine. She speaks to all the world."

When I think about what fiction can do, I imagine Neda in her bedroom, singing along to Googoosh's songs. I think about the life

Neda imagined when she closed her eyes. I think about how she was forced to listen to Googoosh's music in secret, and how she couldn't ever sing in public. There was so much she had to hide. I think about this, and how I, on the other side of the world, was able to blast Shawn Colvin's music in my own car, write her lyrics on my high school whiteboards, free and careless with my American voice.

Eight years have passed since Neda was killed, and the world is no better. In Syria, Bashar al-Assad is still killing his own people. ISIL continues to wage its war of terror. Bodies of Syrian refugees have washed up on Turkey's shores, among them children, some as young as two. Madmen are driving trucks through crowds, gunmen are terrorizing concerts, attackers are bombing crowded train stations, apartment buildings, and markets. When Donald Trump was elected president, demonstrators flooded the streets, marched on the US Capitol, marched all over the world. They protested his rhetoric, his worldview, just as Iranians had done to protest Ahmadinejad's fraudulent reelection.

Meanwhile, white supremacists feel free to spill their hate onto streets, to brandish swastikas in organized marches, to call for rounding up and deporting vulnerable immigrants who so often don't have a voice of their own. Trump, the grandson of an immigrant, has turned his back on our plight (perhaps he never faced us). Through fear tactics, he incites divisiveness in our country by legitimizing the misguided fear of a minority. He withdrew from the Iran nuclear deal so painstakingly negotiated, and he goads Kim Jong Un on Twitter, pushing humanity closer to a world that, if we aren't careful, will indeed burn down.

Amidst these stakes, I safeguard my imagination and return to Neda's bedroom. In all likelihood, her family has moved away, but I like to imagine the same home because it's the closest thing to a shrine that Neda will ever have. In that private space, Neda's mother tends to her things, dusting twice a week, pausing over every article: the notebook half written in, the photographs curling at the edges, pens that have dried out by now in her Mickey Mouse cup. She toils here alone, carefully, deliberately, methodically working against the scrim of dust that, no matter how vigilantly she wipes it away, always returns. Here, among Neda's things, she hears a voice like one on the other end of a long-distance call. It is thin. It is almost a whisper, just beginning to sing.

And I hear it too, but not only in Neda's voice; this song is the song of multitudes. It sings against a kingdom divided, it begins the story anew, and like the fire burning in the torch-clasped hand of the Mother of Exiles, it grows louder. And she is singing too:

Send these, the homeless, tempest-tossed to me,
I lift my lamp beside the golden door!

Fortune-Tellers

Dena Afrasiabi

In the minutes leading up to the arrival of the spring equinox, my parents and I stand around our dining room table, which is covered in a white tablecloth and newly transformed into an elaborate *haft sin*, the traditional Iranian New Year's table. Our *haft sin* had conventional beginnings. My mother grew a curly *sabzi* from wheat germ around which she wrapped a bright pink ribbon. She dug out from old boxes items that she hadn't used in recent memory: Iranian coins from over thirty years ago, a gaudy old paisley tablecloth, little silver dishes she filled with things that start with the Persian letter for *s*, *sir* (garlic), *senjed* (oleaster fruit), *somagh* (sumac), etc.—each symbolic and promising to bring luck to some area of our lives, though we couldn't remember what the objects meant. In our excitement, we kept adding items that didn't belong in a traditional *haft sin*: a paperweight, a small silver bird, a wooden block carved with an inspirational saying, a bowl of chocolates from Trader Joe's. By the end, it almost began to resemble a table at a garage sale. Fortunately for us, understatement has never been a priority when decorating the Iranian *haft sin*.

It's 2015 and the first spring in a long time that we're celebrating Nowruz. For years, we didn't have a *haft sin* in our house. My brother's experiments covered our dining room table: his microscope, petri dishes, journals filled with records of his experiments scrawled out in a shaky hand. Refusing treatment, he believed he could fix his mind himself using science alone. He spent hours in his room reading physics and medical textbooks and listening to classical music, or at the piano composing his own beautiful, frenetic music in minor keys, reminiscent of Iranian musical traditions, the notes warding off the delusions that sometimes took over his mind. That someone had planted a computer chip inside his brain. That he could read other people's thoughts. In fear of what might happen if they let anyone inside the house, my parents closed themselves off from the world: no parties, no holidays, no birthday celebrations. Every time I would visit from Texas, where I'd been living for the past five years, I would stay with my cousin and my aunt. After three years of spiraling downward, hospital stay after hospital stay, he's now at a long-term treatment center a few miles away, and all four of us are slowly coming back to life.

Like a lot of Iranians, we believe that what you're doing at the moment the sun makes its way across the celestial equator sets the tone for the rest of the year. For me, this promise brings with it a measure of anxiety. I turn off my phone and put it somewhere out of reach so that I won't be staring into a screen for those first few seconds of the new year. I laugh for no reason, try not to think negative thoughts, debate whether I should be writing or in the middle of some sort of charitable deed—silly ideas in retrospect. Surely our forebears never intended for us to carefully curate and manufacture the perfect tone. Fortunately, I throw out my ideas in the face of indecision and in the end, the year commences with hugs.

In a photo from our *haft sin* in 1995, my parents and brother and I stand around a similarly long and rectangular table, also draped with a white cloth and decorated with elaborate crystal candleholders, long pink candles, and a bowl of artificial fruit. Back then, we still had a goldfish, a frozen blur of orange trapped inside a bowl. My brother and I stand together between our parents, dressed in our best clothes. My hair poofs in a halo around my head, robust bangs half covering my preteen unibrow. Next to me, my brother's face is defiant and boyish and opaque, his hair is full still and tinted red, and his eyes are clear of the clouds that will later collect behind them. It would be another three years from the time that photo was taken before he'd experience his first breakdown, and an additional ten years would pass before he'd be diagnosed with schizoaffective disorder. But in this photo, those other faces will always enjoy their obliviousness, will always believe that the next revolution of the Earth will bring us only good.

After hugs and exchanges of "*Nowruzet mobarak, nowruzet pirouz*," we pour oversized cups of tea to drink with our chocolates. Dad brings out his set of laminated Hafez cards, stacked inside a shiny black case. One side of each card features an elaborate, romantic painting (most of which, for some reason, include a beautiful woman hugging a forest creature). The other side contains one of Hafez's ghazals. We each take a card from the deck, and it's supposed to reveal our fortune for the year. Though I might pretend otherwise, I want to know what happens next. But what lends Hafez's poetry to fortune-telling—its mystery, its ambiguity—also means that the answer is often unclear. Sure, you can also say this about fortune cookies or horoscopes, but those don't contain literary devices designed with linguistic smoke and mirrors to dance around your attempts to pin down an exact meaning. Despite all this, when I've witnessed *faal-e* Hafez—divination using lines from Hafez poems—before, the person reading the poems has always molded the answer to the question or the wish in such a way that it approximates the experience of a tarot reading. So when I draw a card from the deck, I expect it to temper all the gray areas of my life with some hint of a momentous event in the near future, and I am looking forward to this, despite knowing that the veracity of said fortune is highly questionable. I hand the card to my dad, and he reads it to himself. Then he smiles and looks at me as if it were a winning lottery ticket. "Oh my *Goooood*," he says, grinning. "What?" I ask him, impatient for an explanation. "This is incredible!" He shows the card to my mom, who seems to concur with his conclusion. "I can't believe this," she says. Dad reads the poem aloud in his best Hafez-recitation voice, like someone in a trance. I recognize some of the lines from the classical poetry class I took last spring, in particular one famous couplet from this ghazal describing love troubles and the inherent transience and instability of life. Anyone else reading this poem might have shown a less exuberant response. But my parents are elated. They clap their hands together and say, "Bah, bah," the Persian sound of approval. "It's the very first poem of his divan," my mom tells me, as if this extraneous fact trumps the poem's basic message—that everything is ephemeral, that nothing lasts, that there's no such thing as true security however much we might try to create the illusion of it through love, through shelter, through the outer trappings of success. Later, these lines will provide comfort in that Zen sort of way. But for now, this message is the antithesis of what I want to hear—that the future will bring us stability, that the hospital will help my brother, giving him the life of promise that has seemed so out of reach. My parents' reactions leave me puzzled, searching for clues I might have missed—meanings lost in the constellation of fissures between cultures, between languages. Maybe my parents understand something about the poem that my Westernized mind would never be able to discern. "What does it mean?" I ask my mom. She's still smiling, and my question barely registers. "It's beautiful," she says.

On the Christmas Eve before, my brother stopped taking his medications. He was at the hospital in Irvine and was convinced he'd cured himself with his own thoughts. The psychiatric nurses called my parents in the morning to tell them he'd missed a dose. All afternoon, my father talked to my brother on the phone, trying to persuade him to take his meds. "*Baba joon.* Please, Son," he pleaded, "you need this to get better." After Christmas dinner at my cousin's, my parents and I drove to the hospital to see my brother. On the way there, my father again spoke with him on the phone, repeating the same litany of pleas, losing his temper with the nurses when they told him there was nothing more that could be done. When we got to the hospital, my brother met us in the visiting area, a collection of tables where patients also ate their snacks. Adjacent to the tables, other patients sat on a couch and watched the television flash music videos from the wall. Some patients walked the perimeter of the room, others hovered near us, watching our every move. My brother's eyes were glassy, his thick brown hair stuck straight up, but he looked more lucid than he had in weeks. "I love you, Dad," he said to my father. "Don't worry about anything." Then he got up and left us for his room.

The drawing of Hafez cards continues. My dad selects a new card from the pile, then my mom does the same. My dad reads the first couple of lines of the poem, then sets the card down on the table and recites it from memory. He becomes even more lost in the trance, closing his eyes and moving his head from side to side like a Shirazi Stevie Wonder. For each poem, their reactions repeat in a euphoric refrain: the elation, the grins, the outbursts of enthusiasm. After a few rounds of this unbridled optimism, I leave the table in frustration. I console myself with Trader Joe's chocolates while watching from the couch as my mom picks another card. My dad takes the card from her and when he begins to read the poem, she throws up both her arms and cries, "Hoorah!" This time, I think, there has to be a message, an auspicious sign. I abandon the chocolate and join them again at the table. "What does it mean?" I ask.

In the waiting room outside the psych ward, my mother and I gathered our belongings from the lockers while my father mulled over the words exchanged, the scene with my brother suddenly coming to life. In his tired eyes, I recognized a new kind of happiness, of sated emotional hunger. On the ride home from the hospital, he was lit up and frenzied like someone who had just been visited by the divine. Over and over, he told us the story of what my brother had said to him. "There's a deeper meaning to it," he said. "I know."

My mother looks at me now, still smiling like a triumphant game show contestant. "It's beautiful," she says.

Silkscreen

Omid Fallahazad

Flashing police lights splash blue and red on the walls and windows of our building's entryway. I stay put in the car and try Ra'ana's number again. No response. From where I am parked, I watch the lumbering officer talking into his shoulder mic and buzzing one of the apartments multiple times, but he isn't getting any response either. He gets in his car and drives off, leaving no color behind save for that in the bruised evening sky.

Upstairs, inside our apartment, I deposit the mail on the kitchen counter and snap the lights on. My flared nostrils quickly spot the quartered onion, with its flame-shaped center. I dump it right away. "Onions are sponges," Ra'ana would likely protest later. "They soak up all the viruses from the air."

I, on the other hand, think getting enough sleep would kick that nasty cold out of her system. But she always prefers putting out an onion and guzzling a turmeric drink—her "lollapalooza tea"—and she references the pseudoscientific research done at Harvard on the spice's medicinal miracles. Glasses with yellow residue rings clutter her computer desk next to the stack of blinking hard drives topped with small plates of moldy bread and apple cores. The humidifier runs full blast, and the brown contents of the pot of eucalyptus leaves simmer perpetually on the stove.

As I hang my coat, I see our old briefcase, rummaged through and splayed open on the sofa—her way of looking for things when she needs them. I kneel down on the carpet to collect our documents, which include our Iranian passports and birth certificates, with their official English translations. On impulse, I ruminate over the old photos attached to each document: the younger versions of our faces with deadpan stares; mine, slightly cross-eyed, with my cleft chin, sporting a long-forgotten mustache; hers, pale skin, large Mesopotamian eyes, and an oval face framed in a black *maghnae*—a hood worn as hijab— that, too, a long-forgotten feature. I notice her visa is missing, and so is the copy of our green card application.

I sit still with the briefcase on my lap and listen. I hear a muffled buzzing within the apartment. My phone isn't calling anyone, nor is it vibrating from receiving a call or text. I gingerly walk down the long hallway past Ra'ana's office to the bedroom. I nudge the door open. A strip of light falls on the footboard, which her boot-clad feet are resting upon. She moves her legs like a pair of windshield wipers, motioning me to come in.

"Are you OK?" I ask.

She flashes her face from behind the pillow and then hides it again.

"Hi," a different voice sings from beyond the other side of the bed. I peer over and see a woman sitting cross-legged on the floor. An iPhone illuminates her blushed face and unkempt blonde hair.

"Tammy?"

"Ra'ana had a mishap," Tammy says, batting her eyes. "She's, like, lost her voice, and she might need a few stitches too."

"Her voice?" I put down the briefcase and, sitting on the edge of the bed, turn on the table lamp.

Ra'ana feigns resistance, but I peel off the pillow from her face. Smeared eyeliner makes her look like a charcoal-eyed rag doll. She clenches her teeth while I peel back the bloody bandage to check the small cut under her jaw as tenderly as possible. A few blood drops have stained her collar.

"Tell me it wasn't the police who did it." I reach to unzip her bespattered boots.

"No," Tammy says. "There were these other people . . ."

Ra'ana growls from under the pillow and shuts her up.

I wrestle with the boots, almost falling off the edge of the bed each time one comes off.

"Don't roll over! You'll stain the other side too," I warn her and leave the room to put the boots in the coat closet. As I do so, I hear a soft knock at the door.

"Who is it?"

"Officer McClain from campus police." The uneasy voice seems to be doing its best to sound harmless. "Can I speak with you?"

I turn the brass knob awkwardly, careful not to stain it with my dirty hand.

"Sorry to bother you."

It is the same officer that I saw downstairs at the door. He reads the name off a small spiral notepad, laboring over the pronunciation: "Ra'ana Lotfi?"

"I'm her husband. Is everything OK?"

"I need to ask her a few questions, but nothing to worry about. Is she home?"

"Home? No," I say. "She's probably still on campus."

"I know," he says. "The shenanigans aren't over yet. But you just got home, correct?"

I nod but refrain from saying more.

The officer rips a yellow page from his notepad. "Here's my name and number. If she can stop by my office in person, it'll really make a big difference for her case. The earlier, the better."

I shut the door and rush to the bathroom to wash my trembling hands. For a moment I am transfixed by the streams of pink and brown water interweaving in the porcelain sink. I can hear Ra'ana opening and slamming the chest drawers in the bedroom. When I go to check on her, she is standing in the middle of the room undressed and covered with goosebumps. She has laid some clean clothes on the bed to wear, which, except for the bra, are all items from my wardrobe.

"Why?" I hiss. "Why? Why?" The yellow paper trembles between my fingers.

She snatches the paper and tears it to pieces that fall like twirling yellow flakes and land around her scrawny ankles. Tammy watches us with a tortured expression.

"Put on something else," I say. "You should go and clean up this mess. Tonight."

Ra'ana looks right past me as she adjusts the straps of her bra. I stomp back to the kitchen and stand above the sink full of dirty dishes, the heels of my hands on the counter. Jars are left open here and there. I find their caps, matching them by color or the stickiness of the contents: turmeric, honey, almond butter. It is hopeless, I think. The bread bag is open too, and spilled seeds—sesame, hemp, or flax, or whatever—have covered the stove and filled the gap between the cooktop and counter.

Ra'ana appears from the bedroom, walking with one hand against the wall as if assigned ambulation after surgery. She goes to the bathroom, and Tammy slides onto a high stool at the cluttered counter. "I've never seen her shaken like that," she whispers to me.

I grab three beers from the refrigerator, open and set them on the counter.

"We were all there," Tammy goes on. "I'd say about two hundred, three hundred people, kind of quickly gathering, and . . ."

"Was she holding a sign?" I interrupt her.

"We had a few signs."

"Was *she* holding a sign?"

Tammy gives me a look. We hear the toilet flush.

"Then where the hell did the attackers come from?" I ask. "Were they Trump students or random knuckleheads?"

"No, no." Tammy shakes her head. "They were protesters like us. They were Muslim protesters, all against the travel ban."

"And what? They assaulted Ra'ana out of the blue?"

Ra'ana comes out of the bathroom, glaring at us. The Band-Aid on her jaw, now soaked and darker, matches her skin tone. She climbs onto a stool next to Tammy, facing me. She is wearing one of my company's giveaway blue T-shirts with the picture of a cable drum on it and my old, baggy knee-length shorts. We tried to give away the shorts once, but I recovered them in the nick of time from the plastic bag just before depositing it in the donation box. I feel embarrassed to wear them in front of others, unsure about what that says about me. Even if I am stepping outside to use the garbage chute, I pull a pair of jeans over those shorts. It isn't because of the cheap linen or the frumpy extra-large cut. The American flag print makes me self-conscious. Ra'ana's aunt, a charming, stooped widow, sent me those shorts from Iran, with a tiny box of saffron filaments and a beaded hand fan for her niece. Considering her meager pension and the pinch of humor in her choice of gift, the shorts are too dear to me to discard. But the proliferation of stars and stripes all over the crotch confounds me. I have always marveled at how naturally my Asian and Latino coworkers mount tiny American flags on the roofs of their cars or wear red, white, and blue nail polish for the 4th of July. But the cheap fabric of the shorts, the fake care tag with a blaring logo, and the incorrectly spelled "fredom" printed on the shorts, they all touch me. I imagine an underage, underpaid worker in a moldy screen-print shop in Tehran's sprawling suburb, a boy who holds a squeegee larger than his hand, flashing toxic ink onto to-be-sewn garments, his squinting eyes detecting any bleeding of blue or red. The same hand could have been one of the thousands of raised fists floating over a sea of "Death to America" chants. His eyes could have been a pair of many gleaming eyes reflecting the flames of a burning American flag when his entire school had been bused to attend the anniversary rally marking the capture of the hostages (aka "the nest of spies").

"I'll go with you to the police," I say to Ra'ana.

"Get us something from the fridge first, would you? I can't go on an empty stomach," she says, clearing space on the counter. She instructs me where to find the pairings that she has stashed in the refrigerator-door bins. I put the olives in a saucer and bring a tube of goat cheese and some square-cut *sangak* flatbread. Tammy gets plates, knives, and forks for the three of us.

Punctuated by the clanging of silverware, the two women's telegraphic conversation turns into a subdued evocation of the morning's incident: the contentious crowd, the push and shove on the library steps, the flailing arms and unintended screams. Tammy helps Ra'ana review her interpretation of what constitutes a slap, a punch, or just a touch when consent is not implied. To mask my interest in the story of Ra'ana's fight, I turn on a burner and throw a few frozen falafel in a nonstick pan, snapping the tongs like a bird's bill over the sizzling oil. My heart aches from seeing Ra'ana hurt like this, to think of her being involved in an altercation, and yet I think she is so cruel to dismiss my concerns for her—for us.

From what I gather, there has been a history between Ra'ana's activist group, secular in its DNA, and the other club, a Muslim one. Or maybe more than a history—a rivalry of sorts, a little bit of ill will. Their activism, they both claim, focuses on Middle Eastern issues, but they have criticized and snubbed each other on more than one occasion. The other group has been viewed as "hogging the limelight," but this time, with travel ban rallies bringing widespread attention to campus activists, Ra'ana couldn't stand their verbal abuse anymore.

"'Fuck off!' I told the guy," Ra'ana says. "'You call *me* Islamophobic because I said no to meeting in the mosque? Then I call *you* a misogynist asshole,' I told him in front of everyone."

"You lost it," Tammy says. "You were yelling in his face. Your spit landed on his beard."

"The point is," Ra'ana says, "if in your mosque, men stand in front and women in the back, I have a problem with that. Or if he forces an underage girl to wear hijab to enter a mosque, he is beyond misogynist to me. I told him that."

"I would say," Tammy says, unfurling the goat cheese plastic tube, "his misogyny makes him more of a Trumpist than your distaste for hijab."

"Distaste?" Ra'ana snaps. "It's not just *distaste* for hijab, Tammy. Why don't you get it? Americans are so dumb, even friends like you." Her eyes catch my stern gaze. "And to hell with that police officer," she barks at me. "All they care about is staying out of it. They shit their pants if someone calls them 'Islamophobic.' I'm not going to the police. To hell with it."

"No, Ra'ana," I say. "Get changed, and we'll go right now. That officer wants to help us. Whatever the others accused you of, assault, attack, whatever, Officer McClain wants to help."

Ra'ana slips off the stool, goes to the bedroom, and slams the door shut behind her. Tammy, still aghast from the insult, is over-smoothing a layer of cheese on her *sangak*. I finish my beer and then Ra'ana's, gulping violently. We hear her tapping away at her keyboard in the bedroom.

"Come on, Tammy," I whisper. She doesn't look up. "What if they've caught her on their phones, even a tiny scuffle? She should face the police before it's blown out of proportion."

Tammy looks at me, frowning.

"Who knows what could happen, the way Bannon is running the whole shebang? If Ra'ana doesn't clear her name, they could pressure the school to dismiss her, and then we're screwed. Next thing goes our visa, next thing CBP knocks on our door, instead of Officer McClain, you understand?"

Tammy's expression remains unchanged.

"For us Iranians, it's very different," I say. "Different than for someone like you." I sway my torso nervously but prolong the eye contact with her, hoping she won't misunderstand me or falsely detect sarcasm in my words as an echo of Ra'ana's insult. Iranian vs. American.

"Please," I say, "talk to her before she tweets something self-incriminatory. Or has she already? Just please go talk to her. Tell her I'm waiting."

A few weekends earlier, Tammy had invited us to a postelection gathering at a friend's studio. The friend is a freckled woman whose lucrative commissions mostly come from sculpting life-size figures of black athletes. Ra'ana insisted that we ease the pain of our political discussion by having some therapeutic activity. So the host accommodated us with a mound of clay and a handful of ribboning tools and cutting wires arranged like a futuristic bouquet in a yogurt container. We sat around banging fistfuls of clay on a metal tabletop and fulminating over the election results, FBI director James Comey, and the electoral college.

Gradually, one of the guests, a soft-spoken Egyptian blogger, steered the conversation toward foreign policy. When he quoted

Chomsky, everyone at the table was spellbound. At some point, the blogger turned to Ra'ana and asked her to "enlighten us about your history."

"Our history?" Ra'ana asked. "You mean Iran's history?"

"Tell us about Mossadegh. Tell us how the Iranians felt after the CIA overthrew him."

The more Ra'ana and the blogger bickered civilly over similarities and differences between the Iranian Revolution and the Arab Spring, the more I drank. When they got into discussing movies, arguing about *Argo* and *300*, I left the table. Near an arched window, which let in a flood of sunlight, I slumped tipsily into a velvet chair.

I suddenly felt someone jostle me with an elbow. It was Tammy, sitting sideways on the arm of my chair. "Come on," she said. "Join the conversation."

The other guests were staring down at me.

"What?"

"I was explaining about memory," said Melvin, one of the party guests standing off to the side. "That you can tell a critical event from a lame one by the degree to which people remember its details. You mumbled, 'True.'"

"True."

"Cough it up, bro," he said. "What is tattooed on your brain about the revolution in Iran? Tell us."

"Leave him alone," Ra'ana interjected. I could see her mouthing to Tammy to take away my drink. "We were too young when the revolution happened."

I smirked and rubbed the corners of my eyes. Melvin interlocked his fingers in anticipation, and the others turned quiet. When I spoke, I heard myself sounding reminiscent in tone but starkly different from the suave style of the Egyptian blogger. I described my father as he was a couple of years after the revolution—a young electrician proud of his young family, with a habit of scrupulously maintaining his Volkswagen. Then I talked about our neighbor, Mr. Tavakkol, gray headed and always clean shaven. Whenever we walked past him, my little sister and I always caught a whiff of his aftershave even if it was masked by a puff of his Winston cigarette.

The guests couldn't hear me well. Tammy repeated some of my words louder and with an accent corrective to mine. I went on without raising my voice, and the others shuffled closer, looming over me, walling me in ever more claustrophobically.

I told them about the wintry night when Mr. Tavakkol rang our doorbell late. My mother was helping me with my geometry homework. We could hear the bright exchange of pleasantries quickly fall into grave, whispered tones. After a few minutes, I heard my father saying, "I've got two children, Mr. Tavakkol. I can't. Even one night is too much of a risk." Mr. Tavakkol's hushed voice kept on insisting, and my father kept on rejecting him: "I can't, I can't."

My parents never told me what the old man's request was. But one of the boys at school had heard from his older sister that Mr. Tavakkol's son was a *monafegh*—a dissident—and that the Revolutionary Guard had chased him and captured him after he had jumped off a bridge and broken his leg.

"See, that broken leg made an impression on you," Melvin interjected. "You must have asked yourself, 'Why? Why couldn't my father help his neighbor's son?'"

"But your father *did* help that neighbor," Ra'ana chimed in from across the room. She was wrapping her pinched-rim handiwork. Everybody turned to look at her, but she wouldn't say more. I pulled myself out of the chair and away from the warm bodies brushing against me. I stepped into the shade to finish the story. Blinkless gazes followed me.

The second time Mr. Tavakkol came to our home, it was a few months later, on a quiet summer morning. My sister and I were playing with mud, building a dirt river and dam in our little garden. My father was about to leave for work, but after Mr. Tavakkol spoke to him at our gate, he called his customer and told him, "I can't. Not today." The two men left in my father's Volkswagen van. We could sense something was wrong, the way Mr. Tavakkol drew at his cigarette and ignored our *salams*. My mother didn't answer our questions—it was the grown-ups' business. That afternoon, when my father got home, he pulled inside the yard and closed the gate behind him. He was covered in dust, but not the usual plaster dust of installing fixtures that whitened his nasal hair. He squatted on his heels and told me to hold the hose for him. He washed his hands and face, then took off his boots and socks and rolled up his pants and pulled the hose inside the van. My sister and I peeked inside and saw my father placing his thumb against the hose end, pressure-washing the corrugated floor along the grooves. The spray pushed the pools of water out, and it cascaded like a sheet over the license plate and ran over the hot tiles into the garden to form a braided stream across our mud river and dam. When my father saw us watching him, he told us to go inside. But we had already seen what we had seen: the sheet of water colored the plate pink, and the drops falling from the rear bumper were pink, too.

The other guests remained silent. Was the object of their thoughtful reverence the absent body? Or was it the way my then ten-year-old mind had to stumble upon it based on a bloody license plate? As a young boy, my flights of horror had nothing to do with ghosts or skeletons. The images I saw in the middle of the night were grainy, phantasmagoric pictures of a body lying inside the van while my father followed Mr. Tavakkol to an unmarked burial site. Years later, as an adult, my mind would masochistically leaf through an imaginary photo album of the man's execution, him in a long leg cast being carried on a stretcher to the prison yard at daybreak. They place him on the ground next to the other prisoners who are already lined up against the wall, blindfolded. He has to raise his head to let the guard blindfold him too. The last thing he sees is one of his comrades shifting his weight as if annoyed by the delay, and he hears the older guard, who is assigned to him, discussing with the other guards in the firing squad the unusual angle that he has to aim at to fire. A young guard volunteers to switch places with the older guard, and soon everything is quiet. Everything proceeds like normal.

Tammy comes out of the bedroom, expressionless. As disoriented as that memory always makes me feel, it has made me certain of one thing: during times of unrest, there is always a point of no return to any decision. There is a trigger mechanism of sorts that exacts one's fate unless the sequence is interrupted in time.

I walk to the bedroom door and shove it open with my shoulder. Ra'ana turns around in her swivel chair, alarmed. The large computer monitor behind her shows a headshot of a young woman wearing a veil made of the American flag.

"What are you up to?" I ask her as I squint to read what she has posted in the comments box below the picture: "Inviting the administration and the dean to wear hijab in solidarity with those students and professors affected by the new travel ban is not a non-event. Far from promising, it is an invasive act that undermines women's struggles in many places, including in my homeland of Iran, in which hijab is imposed on women and is a form of oppression."

In one quick move, I sweep the keyboard and mouse off the table, sending them flying to the corner of the room. I pull Ra'ana out of her chair and into the hallway. Tammy screams, and I feel as if my blood is boiling inside my head. I snatch Ra'ana's purse from the table and grab my own long coat to drape over her shoulder before opening the door.

Waiting for the elevator, I reach inside her purse and find her phone, dead. And there is a copy of our green card application there, folded.

"What did you plan to do with this?" I ask. "It's like everything's a prop for your protest, huh? Were you going to shred our legal papers in public to prove that you're protesting? Or maybe you want to burn this in front of the reporters like Gandhi burned his British passport?"

"If you push or grab her one more time," Tammy warns me, approaching us in the hallway. She follows us into the elevator.

"What?" I laugh. "You'll call the police?"

"Stop it, Tammy," Ra'ana tells her.

Tammy stays quiet during the elevator ride and the walk to my car. I keep on fuming, patchily referring to the sacrifices Ra'ana and I had to make during our first few years in the United States—the loneliness, the emotional deprivation that we weathered before we could find any friends.

I open the passenger door for Ra'ana, but she jerks her elbow out of my hand and says, "I can't go like this." I look at her. Even if the long coat were buttoned, you could still see the American flag shorts. She starts back toward the entrance to our building. I grab her by the elbow again.

"Let her go," Tammy warns, "or I call the police."

Ra'ana gently frees her arm.

"Five minutes, Ra'ana," I say, and then to Tammy, who is glaring at us, "What?"

Tammy clenches her phone in her fist. In the unmatched lighting of the parking area, our elongated shadows crisscross. I tuck Ra'ana's purse under my arm.

"Do I really care if someone decides to protest using a hijab?" I say with a checked vehemence. "I honestly don't give a damn. And Ra'ana shouldn't either. That's irresponsible of her if it costs us her degree. If the school deems her a troublemaker and drops her from the program, Immigration will reject our application too, and then we're finished. You understand? They deport us. None of you liberal friends would move a finger to help us if she's labeled Islamophobic. We'd be banished."

The "liberal friends" comes out with a nasty tone.

"Ra'ana doesn't have to put up with the way you treat her," she says. "She hates wearing hijab, but then she lets you drag her like that out of her room and force her to do something she doesn't want to do. She told you that she doesn't want to go to the police. She obviously needs help."

I smirk as I head back toward the entrance.

"Where are you going?" she asks.

"To help my wife," I say.

Upstairs, the warm air of the dimly lit apartment carries the din of a crowd played on a computer speaker. It is coming from the bedroom. Ra'ana is sitting in front of the computer with the wireless keyboard and mouse reactivated, the coat still draped around her shoulders.

I stand in the doorframe and watch the jumpy footage with her. It is a mishmash of cheers and camera jolts until the handheld device steadies and frames a crowd in front of the campus library. People spill down the steps to make room for the speakers. A lanky bearded man, slightly stooped and with one hand casually in his pocket, addresses the protesters with a megaphone. He is generous in his use of the word *inshallah*—if Allah wills.

"That's her," Ra'ana says under her breath.

"Who?" I ask. "The man that you assaulted?"

"No, *her*," she says, pointing at a woman next to the lanky man. "The dean."

Students rattle their keychains and throw their water bottles up in the air. Their gazes and attentive gestures converge on the formally dressed woman, who has clambered up on a table with the help of the students and now gives them a thumbs-up.

"Who cares about the dean, Ra'ana," I say. "Tell me where to find the guy. He's the one who has gone to the police. Tell me how we can turn him around . . ."

"Shush!"

I keep watching with her: like an improvised bucket brigade, students are passing along a large American flag until it reaches the dean. They help her to drape it around her head and neck like a scarf, correcting her until her makeshift hijab is perfect. Their cheering and clapping wane and glowing phone screens mushroom all over the place, but whoever was streaming the video stops recording.

"OK," I say. "You tell me then, what do we do if we're not going to the police?"

"That man," Ra'ana says, "he's got the dean on his side. I was the one who talked her into it, to put out the statement."

"What statement?"

"That the school won't comply with the travel ban, which ironically will benefit someone like you, who thinks protesting is absurd."

I bite my tongue. Her eyes remain glued to the picture of the crowd and the placards that have popped up in the jungle of phone screens. I think about those students, those kids who are holding up the signs. What have their lives been like? For them, the biggest change after finishing high school and starting college may have been what they see through their windows when they get up in the morning. They may have simply swapped one well-manicured lawn for another: the front lawn of their parents' home with the lawn on their campus quad. What next? Maybe feeling homesick for a couple of weeks, until they stumble upon a crush-worthy liberal professor. The professor deliberately or unwittingly trifles with their emotions. The professor gives out custom-made activist wristbands. By their second term, they are the professor's acolyte, following him or her from one event to another to make history. Their fervor, I want to tell Ra'ana, sickens me. It reminds me of a fifth-grade classmate of mine in Iran and his zeal for martyrdom. One day he showed up at a make-shift recruitment center and when they asked him for his birth certificate, he showed them an altered photocopy. He swore on the Koran so vehemently that they believed his lies about his age. They enlisted him as a kitchen worker, but he ended up sneaking to the front lines. They said when he marched as a soldier with a Kalashnikov slung over his shoulder, the muzzle left a track in the earth—that's how small he was. There were stories about child soldiers walking single file into the minefield, stories about RPG shooters who cut their brake cables so they could go kamikaze with their motorcycles on Iraqi tanks during the Iran-Iraq War. Why shouldn't I be skeptical this time? Ra'ana's altercation on the library steps has left a cut on her chin and brought cops to our door.

"Help me change," she says.

The door buzzer goes off, unremitting and rude, but we pretend we haven't heard it. I take the coat. The American flag shorts drop to her ankles, and she lifts one leg at a time for me to pull them off. She tells me to pick a pair of jeans from the overflowing laundry basket. I kneel down and hold the jeans for her to put her legs in them.

"I'm not going to beg anyone," she says.

"If we have to . . ."

"Don't expect me to beg," she cuts me off.

"Then I'll do the begging."

We have both grown stiff and agitated. A loud knock rattles the apartment door.

"Open up, please," a man's voice booms. "It's the police."

I spring up, and Ra'ana loses her balance and falls on the bed face down as if tackled.

"What happened?" I cry out.

The cut on her chin is bleeding now. I want to fix the bandage, but she pushes me off. I rush to open the door.

"Officer McClain?"

Before he can say anything, Tammy shimmies between us and runs to the bedroom. McClain steps in and positions himself between me and the corridor to the bedroom.

"Just to be clear," he says, "I received a call regarding domestic violence, so we have to follow a certain protocol."

The shorts are slung over my shoulder. Flabbergasted, I bunch them in my hand like a bartender's towel and nervously clean my fingertip and the blood-stained doorknob. My answers to his questions are monosyllabic. I avoid eye contact, but I can see his bulged reflection in the polished brass of the doorknob, his hand resting on his holstered handgun. The two women emerge from the bedroom. McClain introduces himself to Ra'ana and asks her if she feels safe.

"I'm safe," she says, "but not because you're here."

"Excuse me?"

"I'm much safer here than I am outside," she says. "The cut on my chin is from this morning, from outside."

"Your voice, too?"

"That too."

"Well Ms.," McClain says. "I came here an hour ago, and your husband told me you weren't home. Not true, though, as I found out." He vaguely points at Tammy. "Can we please speak in private?"

I offer to step outside, but McClain wants me to stay. I throw my arms in the air, then take a seat on one of the kitchen stools. The three of them step into Ra'ana's office. I wonder how Tammy's presence seems not to be an issue for the officer. I eavesdrop over the dishwasher's hum.

Their conversation about the morning incident quickly turns technical. Tammy keeps offering solutions, but Officer McClain dismisses her with "Yeah, buts." He explains that an occurrence witness won't work because the accuser can outweigh Ra'ana's with his own witnesses.

"It is very difficult to drop an assault charge," he says. "But if you obtain a sworn statement from the quote-unquote victim to correct what he has said before, well, that would certainly help. The sooner the better."

Ra'ana's words are indistinct.

"That would be very tactful of you," McClain says. "Very diplomatic. If you think that the dean is willing to mediate between you and him, that'll make a world of difference."

I don't want to listen anymore. I leave the apartment and take the elevator downstairs.

Officer McClain's car is parked alongside the curb. I walk to my car and reach in and grab a cigarette from the glove compartment. I spin-flick the lighter and light the cigarette. The puff of smoke rises into the overcast sky.

I wish I had the power to holographically evoke our past for Tammy and McClain, or even to project a hazy footage of it on the facade of the campus library so they could all see, friends and foes. As much as they have grown tired of hearing about my past and its predicaments, I want them to see this memory—to see both of us, Ra'ana and I, young-faced college freshmen, sneaking out of our respective single-sex dorms in Tehran one day, butterflies in our stomachs. It is a pleasant day, with a blue sky. Blooming wayside shrubs are dripping from having recently been watered by park workers. The park regulars, retired old-timers, are arriving one by one, cheerful and chatty. A brightly dressed couple, engaged or newly wed, is snacking on sunflower seeds in a paper cone. Ra'ana walks along the edge of the fountain, making the bathing sparrows dart off. She thought a public rendezvous would be the safest—the easiest situation in which to prove our innocence in case we were caught. Her hand-knitted headscarf is meticulously beaded, sparkling in the sunlight. When I tell her about my ear-cleaning OCD, she can't control her laughter. She laughs a little louder than our whisper, a little louder than the *plop* sound of the tiny pebbles I throw into the water, a little louder than the ripples slapping softly against the fountain wall. That is enough to bring a group of plain-shirted Basijis right to our foot, like summoned spirits. And there, Ra'ana is not tactful, not diplomatic at all. She could pull her scarf farther forward and tuck her hair under it better. She could cast her eyes down as I do and repeat my words, saying that we are sorry for "being a disgrace to our martyrs' blood." Instead, she snaps at them. They make me sit on the ground with my back to her. I listen to her wrangling with them. I can't turn. They have the youngest member of their group, a teenage boy, holding a Kalashnikov pointed at my sideburn. The more they tell her to shut up and cover her hair, the more she yells back at them. She screams obscenities, blasphemies. I stare sideways at the worn muzzle and listen to their struggle. Her voice turns to a groan, but soon the groan is muted. The only sound is from the men, short of breath, fuming and spewing expletives.

When they finally leave, they dart off in different directions like a gang of petty criminals. I want to help Ra'ana, but her eyes beg me not to, as if pulling out the bunched beaded scarf from her bleeding mouth is going to be a slow labor, best to be left to her wounded throat and scraped palate to regulate it, one bead at a time. She wears the same bloody scarf to the emergency room.

And here she is again, now, meditatively coming down the steps in front of our building with an air of inner pain, like that day in the park in Tehran. Officer McClain approaches his car and gets the door for her and Tammy. But Ra'ana walks toward me first.

"Isn't this what you want?" she says. "To clean up the mess?"

I drop my cigarette and step on it. "I'll follow you in my car."

"What for?" she says and goes back to join them.

The three of them get into the police car. Officer McClain waves as he drives by. The flashing blue and red lights become evanescent from every surface surrounding me. I sit in my car and start the engine.

Hookah, Once upon a Time

Poupeh Missaghi

It is Saturday night in Rockville, Maryland, at Z's place. Z sent an email a week ago inviting everyone for a night of wine, kebab, hookah, and poetry reading. The wood is burning in the fireplace. B is smoking a cigarette on the balcony. Z is making tea in the kitchen. M is in the kitchen too, busy preparing the hookah, putting in the tobacco, just brought by A's brother from Saudi Arabia (he was there on a business trip), bought in a local bazaar, mint-flavored—not artificially but with fresh mint leaves. The scent already fills the air in the kitchen. The charcoal is burning on the stove. B finishes his cigarette and walks in, closing the sliding door behind him. He turns to A and asks whether he remembers K. A says of course and takes a sip of his wine.

We had such a great night together, unforgettable, that night we spent in the prison cell, my last summer in Tehran before I moved, A says. We were all at a party at H's, pretty drunk. Poor K. He was at another party and we called him, insisting that he join us. He said he might not come, and we said no, you should. He came and only fifteen minutes after he arrived, the morality police came. They took us all. Ten guys and eight girls. I have never laughed so hard in my whole life. We just took the party to the prison. We made jokes. We played games. All night long. We recounted memories from childhood and school and girls. We made friends with the prison guard and sent him out to buy us cigarettes. The girls had not taken it so easily, we found out later on. Their cell had been on the other side of the hallway. They had become touchy and snappy. The female guards had not been nice to them. The blankets had not been clean enough. They were so mad at us when they saw us in a good mood in court the day after. What a night.

N remembers the night. I can't forget my dad's face when he entered the police station the morning after. He had never set foot in such places, to put it in his own words. He was acting as if he were in charge of himself. And of everything else. But the way he talked, I could see how nervous he was. Poor guy. So unlike K's father. He joked his way around with the officers. T's mom was hysterical, crying, shouting, you don't have the right to put my girl in there, you can't, and the officer gave her a look, a distant cold reproachful look, and said we do, we can, she was drunk, wearing inappropriate clothing, hanging out with guys, dancing, drinking, and if you don't calm down, I will have you thrown out of the station. She sat there and didn't say another word for the whole court session. It was fun seeing her like that. The way she had always been hard on T. The woman could not let go of her discipline. T had by then been living on her own in London for a few years, getting some kind of degree. Back in town, she was thinking of maybe moving back to Tehran because she was not feeling quite at home in London. She had even started looking for jobs. That night in prison and her mom's cries pushed her to make up her mind and return to London. From then on, she just came back for short visits.

I think the first time I came face to face with the morality police was at your wedding ceremony, B says, addressing C, but of course they did not take us that night. Z hands C a cup of tea and asks her to tell the story. As the bride and groom we were permitted to go home, because nothing should have interrupted our first night of wedlock. They took our parents and a few of the guests, because of the sinful party that the ceremony was, but let them go after a few hours, C explains. B continues, I remember I was so drunk that by the time I realized the police were there and looked for my girlfriend to warn her, everyone was already aware of the situation, trying to find a way out. She shoved a cucumber in my mouth and then forced me to smoke the cigarette she had just lit, but with all the drinks I had had, I doubt any of that did anything to help hide the scent of alcohol on my breath. She had one of the tablecloths wrapped around her to cover up her bare legs and shoulders. I don't remember much else.

How she left or how I ended up waking up the next morning behind a car in the rear end of the parking lot.

M comes out with the hookah and puts it on the floor, on a tray next to the fireplace. C takes a couple of cushions and arranges them on the carpet and sits down on the floor, waiting for M to hand her the hookah. B puts a dish of sweets and a bowl of pistachios on the tray and sits down.

What about K? A asks.

Nothing, I just found him on Facebook today, B says.

For me the most absurd confrontation with the police was on election day, the first time Khatami ran for president, N says. How long ago was it? N wonders out loud. Don't even count, C says. N continues, pouring more wine into his glass. They arrested us just as we turned from our alley into the main street. Me and two of my friends. They stopped us at a checkpoint on the pretext of our music being too loud in the car and made us wait, for almost two hours. The officers busied themselves with one thing or another to kill time as we waited in the police van. By the time they sent us to the station, and by the time our parents came and brought us out, there was just half an hour left to the closing hour of the polls. We rushed to the nearest polling station. The mosque was just two buildings away. The guys waiting in line in front of us were the officers who had stopped us at the checkpoint. We threw in our ballots one after another.

Z offers another round of tea. She goes out of the room and comes back with a couple of poetry books from her library. She puts them next to the dish of sweets. She sits down and reclines on the cushions.

C takes the hookah from M. M never hands it around willingly. C takes in a deep puff. She exhales. Mint-scented smoke rises above the fireplace.

... X was arrested making out with his girlfriend in a dark corner of the Caspian Sea beach and condemned to twenty lashes. The girlfriend was freed by her father's intervention and a fine.

... X was arrested in the fruit market because she was wearing sandals showing off her feet and red toenail polish. She spent an hour in the police van, three hours at the police station, and was freed by paying a fine and signing a letter of repentance.

. . . X was arrested with three of his friends on their way to their country house for the weekend because one of the guys had had two prostitutes drive there to meet up with them, and the girls had been stopped and had talked a little too much. X's car was stopped half an hour after the girls'. The guys spent three days in a prison cell in a little town on the road. Each received twenty-five lashes and paid a fine.

. . . X was arrested along with several other female activists during a protest to collect signatures demanding changes in family laws. Nobody knew of her whereabouts for a few days. X spent a few months in prison.

. . . X was arrested a few nights before a student protest in front of the city university. X was one of the main organizers. The government canceled the protest for security reasons.

C hands the hookah to B. M asks if anyone wants more tea. The fire continues to burn in the fireplace. Z asks whether they are going to read any poetry tonight.

Think of the Trees

Leila Emery

> Think of the rain licking up
> its dirt. Think of what it means
> to be clean. A girl, swallowed
> whole in the word *should*,
> the moon settling her shoulders
> like milk. A tide pool, brimming
> with light. Think of the deer,
> the men. Think of the way this
> was never skin.
>
> Emily Zhang, "Exorcism"

"Have you been saved by Jesus, honey? Or are you one of those Muslims?"

How to respond to pretty, blonde mothers with southern accents dripping with genteel honey? At ten, I knew nothing about Muslims. In our house, Jesus didn't dominate, but Sunday school had taught me that God was kind. That He was good. That He was forgiving.

When I asked my mother what it meant to be Muslim, she spoke not of prayers but of symbols. The times when she would leave her home in Tehran to visit the Caspian Sea or to travel back to school in England after being on Christmas holiday, her father, my *bababozorg*, would hold a Koran over her head for protection. For safe passage. But the Koran didn't make other appearances, either in our home or in her stories.

The best stories were about warm summer nights in Tehran spent sleeping on rooftops under a star-scattered canopy. Tea the color of almonds, always at the ready, poured from a samovar into clear glass cups, to be savored with the eyes as much as with the mouth. Lazy springtime picnics during Nowruz—the fruit so luxuriant on the trees that it resembled jewels ready to be plucked. Her voice, wistful and soft, would inevitably trail off, envisioning that time as though speaking of a fairy tale. Those trees. Always the fruit. These images were her refuge—a moment in time she could escape to. The time *before*.

In the subsequent years, the othering of my identity by my classmates formed a hard carapace around me, toughened more intensely by my projecting a slightly fraudulent image of myself. That new girl with the dark hair—where is she *from*? I could have been "from" anywhere. Was there power in that?

There was a boy who also could have been "from anywhere." A fellow chameleon, his hair shone like black gold under the football lights and he strode through the halls with undeniable swagger. Confidence was its own kind of carapace, and I envied his. Walking hand in hand with me through an abandoned park, the long fingers of fading afternoon light streaming through the trees, he would whisper, "My Persian princess," his wry smirk easily mistaken for a smile.

Under the pretext of meeting his family and sampling his mom's famed rice—"Don't your people like that kind of thing?," he'd tease—I skipped ballet rehearsal and rode to his house in his candy-red car, hoping I could leave before my parents discovered I wasn't where I was supposed to be. Entering through the front door, I was hit by the overwhelming stench of stale beer. No family. No welcoming hugs. Only the cacophony of dogs barking from somewhere behind the house. "Can't we just talk?" No. Instead, the blanket with the sandpaper texture, the smother of cigarette breath, the echoes of "You'd better pray" ringing in my ears. I closed my eyes and tried to find God in the darkness, but it was too late. No version of "no" could save me.

In the time after, the Persian Princess moniker became a dreaded shadow, creeping up behind me in the cafeteria, running alongside me in gym class, always followed by shrieks of hilarity from my classmates. From former friends. From *him*. Even their hands were laughing. They *knew*, and now my mystery, my otherness, my shame had converged. I was hated, and I now had a name and a story beyond my control.

Although home was a refuge where those echoes couldn't reach, and despite knowing that my parents wouldn't react with anything other than compassion, I nevertheless decided to keep what had happened from them. Retreating to my room, I'd sleep for hours, willing myself to wake up and be someone—anyone—else. Sensing that my somnolence was a sign of something more than just typical teenage sleepiness, my mother would stroke my hair lovingly. "This too shall pass." She'd tell me of the times when she, too, had wanted to be somewhere else. A different time. Another life. "I'd think of those trees," she'd say. "Think of the trees. The fruit."

A friend—a fellow outcast—invited me to her church. She seemed to be happier than I was, or at least more comfortable in her own skin, so I accepted the invitation. The youth pastor had a kind face and gentle voice, and when he told us to close our eyes and ask ourselves whether we were happy with who we were, to closely examine whether we wanted to be better—to be *good*—I raised my hand. I was not happy. I was not good. I did need saving. In his office later that evening, he said that Jesus could fix me if I would accept Him. The pastor's voice had hardened, and I began to wonder if I had slipped into an identity not my own. But wanting so desperately to believe, to be *pure of heart*, to be OK with my reflection in the mirror, I grabbed hold of what I thought was salvation.

As my parents and I sat down to dinner one night, the youth pastor came by the house unexpectedly. We invited him inside, and my mother filled his plate with Persian rice and pomegranate *khoresht*, happily giving him second and third helpings. Between several glasses of wine, his silver tongue painted a picture of an all-American upbringing. The parades. The baseball games. His debutante mother. Was this meant to impress us? Intimidate us? When I walked him to his car, the pastor's voice again had an edge to it. "I didn't realize you were part Iranian. I didn't know. You looked like you could be from anywhere." I was told that it was best if I not return to church. I couldn't be saved.

My mother's stories from her childhood in Iran are idyllic, especially these days. For her, that carefree time, that country such as it was, no longer exists. I have clung to her stories my whole life as though they were my own. I have tried to discover parts of myself within them, hoping that in doing so, I could find out how to *be*—all the pieces finally joined, a pomegranate puzzle. Instead, when those shadows— those ugly echoes and their accompanying violences—find me again, I think of the mirror on our Nowruz *haft sin* shining brightly on my mother's face as she smiles down at me, ready to welcome a new year with small, cloud-like cookies. I think of the Persian I'm starting to learn after all these years, the weave of its lyrical curves around my ears like the curl of a cat's tail—soft, nearly imperceptible. And I think of sitting on Persian carpets given to us by my *bababozorg*, their reds and browns slightly faded, as I wait for stories of jumping over fire.

Pushing the Boundaries

Dena Rod

"*Yekee bood, yekee nabood. Gheraz Khodah, heech-cast nabood.*" That's how you begin children's stories in Persian. "There was one, there was no one. Besides God, there was no one else." Despite its religious connotations and my parents' unfavorable stance on Islam, that's how they would tell me fairy tales when I was young. But this story is no fairy tale, which is why it begins a bit differently.

Being part of the first generation of Iranians born in America, there's a constant battle for me between fully embracing American culture and holding onto Iranian culture. Is there an innate way to be Iranian? Is it in how you dance? Is it in the way you speak? Is it in not knowing how to cook rice other than in a rice cooker? Or is it in loving another girl with all your heart? And can you still be Iranian if you're queer?

I'm twelve, and Chloe keeps insisting on holding my hand during gym class. I don't know why, but I like the way our tactile comfort makes everyone around us ask if we're dating. She says no, but her holding my hand makes me happy. I stare at her in class, noticing how the sunlight shines in her light brown hair, and I realize that I'm in love with a girl. This feels different because I've always liked boys. This difference is compounded by the fact that I'm fatter, hairier, and browner than my middle school classmates, so I'm already uncomfortable in my own skin. Liking girls is just another nail in the coffin that is my lack of social capital in middle school. I don't need another characteristic marking me as different.

At the Harvest Festival that fall, I "marry" a different girl at the "wedding booth." It's Katie, a blonde girl from a large Catholic family. Somehow we both ended up without boys to marry. Fancying ourselves budding feminists, we decide to marry one another. We exchange cheap rings that the school provides, and I tell myself that my racing heart has more to do with the sugary kettle corn I've eaten than the idea that maybe marrying a girl would be much nicer than marrying a boy.

I tell my best friend, Ana, that I have a crush on another girl, Chloe, because you tell your best friend about your crushes in middle school. She tells me my feelings are a sin against God and that I'm going to hell. Somehow we remain friends, and I don't tell anyone else about liking girls as much as boys until I'm nineteen years old and a sophomore at San Francisco State University.

"I'm bisexual," I told my mom on July 31, 2009. It was Harry Potter's birthday. I had picked that day to come out to my parents because it felt right to do it on a date that had always given me comfort. I had just come back to town from college, and I had built up this weekend as The Weekend I Am Going to Come Out! It was going to be hard but ultimately fine, I told myself. I wanted to tell both my parents in person. My dad, however, had other plans and decided to go to a poker game with family friends.

My mother plied me with basmati rice topped with saffron and *khoresht sabzi*, a thick herb-based stew accompanied by *sabzi khordan*, sweet fragrant herbs. Afterward, she suggested a walk. I wanted to wait for my dad to come back so I could tell them both, just as I had planned, but I couldn't keep my secret in any longer. After dating women the past year in the wake of an epic breakup from my high school (male) sweetheart, I found that the words bubbling in my throat couldn't wait any longer and spilled forth.

"I finally realized that I've always had these feelings inside, and I'm just now starting to believe that it's OK and I don't want to hide from you anymore," I said, staring straight ahead but unable to look her in the eye as we walked down a trail near our house.

"But it's not OK," my mother replied.

These four words crushed me. With these four words, in the

landscape of my mind, my mom seemingly transformed into all those "Yes on Prop 8" voters (even though she'd voted "no"). I lost it. I took her to task for her homophobia, and, leaving a wake of devastation behind me, I ran away from the trail and past my house on Esther Drive. My friend Courtney, my first-kiss-turned-best-friend, picked me up in the parking lot of Navlet's plant nursery down the street. I stayed at her house that evening while she practiced for her flute recital, and her mom made me lavender mint tea in a chipped opaque mug, so different from the clear glass cups Persian tea is served in. I'd known Courtney and her family since she and I were eight, and it felt fitting that this was where I ended up, in the arms of soft, suburban whiteness.

The fear of every worst-case scenario being realized coursed through my body. My cell phone would be cut from the family plan. All my soccer trophies, swim ribbons, prom dresses, and yearbooks would be tossed in the trash. I wouldn't be able come back to our house for school breaks. I would be estranged from the rest of my extended family. Indignation then began to intermingle with fear. Didn't my parents move to the United States so that their children could live a life of freedom? Didn't that include the freedom to love anyone I wanted? For me to become anyone I wanted to be? For me to become the person I *couldn't be* under the thumb of Islamic fundamentalism?

I went back to the house later that night, and my dad was waiting for me on the couch in the dark. My mom had called him and told him the news. He'd left the poker game early to deal with this turn of events.

"I don't care about your being bisexual," he said. He explained that he cared more about how I'd treated my mom. I apologized profusely, and we never really spoke about my sexuality again until I started dating a girl from Texas named Diana. But a chasm had formed between us. My sexuality felt tolerated rather than embraced—just another one of the differences between my parents and me.

Coming out is not a singular process. Ever. You can never do it just once, because with heteronormativity, everyone assumes you to be straight. Coming out to my mom in 2009 was only the beginning.

Since then, I have constantly come out about my queerness to strangers on the street, or cashiers taking my coffee order when I'm holding my wife's hand, or, before I was married, when I first met people and they assumed the fiancée I spoke of was male. Now, it's always an act of coming out when I say "my wife," and there is no misunderstanding anymore about the differences between *girlfriend* and *fiancée*.

This protracted coming out also translates to my extended Iranian family. I remember constantly checking in with my parents about which "aunts" and "uncles" I could be honest with. They're not actually related to me by blood. When my parents first immigrated to America in the early 1980s, fresh off the heels of the Islamic Revolution in Iran, they had each heard about the thriving Persian expat community in Northern California. When they met at a wedding in Oakland in 1986, their individual journeys converged. Settling here in California, they imported a desire to belong to the type of community an Iranian village had provided for them back home. These women and men raised me and looked after me as I grew up, gave me advice when my parents couldn't, and tried to prevent any boys from breaking my heart.

Introducing Diana to my parents felt like coming out all over again. My palms were so sweaty I couldn't even hold her hand. We were at a barbeque held at the house I'd grown up in, where my dad was grilling *jujeh* kebab. There weren't very many of my Iranian aunts and uncles there, mostly white work friends of my father's. Even so, I felt like I couldn't be affectionate with Diana in front of them. I recall looking longingly at the other partygoers, who were effortlessly showing affection to their significant others. I've now been with her for nearly a decade, so these days, I don't hesitate to reach for Diana's hand in front of my parents. However, I sometimes think about what the social and political consequences would be if I were to reach for her hand walking down the streets of Tehran.

"Does *Amu* Mehdi know?" I asked my father once about one of my "uncles" unrelated by blood but knit into our family by distance and circumstance. "Does Aria? Does Khosroh?" Persians like to talk. Even though I didn't speak with my extended family often and knew that they were too polite to say anything to my face, they likely already knew this piece of family gossip and had said something to my parents. They were more proficient in Farsi than I was, and with my American accent being the family joke (I spoke Farsi "like a Turk," my dad said the time I tried to say *sofreh aghd*—the wedding altar set up in front of a bride and groom—with its hard *gh* sound not found in English), my communication with my extended family had all but ceased because of my discomfort with the language and lack of understanding of what my family was saying around me.

"*Amu* Mehdi knows, Khosroh knows, Aria knows . . ." My dad rattled off a list of my entire extended family in Northern California. A prickly hot-cold feeling came over me. The only person I'd taken the time to tell directly about my bisexuality was Uncle Rasool, who embraced me with open arms and understood completely. The reality that my entire family knew about me and Diana without my consent felt terrifying, but surely nothing was amiss since my dad said all of this so nonchalantly.

"It's a different country, a different culture," he said. "We have to adapt."

This sentiment made me want to protest. I would've been just as queer growing up in Iran, albeit much more closeted. My bisexuality wasn't an American influence—it was part of me that would've been the same in Tehran or San Francisco.

Yet my father's words sowed seeds of doubt. Adaptation can also feel like assimilation, especially when it comes to growing up in America. At times, it feels like my relationship with Diana is proof of how far I've strayed; here I am married to a white woman from Texas whose heritage is as middle-America as you can possibly get. Would I have these same feelings if I had been born and raised in Iran? Would my queerness have spurred me to leave the country, as my parents' political beliefs had them? Tracing these threads sometimes seemed as if it could unravel my sense of being Iranian, especially when my dad would "reassure" me that I was a child of America, not of Iran. However, if that were true, the diaspora wouldn't be calling me as it does now.

Diana proposed to me on the top of Twin Peaks. It was May 13, 2014, one of those rare hot days in San Francisco that makes everyone lose their minds and go out for ice cream. The entire city sprawled below us, with nary a cloud in the sky above as she asked to me to marry her. The only clouds that day were those in my head, as I kept wondering how I was going to tell my parents.

The anxiety I'd felt about coming out to my parents was nothing compared to how I felt about telling them that I was going to marry a woman. But after five years of getting to know Diana, my parents supported me, loved me, and congratulated me when I told them the news. The chasm regarding my sexuality felt smaller than it had in years. As I debuted my engagement ring on Christmas—seven months after we had actually gotten engaged—my dad asked me why I looked so scared. "All right, congratulations," he said, a smile crinkling his eyes in a way I couldn't read.

The fact that I don't know how to have an Iranian same-sex wedding poses a challenge. Despite getting married at San Francisco's City Hall weeks after the 2016 presidential election, I still want a full Iranian wedding ceremony. Our wedding was small and planned in only ten days, as we literally ran to the altar to protect ourselves from the upcoming onslaught of the Trump administration. From my Iranian family, only my parents were in attendance. For reasons unknown to me to this day, my mother said she didn't know whether she would come to the ceremony. After all, getting married is often seen as the most important event in an Iranian woman's life.

Nevertheless, after two years of marriage, I still want to sit on a bench in front of a *sofreh aghd* as our closest family members grind sweet sugar-cone snowflakes over the canopy above our heads. The rituals, the food, the vows—I still yearn to partake in this tradition even though I have discarded so many others in the name of assimilation.

The consequences for being openly queer are dire in Iran, where homosexuality is punishable by death. I have never been to Iran, but I feel an intense need to go despite my misgivings. Yet with every word I write, the possibility grows slimmer and slimmer. My parents have always discouraged me, telling me to go anywhere else on earth. "Go to Dubai, go to India, fuck, even go to the Emirates, just don't go to Iran," my dad always says. The sentiment is understandable, as they can't accompany me if I go, so they'd be helpless to assist me if anything untoward were to happen. Yet I can't deny my desire to see Shiraz, the town my dad grew up in, and Abadan, where my mother grew up. I need to see the ruins of Persepolis and Dena, the highest peak of the Zagros Mountains, which I'm named after. But how am I supposed to travel to the villages where my parents grew up, in a country I've never been to, and not bring my wife? How could we take such a life-affirming journey together and not display any affection toward one another?

Homosexuality is an open secret in Iranian society, told in whispers rather than in marched parades. Discovering my queerness has taken place against a backdrop of American protests, the legacy of the Stonewall riots begun by transgender people of color in New York City, and efforts to claim queer identity "loud and proud." Among Iranians, those of us who come out despite our family's wishes for a glass-closeted existence are seen as rocking the boat, advised not to tell anyone outside a small circle. Uncle Rasool always encouraged me to speak openly about Diana to the rest of my extended family. He was the only one who insisted on meeting her when he came back to California to visit from North Carolina. "You need to be public about this," he advised. "We're in America. There should be no more living in shame."

But will my decision to live a more authentic life prevent me from seeing Iran? I don't know whether my extended family still living there knows about my queerness. How could I ask them to sponsor a visa for myself and my wife, knowing it might put them in danger with the Iranian government? How could I properly see the country with a state-mandated tour guide watching our every move? Would having a white woman accompanying me prevent access to spaces that I would otherwise be able to enter?

I'm constantly navigating what it means to be queer and Iranian and American. Since the 2015 US Supreme Court decision declaring same-sex marriage a right in all fifty states, I've found that LGBTQ rights are often seen as a Western import to the rest of the world. At times, Iranians see queerness itself as a colonizing force, and those in other Middle Eastern cultures resist acknowledging same-sex attraction. Coming out is only one way I have combated this cultural assumption. It's difficult that this is seen as a militant challenge to the status quo, when really it's just me being myself and not wanting to be inauthentic as people get to know me. I've often had closeted cousins ask me how I do it. I'm at a loss for an answer. I don't know any other way to be *me*. Just being myself is seen as a radical act.

Traditionally, Iran's condemnation of homosexuality has focused on male homosexuality. The erasure of women from Iranian society extends to homosexuality. Defining my own Iranianness against this background is an "up a San Francisco hill" battle. Even in San Francisco, many of the Iranian queer groups are overrun by the patriarchal forces present in the Castro, which is predominantly cis, white, and male. As a queer woman of color, I have waited hours to get served a drink at the popular dance clubs down on Eighteenth Street, ultimately giving up and asking one of my gay male friends to order my Midori sour for me. When I first moved to San Francisco, I thought the city's reputation for being gay, open, and welcoming extended to everyone in the LGBTQ community. However, the dearth of bars, clubs, and spaces for lesbians and other letters in the LGBTQ acronym made it clear that it was only for gay men. The lesbian girl bars closed when I was just a child, and we, as a culture, settled for "girls' night" once a month at bars like QBar or the Cat Club. I once asked someone for a cigarette outside of Badlands multiple times before he would even acknowledge my presence. Then he disdainfully flicked ash toward me instead of giving me one. I often meet Iranian gay men, flashy and fabulous, peacocking in a way that reminds me of my uncles, but there seems to be a dearth of queer Iranian women in this city. I can count them on one hand.

I researched queer Iranians in the James C. Hormel archives in the San Francisco Public Library and found only *one* primary source written by Iranian lesbians. The newsletter, *Hasha* (Persian for "denial"), had two issues printed in English and Persian, in spring 1994 and summer 1994. The women who wrote and produced *Hasha* wrote under pen names about the Islamic Republic's genocide of homosexuals after the revolution, the pushback the academic community gave to LGBTQ rights at conferences, and the relief at finding others who were like them. There were no other *Hasha* issues to follow up on, and I have no idea who wrote these two, whether they are in the Bay Area, or even if they are still alive. I want to carve out a space for my dual identities—so that those who are like me can reach out and hold on, can know that they're not alone, so that we may create an Iranian queer community in places where we're told that we don't exist.

I see the vibrant queer communities in black and Latinx circles, and I feel a particular longing for the cultural hybridity of language and dance that is seemingly not present in other queer cultural spaces. Take drag ball culture, for instance, with its own vernacular, events, and "houses" that are really chosen families for queer black and Latinx people. There is a distinct cultural identity. No such thing exists for Iranian queers. We simply haven't been visible in America long enough to cultivate our own culture.

I take the words of Audre Lorde to heart. Born in Harlem to Afro-Caribbean immigrants, Lorde was a poet, and in her biomythography she refers to "old living in the new way," meaning that we bring old customs from the home country into our new one. Lorde, a lesbian at a time when it was seen as politically inconvenient for the civil rights movement, traced her lineage of same-sex attraction to *les amies* in Carriacao, women who lived and worked together when the men would set sail from the island. These women, self-sufficient and hardworking, didn't need the men when they came back to Carriacao. "Old living in the new way" described how Lorde loved in her lifetime while also honoring her Caribbean heritage. I envision Diana serving me black tea in a clear glass mug, kissing me on the forehead, and me cooking basmati rice in a rice cooker, sumac sprinkled on top, as diasporic new living in the old way. The mountain I'm named after is waiting for me, and we will make it there together—in our way.

Uninvited Guest

Roia Ferrazares

The massive flat-topped steamer trunk was delivered to our house by truck one brisk day in October 1975, an unusually windy day that made the purple flowers of the jacaranda tree in our front yard tremble with anticipation. Made of dark-green lacquered wood, the trunk was an imposing figure crowned by an array of large iron hinges and bound with what was now shredded rope around its belly. There were stickers with messages slapped on its faces, mostly in foreign languages, and one in English plastered to its top with our Oakland address on it in my father's careful script. This was the mythical trunk that my parents had sent ahead before our return from Iran four years before. They had long since considered it lost—forms were filed with the shipping company, shipping clerks had been on the receiving end of my mother's wrath—and yet here it stood, like a forgotten relative on our doorstep, after having travels of its own.

It must have taken both my parents to lift it over the threshold of our front door. I imagined them holding the iron handles, surprised by the smoothness and the weight of them, and then, with a noisy heave, bringing it inside. They would have carried it slowly through the dark hallway and down the carpeted stairs to our rumpus room, calling out to each other when they turned the corners. But I wasn't there to see any of that. It was already enthroned in the deep brown shag carpet of the rumpus room by the time I got home from school, and it lay in waiting to be opened, finally still and finally home.

The room was cool and shadowy in the late afternoon when my parents led me down to meet the mysterious guest. Our black upright piano, with its bench settled underneath, stood against the wall next to the old Zenith TV sitting darkly on its rolling cart: both sat waiting for me to awaken them from sleep—my typical afternoon routine.

But that trunk, surrounded by our big corduroy pillows, that was new—unexpected, uninvited, even. All else was forgotten.

The trunk tickled my memory in a way that made me irritable. It was a curious reminder of the half of me that was an odd color and that smelled of celery stew and rose water, the half of me that I usually tried to ignore in an effort to fit in at my lily-white school. My year in Iran when I was three and four was like a closed chapter of one of my father's library books—black-and-white pictures of artifacts and statues, flashes of memory, paper schoolbooks and pots of steaming rice; the bright orange of a glass of fresh carrot juice. Iran was a nursery rhyme that I didn't understand, but whose unintelligible syllables and phrases were always accessible on my tongue. Iran was the sound of my mother's shouts into our pastel blue princess phone on New Year's Day; her voice heard in the kitchen desperately reaching, searching, shouting in the language that was familiar yet incomprehensible to me now. Iran was the phone inevitably handed to me by my mother, tears streaming down her face, to hear a tinny distant voice calling my name in answer to my small hello. The awkward silence when I didn't know what else to say.

And when this steamer trunk was finally opened, it brought forth all these feelings of awkwardness and estrangement in a flood that made me breathless. My third-grade reader and binder were set aside on the piano bench as I watched my father cut the thick rope with our kitchen knife, letting it fall away to expose the hefty padlock that had been hidden underneath. Within minutes he produced the key, as if it had all along been kept at arm's reach, and the top was lifted, too heavy for me, to rest on its hinges. The smell of stale air mixed with mothballs lingered in my nose as I stretched my neck to peer inside. Its dark gut was still and full, so large it could have swallowed me whole.

My mother, chatty and exuberant, welcomed each item from its depth as she gingerly removed them—small rugs with bright patterns, a tiny sheepskin hat that I could hardly believe I had ever worn, an ornamental samovar with matching teacups the size of thimbles, clothes too small or too big, wraps, shawls, and stiff, beaded shoes of gaudy colors that were awkwardly narrow. Initially I stood away and poked at these things with outstretched fingers, but, with an insistence that could not be ignored, my mother bid me to remove my jeans and T-shirt and I found myself in their midst. Everything was scratchy against my skin, and old, and carried a smell so strong it assaulted me and seeped around the far corners of the room, but the items brought those familiar tears to my mother's eyes, induced by feelings of nostalgia for a faraway home fading from her memory. Once released and back in my familiar clothes, I gladly disappeared into the kitchen to make her a cup of strong black tea and leave her with these unwelcome guests. I stole peeks at her melancholy profile as I waited for the kettle to whistle.

When my mother was satisfied that she had unfolded each item, caressed each with nostalgia and longing, and then refolded each with the same creases, she began returning them to their waiting vault. The trunk, witnessing this whole scene, was eventually closed with a slam and my mother sprang up from her squat refreshed, with a light step.

Both of my parents seemed to welcome this trunk home. As for me, I was awash with relief when it was all over: the foreignness of these things only served to remind me of my own unexplainable foreignness. Friends at school didn't know me as Persian or as Italian, even though I was half of each. They didn't think of me as "mixed-heritage" or even as "ethnic," nor did I know them as Greek, or Portuguese, or Swedish. There was an unspoken understanding in the schoolyard that we never spoke of such things. I was just Roia, like the boy's name Roy with an *a* at the end. In order to conform I needed to make my world smaller, more generic. While my goal was to avoid drawing attention to myself, my bushy brow, hooked nose, and olive skin were becoming more accentuated the older I grew. They were my daily reminder that there was something different about me. Looking back, I know now that my ability to hide my ethnicity was contingent on the ignorance of those around me. No one knew where Iran was on the map in 1975. The years and world events that followed me into junior high would change that.

The green steamer trunk began a new chapter among the boxes in our cold garage, subjected to a sedentary life in a small patch of light from a dusty window, wedged behind my old tricycle and boxes of clothes. Occasionally, I would think about it and even steal away to the garage to remind myself that it was still there. But largely I felt more at ease with its place there, hidden and unseen.

Eventually, the intensity with which I sought to hide as a child was met by an equally intense will as a young woman to understand more about where I came from. Through books, films, and the relics that the old trunk returned to us, I began to feel more connected with my past, and with my ethnicity. And as I grew older, my hooked nose and bushy brow instead told me a different story about myself: I am both uncommonly beautiful and beautifully uncommon. It is no accident that I now own my own steamer trunk, a distant cousin of the one that arrived that day in 1975, and in it I keep many of the original relics it returned to us. I need only bury my nose in a tiny sheepskin hat to feel a flood of memory wash over me, and with it I feel pride and contentment that I am an Iranian woman. The trunk, once a nettlesome "auntie," along with its lessons, had become a treasured family friend.

CODING/DECODING

The Name on My Coffee Cup

Saïd Sayrafiezadeh

The busiest Starbucks I've ever encountered is located on the New York University campus—with an average wait of almost twenty minutes—but I'm such a regular there that the baristas frequently make my coffee before I've taken my place in line: decaf quad espresso ($3.21). They know me so well, in fact, that they've eliminated the most contentious aspect for me when ordering a cup of coffee at Starbucks, namely, the perpetual misspelling of my name on the side of the cup. The mutations have been many, and they've often been egregious—"Zal," "Sowl," "Sagi," "Shi," and so on. And then once, incredibly, several years ago, at a branch in the financial district: "Saïd," diaeresis added, prompting me to seek out the barista, whose hand I grasped with deep feeling but who, frankly, seemed perplexed that anyone would have difficulty spelling my name. He was Latino, I think, and he told me that he had a best friend named Saïd, spelled identically, which would explain his astuteness. Never mind the backstory, I was delighted by the outcome. I photographed the cup for posterity, and then, for good measure, tweeted it for the world to see.

Until that moment, I'd always recoiled when asked for my name by a barista—an innocent question for a simple transaction, but one that harkens back to traumatic days growing up in Pittsburgh, where my name caused controversy and consternation for people who, if they weren't black, were mostly descendants of immigrants from Germany, Italy, or Ireland. When I was in sixth grade, there happened to be one other boy in my school of Middle Eastern extraction, whose name was Hassin but whom everyone called Hi-C and who had the further misfortune of having an accent. I remember that the boy had wanted to be friends with me but that I'd avoided him at all costs lest his foreignness reflect back. My own apparent foreignness was misleading, considering that I'd been born in Brooklyn, and I did my best to try to mitigate it when I could—that is to say, always—but there was no getting around the fact of my name, which was occasionally brought into the spotlight by substitute teachers, who mangled it when they tried to say it, to the amusement of my classmates, reminding them that there was someone of abnormal ancestry sitting in their midst. Thirty-some years later, I might have been able to endure the painful and momentary mispronunciations of my name shouted in Starbucks, but it was the misspellings, perhaps because they were written in harsh black ink, that seemed as if they would last forever.

But after that wondrous occurrence at the Starbucks in the financial district, a profound shift took place inside of me, revelatory and liberating, and I began to openly acknowledge misspellings of my name, even to look forward to them, so that I could photograph and tweet the results—in essence, preserving them forever. For the record, there are several acceptable ways to spell Saïd—"Saeed," "Sayid," "Saeid"—but I accept only one, with the diaeresis included. A high standard, I suppose, but we should each have high standards when it comes to our name. As a rule, I never offer the barista assistance with the spelling unless it's requested, which it seldom is. There have been a few instances when my instructions for "two dots over the *i*" have been transcribed as three dots over the *i*, which is cute but wrong. When I was four years old, I would draw pictures where the *i* did indeed have three dots, and those three dots then became parts of a smiley face. That was back when my name was a playful thing for me and I marveled at its unusualness, but that playfulness is gone.

Not too long ago, a Twitter follower, perhaps growing weary of seeing Starbucks misspellings from all over the United States, suggested that I could easily resolve the dilemma by providing the baristas with a different name. Bob, for instance. Strangely, this hadn't occurred to me. Nor had it occurred to me that even common American names might be undergoing problematic interpretations at Starbucks. Henry, I've since heard, becomes Avery. Amy becomes Jenny. The advice struck me as sound, but I hadn't hung on to my name all these years in order to now become someone named Bob, even for the sake of a momentary convenience. The time for being Bob was 1979, during the Iran hostage crisis, when having a name like mine was a badge of shame and criminality. But the name had been the single constant connection to my Iranian father, who'd abandoned me when I was nine months old, leaving me alone with my Jewish American mother, Martha Harris. If there was a time for transformation—or obfuscation—it was then.

I would be remiss, though, if I did not acknowledge that there have been a few occasions when I did, in fact, change my name for the purposes of obfuscation—or obliteration. The first was when I was about thirteen and had to deliver the afternoon paper to an elderly woman who lived behind one house in another, smaller house that resembled a shack. She'd signed up for the paper as a new customer, but something kept going wrong with the circulation department's process of conveying the correct address to me—perhaps because it contained a ½—so my dispatcher finally demanded that I make a special delivery and hand her the paper in person. It turned out that she was nice but lonely and she wanted to spend time talking with me, but I was frightened of her because of her age and the condition of her home, so when she asked me my name I told her it was Steve. I was amazed that she couldn't tell I was lying. After that, I was always Steve with her, which felt to me like a terrible betrayal of everyone involved, including my father—but there was, of course, no going back. When I collected the weekly payment, she would pay me with a handful of coins, since she was poor, and she never tipped but she would always say, "Thank you, Steve."

The second time I gave a false name was about fifteen years later, when I was living in New York City, hoping to become a professional actor and having no success. Apart from an occasional call to audition for the role of a taxi driver or a deli owner, the phone never rang. At some point, I managed to arrange a meeting with a casting agent, and the first thing she asked me was whether I'd ever considered changing my name. It was a fair question, I guess, but I felt insulted. "You're sitting directly across from me," I said, "and can see that I could easily pass for Italian-American." I was basing this on a moderately ambiguous ethnic quality in my face, which people had speculated over the years could be Italian or Greek or "anywhere in the Mediterranean." But I hadn't formulated this concept as tactfully as I could have, and now it was the casting agent's turn to be insulted. "Why would I call *you* for an Italian-American role," she demanded, "when there are a hundred thousand Italian-American actors?" To this, I had no response. "If I send you out for an Italian-American role," she said, "that's trouble . . . and I don't want trouble." She was earnest and annoyed. It was also clear that she'd lost any interest in helping me. "Change your name to Joe Kelly," she suggested, "and I can get you work." And then she concluded with this powerhouse line: "Until then, I'll call you when I need a terrorist." At that, the meeting was effectively over.

She never did call me in need of a terrorist, a role that I most likely would have accepted. And after a few years had passed and my career had continued to stagnate, I finally took her advice and had five hundred headshots made with my face and the name Anthony March Harris, a clever amalgamation of names belonging to my mother, my cousin, and a childhood friend. I thought it had a nice ring to it, but unfortunately it also put me in competition with every other white American male actor, an even more daunting subset. The one audition I landed, a shaving-cream commercial, seemed exceptionally promising when the young female assistant director, before turning on the camera, remarked, "You look like my ex-boyfriend." I'd never heard this before at an audition, and I took it to mean that she found me mildly attractive and that my odds were good. With the paranoia of my ethnic psyche running in the background, I assumed that my commonplace name was partly why she'd managed to see a resemblance. Either way, I didn't get the part, and not too long after that I gave up acting for good and threw away my several hundred remaining headshots.

Lately, I've begun spending even more of my afternoons—and sometimes evenings—reading in the lovely New York University Starbucks location. At its enormous windows facing Washington Square Park, in one of its chestnut-brown armchairs, I sit there with my noise-canceling headphones on, undisturbed. It's something of a dis-appointment that I'm only able to tweet a photo when a new employee is hired, one who invariably butchers the spelling of my name, but so be it. Just the other day, the eternal line of college students notwith-standing, one of the baristas took the time to deliver my cup of coffee to me. It was such a sweet gesture. The type of small-town fellowship that people lament the modern age for having eradicated.

Negotiating Memories

Amy Malek

There were sequins and scraps of red and green faux-silk fabric all over the dining room. I was six and had tried to push the big black pedal of my mother's sewing machine one too many times to be allowed close to it again. But from my perch at the kitchen counter, I could watch my aunt and grandmother working, as they had been for several days, on a costume for me. An *Iranian* costume, I'd been told.

One of my favorite storybooks at the time was one handed down to me by my mother: *Dolls of Other Lands*. It had been one of her favorites as a child growing up in 1950s Ohio. In it, little Barbara played with her impeccably dressed dolls from places like Greece and Japan. I had envied Barbara as much as I envied her dolls and their elaborate and colorful costumes. There were no Iranian dolls in the book, but my grandmother had brought me a doll from Iran, and I imagined I would get to look just like her. My doll wore a sequined headband over her dark hair and a colorful vest over a full skirt, which she wore over black pants. I was excited about getting to wear my grandma's version of it. I was going to beat Barbara at her own game.

While my grandma and aunt worked at the dining room table, my mother and I sat together at the kitchen counter for what felt like hours, practicing: "CHAHARSHANBE SOORI IS A CELEBRATION OF IRANIAN NEW YEAR."

She had carefully written these words in big capital letters on index cards for me. It was the speech that I was to give on behalf of my kindergarten class, which would be representing Iran at our elementary school's 1987 International Night.

"ON THIS DAY WE JUMP OVER LITTLE FIRES TO TAKE THE FIRE'S HEALTHY REDS . . ."

While I practiced reading from the cards (a skill I had only just started to acquire), my mom traced out a large, curvy figure in pencil on bright orange construction paper.

". . . AND GIVE IT OUR SICKLY YELLOWS. THIS IS HOW WE START THE NEW YEAR CLEAN AND PURE."

She cut out two of these large orange shapes and then traced and cut two red ones as well. "AS WE JUMP, WE SING, 'SORXI-YE TO AZ MAN, ZARDI-YE MAN AZ TO.'"

My mom corrected me as I sounded out the big English words; my aunt corrected me from the dining room as I stumbled over the big, unfamiliar Persian words. My mom taped the red and orange flames onto a brown construction-paper base and stood the little fire up on the counter with a big smile. "We're ready!"

The next day, I brought the construction-paper fire to school, and our class went to the cafeteria stage to practice our performance. Rehearsal went without a hitch: my class of thirty-something students lined up on stage as I went up to the mic, Iranian flag in hand. I read my speech as my classmates jumped over the paper fire one by one. The only thing missing was my costume and the audience full of parents, teachers, and students who would be there that evening.

The costume was perfect, and unlike anything I'd ever worn. A green silk vest and a short, red silk skirt were set off by flowy black harem pants; both my vest and skirt featured a red sequin trim that caught the light just right. And my favorite part: a red- and green-sequined headband that formed a crown over my long, dark hair. It was even better than my doll's costume.

We arrived at the crowded cafeteria that night, me in my costume and my family carrying bags full of items from our home for our class's display table. Underneath a homemade construction-paper flag of the Islamic Republic of Iran, likely crafted by a schoolteacher based on the World Book Encyclopedia entry "Flags of the World," our table was essentially our living room reconstituted on a school lunch table. On it, my father, mother, grandmother, and aunt carefully arranged a Persian rug, a printed cloth, a brass ewer, an example of metalwork from Isfahan, a couple of vases, several books, a miniature painting, a pair of handcrafted traditional shoes, and my Iranian doll, dressed in her traditional clothes. My family sat behind the table, prepared to answer whatever questions might come their way.

As the youngest grade in the school, my class was slated to go on stage first. I scanned the room nervously, straining to see my class-mates and friends before it was time for us to perform. *Maybe I just can't see them behind all the adults.* We walked the length of the room, taking in all the other grades' tables, representing Brazil and Mexico and India and South Korea. But in the crowd milling about the room I saw only older kids I didn't recognize, parents I didn't recognize, and a few teachers I barely recognized. *They're probably in traffic. Maybe they're rushing here like we were and can't find a parking spot.* My kin-dergarten teacher, Mrs. Milne, was chatting with my parents, and this meeting of my favorite adults was thrilling. She complimented my costume, and we took a photo together. I was beaming with pride and nervous excitement, anxious about what was going to happen next.

I was six years old when I was first asked to represent Iran to an American audience. Until that evening in March 1987, I had had no reason to think that doing so could be anything other than fun and exciting. But a lesson was on its way, one I wouldn't fully recognize for another decade and a half.

Before starting school, I had understood my Iranian-American fam-ily in the way young children generally understand their families: we were normal. I understood that my mom and dad and I would drive to rural Ohio to visit my mother's family each winter, walking through cold air on farmland that her—*our*—relatives had worked for at least a century. Each year, I got to "drive" a giant tractor with my cousin, eat my great-aunt's chocolate-covered buckeyes, and play with my way-cool teenage cousins (and their way-cool toys).

I also understood that, unlike our traveling to visit my moth-er's family, my father's family would visit us instead. His parents and two of his sisters had visited our Atlanta three-bedroom split-level on separate occasions, each staying for long stretches, bringing all kinds of new treats and gifts like my doll, and speaking another language. I understood that this language somehow corresponded to the poster of Persian letters my dad had hung in my room, on the wall across from the English letters my mom had hung on the wall over my bed. But I didn't understand then that my father's family members traveled halfway around the world to be with us, nor that by the mid-1980s a relentless war would lead my grandparents to decide to immigrate permanently. I did not yet know that my aunts and my cousin would soon flee the same war and join our growing household, too.

My parents were careful to bring their cultural traditions into my life from an early age, and, despite whatever contradictions others might have seen in them, I saw them as fluid and normal . . . at least for the first several years of my life. We celebrated Nowruz with a traditional *haft sin* table decorated with colored eggs that would reappear in my Easter basket soon after. My Christmas memories are punctuated by recollections of my mother teaching both me and my Iranian grandmother how to make sugar cookies, of decorating the Christmas tree with my mother's family heirlooms, and of attending midnight church services. At church, while my mother celebrated the birth of Christ, my devout Muslim grandparents were honoring the birth of Hazrat-e Isa. The next day, after we tore through our presents, my mother would teach my grandmother how to make her favorite Christmas dinner dishes—squash casserole, sweet potato casserole, all the casseroles. They did this sharing of recipes year round, and my mom's favorite dishes would appear on our dinner table later in my grandma's altered forms: Prunes and hard-boiled eggs showed up in traditional southern meatloaf. Plump raisins dotted an otherwise classic pound cake. And my hamburgers began to taste more like a Persian *kotlet* in a hamburger bun. As my family grew, my six-year-old understanding of it did as well, but the blending of cultural forms that I was experiencing at home was not yet a difference to hide or even to mark; we were normal.

At school, though, I was different. I started noticing some of those differences slowly, while others were pointed out for me, not so slowly. And as I continued through school, in an effort to belong, I would take on the preferences and shared experiences of my peers.

This was a privilege my Korean, Mexican, and Indian immigrant class-mates didn't necessarily have. Unlike their mothers, my 100 percent American mom carefully packed my 100 percent American lunchbox each day with the comfort foods that my classmates also craved—peanut butter and jelly sandwiches, cheese puffs, chocolate chip cook-ies. I ate what most of my classmates ate and spoke how they spoke. We watched the same cartoons, played the same games, coveted the same toys at Christmas. But while these commonalities and my first name tied me closely with my classmates (I was named Amy in honor of my maternal grandmother), my eleven-letter, unfamiliar last name had marked my difference from the first day of school, and during every morning roll call thereafter. Little differences like this began to accumulate and, after realizing that my family and I weren't "normal" in the ways required to fit in, my kid mind saw these foods, cartoons, games, and toys that I loved as tools that I could also use to at least approach inclusion.

But in kindergarten, these weren't yet my concerns. My best friends were two blonde, blue-eyed girls, but also a Laotian girl who I didn't learn was Laotian until third grade. In kindergarten, I just knew she was a good friend and the best artist in the class. Mean-while, my beautiful blonde kindergarten teacher was my favorite lady outside of my family. Mrs. Milne was a schoolteacher of the 1980s, a period marked by early (and often experimental) approaches to multiculturalism in the United States. Our elementary school, one that would later win awards for excellence in the state, was diverse, particularly by 1980s Atlanta standards. Not only was that diversity brought about by minority-majority busing, still mandated by the desegregation laws of the civil rights–movement era, but the outlying neighborhoods were in flux as immigrants like my family were buying older homes and renting apartments, starting their ascent toward the middle class and their version of the American Dream. As a result, in my school, the white, neighborhood kids and black, bused-in kids found themselves joined by an array of immigrant children: my Lao-tian friend, a boy from Nigeria, several kids from South Korea, a girl from Thailand, a boy from Mexico, a girl from Ukraine, and so on.

And then there was me, a "half-Iranian" girl whose teachers always seemed to remark that she must look like her daddy.

Perhaps it was this growing diversity, beyond the black/white historical divide of the American South, that caused our principal to start our school's international night, where a PTA meeting would be augmented by an optional evening assembly. At the event, each grade would represent a country, display a table of arts and crafts and other items from that country, and present a class performance (a song, sketch, or dance). During my eight years at the school, the growing diversity of the student body led this annual event to eventually outgrow the cafeteria. In that time, my grade was chosen to represent Iran twice. I thought this was an amazing coincidence.

That first year, in kindergarten, I can only imagine that those in charge saw an opportunity to have Iran represented differently than what had been displayed in the media between 1979 and 1987. It was, after all, fresh in the minds of most Americans that Iran had held fifty-two Americans hostage from 1979 to 1981, a crisis that created a relentless US news cycle. Should any Americans have deigned to forget this ultimate Iranian aggression, the news each evening of the ongoing Iran-Iraq War was there to remind them of this continued enemy status (recall that the United States supported Saddam Hussein's Iraq against their mutual Iranian enemy, including through the supply of chemical weapons, to the great detriment of Iran's population).

Perhaps most fresh in the minds of Americans in March 1987, however, was the Iran-Contra affair. On March 4, 1987—mere days before a small Iranian-American girl in Atlanta was scheduled to give a speech to her elementary school about Iranian culture—President Ronald Reagan held a nationally televised Oval Office address to comment on the allegations that the United States had sold arms to Iran in exchange for the release of American hostages in Lebanon. Whether people watched this address and the continuous coverage of the ensuing congressional investigation into Reagan and Oliver North or not, American attitudes toward the Islamic Republic of Iran and its people had changed very little since the hostage crisis. In 1987, Iran was still, without a doubt, America's sworn enemy.

Given this political climate, and what my father had experienced in the United States in those intervening years since unexpectedly leaving Iran for the last time in 1979, my parents saw the same opportunity in International Night as my teacher likely did. My family took on the task of coming up with a class performance and putting together a table to represent their Iran to a large room of their neighbors. If the internet had existed then, maybe my family could have known that Iranian families more or less like mine in cities more or less like Atlanta were steeling themselves in similar multicultural-ish elementary school settings, trying to positively represent the country from which they too had fled. Instead, my family moved forth in relative isolation and used whatever they had at hand: mementos, memories, and the belongings they'd carried with them in stuffed suitcases.

Through our participation in International Night, my parents thought, maybe my peers—and their parents—would learn about the Iranian New Year and augment whatever else they'd heard about Iran and its "crises" with this newfound, personal cultural knowledge. I had no such lofty goals and didn't know enough to know of theirs. I was just nervous about reading from my mom's carefully written cards in front of all those people. And excited to wear my new costume.

The performance was about to begin, and I was growing anxious. There was no sign of my classmates. *Am I going to have to do this all alone? Where is everyone?* It didn't make sense. In the first half of the school year I had made friends with several kids in my class. *Why haven't they shown up? Didn't they like what we practiced earlier? Aren't they as excited as I am? Did I do something to make them stay home?*

Finally, at the last moment, a girl from my class rushed over. Monica was truly a sight for my sore eyes. She was the only classmate who showed up that night, and I couldn't have loved her more in that moment. Monica and I performed the routine by ourselves, me reciting from my mom's notecards, both of us jumping over the fire again and again.

I don't remember the performance, nor the crowd, nor their reaction, nor what my parents told me afterward about why no one else had jumped with us. I only remember, vividly, that none of my friends had shown up—except for (wonderful, brilliant, godsend) Monica. I struggled to understand what I had done wrong. Why had my classmates abandoned me?

I have often wondered about that evening. As a college student majoring in Middle East studies some fifteen years later, I found the snapshot of me with Mrs. Milne in my parents' boxes of family photos. Finding that photograph and several others of my family in front of our living-room-on-a-cafeteria-table, I was suddenly struck with the memory of that evening. Now equipped with a sense of twentieth-century history and politics, it dawned on me that it wasn't likely that all thirty-something of my kindergarten classmates had been stuck in traffic, nor that they had decided I was awful, nor even that they and their families had all happened to have other obligations on that evening in 1987.

What must their parents have thought when their child brought home a note informing them that their kindergarten class would be representing the Islamic Republic of Iran? What did those parents discuss with one another about it? What excuses did they give their children to explain missing the performance? What did they say to Mrs. Milne and her co-teachers about this choice to ask American six-year-olds to represent the culture of America's sworn enemy?

I can't know the answers to those questions, or why my classmates weren't there that night. But I do often reflect on how the memory of that experience has become a touchstone for me, something I return to again and again in trying to understand how my childhood memories reconcile with what I have read about history. I recently asked my family about that evening, trying to fill in some blanks. My grandmother, now in her nineties, doesn't recall it vividly. My mother and aunt fondly remember the costume but few other details. My father remembers preparing the table and why he felt it was important to do so. He also remembers a few "side-eyes" he caught from some of the other fathers that night, glances he filed away as just another occurrence he was by then used to experiencing.

In fact, no one else in my family remembered that Monica had been the only kid to show up, until I showed them the photo. Even more surprising to me, my mother wasn't at all convinced that some of my classmates' parents likely had balked at the thought of their child celebrating Iran in 1987.

Why has this memory been such a touchstone for me, but a forgotten blip to everyone else? How can our interpretations of the same event be so dissimilar—one teeming with importance, the other verging on irrelevance?

We all interpret and reinterpret our memories in light of new information. But for Iranian Americans and other diaspora kids, that new information is not necessarily a previously undisclosed family secret or a parent's migration story. It's also what we see on the news and read in history books. My youthful interpretation of that 1987 evening (that I had clearly been rebuffed by my entire class, save for one) had shaped my sense of self as much as my young adult interpretation (that my classmates' parents had rebuffed a celebration of America's sworn enemy), under the influence of newly acquired sociohistorical knowledge. What I've come to realize is that it doesn't really matter which interpretation is closer to the truth, nor that others don't interpret that evening the same way I do.

That's the thing about memory and negotiating identity as a second-generation diaspora kid in America. Second-generation children are often called to represent countries and cultures that they themselves may not yet understand. And as cultural theorists have long examined, we often have conflicting experiences that others may not see or feel: feeling that we belong neither here *nor* there alternates with feelings of belonging both here *and* there. That could mean feeling alternately included and excluded in the only home one has known, while also feeling attachments to a place one may never have experienced and may or may not be welcome even to visit.

These alternating senses of belonging and exclusion can make for a lifelong negotiation that requires some messy memory work. It can be a familiar, comforting feeling of belonging among co-ethnics, or it can be a weird, not-normal feeling in a kindergarten class, one that you wrestle with interpreting decades later. Iranian Americans have grown up negotiating these kinds of experiences and memories in a constant (though not always conscious) process, where geopolitics and personal identity are always intertwined. I didn't see myself or my heritage in my favorite storybooks. Instead I saw what I was told was my father's homeland on news programs, and it wasn't much like what I saw in our family photos.

In the summer of 1987, just a few months after my first confusing experience of representing Iran, I sat with my father as he watched the TV broadcasts of the Iran-Contra congressional testimony. We often watched the news together, and I awaited his reaction to know how to interpret what was happening in our world.

With siblings and extended family living far away in the midst of a long war, my father sought news of Iran anywhere he could get it. He read newspapers, watched the nightly news each evening, and spoke on the phone to his family as much as possible. I didn't know then that he had been working tirelessly to reunite our family. All I knew was that if I was watching TV while he was elsewhere in the house and someone uttered "Eye-ran," I should call him quickly: "Daaad! It's about Ee-rahn!"

Sometimes I was right, and the mention was news of the Iran-Iraq War; other times, it was just someone speaking in past tense about having run somewhere. I'd learned not to assume I could tell the difference.

Even when we don't know enough yet to realize it, we are always negotiating our belonging in multicultural America.

In Praise of Big Noses

Persis Karim

Until my adolescence, I avoided thinking about my nose. As a child growing up in the San Francisco Bay Area suburban town of Walnut Creek, I was aware of the ways that my difference was cast in both my name and my appearance. Beyond the constant butchering of my first and last names, "Paris," "Parsis," "Purses," "Perees," I often faced that singular question: where are you from? I had inherited most of the features associated with my father's Iranian appearance: large brown eyes, thick dark hair, long eyelashes, plentiful eyebrows, and olive-colored skin. My mother was from France, but she, too, had dark hair and brown eyes. Although my father was a handsome man, his exceedingly large nose and well-sized ears were an inescapable part of his distinctively non-Anglo, foreign look.

When my father's two daughters Cima and Lily, my half sisters from his first marriage in Iran, arrived in the United States, I was still a young girl. I could see in their faces something of how they both resembled and didn't resemble my sister Avesta and me. But as Avesta approached her teen years, I began noticing her increasingly self-conscious comments about the size of her nose. My father's sister and her three daughters had come in the early 1970s from Iran, and at the various family gatherings we attended at my aunt's house, I noticed women—some my cousins, others friends of my aunt, who came to her Nowruz parties—with bandages on their faces. When I was about eleven or twelve, I finally mustered up the courage to ask one of my cousins what was going on with the large white bandages across one woman's nose and the black and blue bruises under her eyes. She leaned into me and whispered, "They've just gotten their noses fixed—it's a nose job." I had seen enough to surmise that it was an Iranian female practice that might one day be visited upon me, but I hoped I would be spared this seemingly regular female rite of passage.

Later, when I asked my father about these women's wounded faces, he blurted out, "Well my dear, in case you hadn't noticed, we've got a few people in this family with pretty big noses." He smiled and pointed to his own.

As a teenager, I became aware of the bountifulness of my proboscis and wondered if I would be next. Indeed, I was processing how much more beautiful my half sisters were, and I wanted to look like them. Without ever asking them or speaking about it, I knew that they had participated in the ritual of nose reduction. Theirs were petite and well-proportioned noses, even a bit Anglo looking. One of my two half sisters even had a slightly up-turned one that looked more like Audrey Hepburn's than my budding Barbra Streisand nose.

The contagion of nose-reduction operations in my extended family seemed more and more prevalent with each passing year. First it was my oldest cousin, then her younger sister, then a sister-in-law, then the daughter of my father's distant cousin. It was the mid-1970s, when Iran and the United States were close allies and when there was relative ease of movement between the two countries; plastic surgery had become big business in Iran. The influx of Western culture, the importation of beauty products from the United States, and the influence of American movies and television had transformed the landscape of aesthetics and beauty in that country. Iranian women sought to be more beautiful by bleaching their hair blonde, fixing their noses, and wearing shorter skirts. And they seemed to bring that aesthetic with them when they immigrated to the United States. Iranian women were beautiful to me. But apparently they wanted to be just exotic *enough*, with large brown eyes and voluptuous lips, but with small, perfectly sculpted Anglo noses. Some of the noses were petite and perfectly triangular, while others were slightly upturned like my sister's. Mostly I noticed that these noses all looked alike—as if they'd been reworked by the same plastic surgeon, who had taken away nature's unique character from each of their faces. But I also noticed how much their noses looked different from mine. And it began to bother me.

Around my fifteenth birthday, during that awkward phase when most adolescents' features appear scarily large and unsettled on their still-childlike faces and bodies, I realized I was being recruited into this cult of Iranian beauty. The first occasion was at my aunt's house, when she told me that I should pluck my eyebrows a certain way and put on makeup, then followed that with the casual comment that I should "get my nose fixed" so that I could "become more beautiful." On another occasion, my sister Lily gave me a lesson in upper-lip depilation and gently suggested something similar: "You are beautiful, but you know, we Karims have large calves and large noses. You can't do anything about the legs, but the nose you can fix."

Several months after that conversation, I became more aware that the odds were against me when I overheard Avesta speaking quietly behind a closed door with my father about his offer of financial support so she could get "the operation." It was sometime around her twenty-second birthday. I knew that she had felt increasingly self-conscious about her nose and though she possessed some of my mother's features—fairer skin, lighter, curlier hair, as well as my mother's very petite build and the gene for green eyes—her nose was decidedly a carbon copy of my father's.

In the days after my sister's surgery, I saw her only once in the white bandages and with black and blue lines under her bright green eyes. I remember that, for the most part, she retreated to her apartment to recover and heal and we didn't see her again until a month had passed. She came to the house and without saying a word showed off her new nose as if it were a brand new car. Her new petite nose seemed to make her happy, and she now held her head high. I remember how it struck me as odd. I felt both embarrassment and shame. For her and for *me*. I wanted to like my nose. I wanted not to feel the pressure to do the same thing she had done. But for her, the operation had been a double success: she was more aesthetically aligned with American beauty norms and she had, in effect, eradicated her Middle Eastern heritage, a part of herself with which she was never comfortable. She had also participated in a rite of passage that she shared with our other two sisters, and despite our age difference and her emotional distance from them, it was a way she belonged and I didn't. I was now the only one with my original nose.

I managed to avoid the topic of the nose job until around the time I turned seventeen, when my father, who was acutely aware of the long-standing tradition and the rising costs of the operation, asked me whether I wanted one. He told me that along with savings he'd been putting aside for my college education, he'd also saved an additional $3,000 in the event that I wanted to join my sisters in the nose-reduction club. Although I appreciated the gesture, deep down I was distressed by his offer.

"But do you really think I need one, *Baba*? Do you also think I'm not beautiful enough?" He laughed and responded by saying that I looked like him and that as his daughter I would always be beautiful in his eyes.

"But do you think I have such a big nose?" I pleaded again. "Your nose is a smaller version of mine," he said and, in his usual philosophical and pragmatic way, followed by saying, "I regard the nose as a sign of character, and on you it is part of the total aspect of your beauty. But what is inside you is what ultimately determines how others see you. You are beautiful, my *Souski*"—his nickname for me, which means "little black bug" in Persian—"but it is up to you to decide if you want this or not." I was relieved that he didn't pressure me and that he allowed me to consider the decision myself. My mother never said a word to me about it.

After thinking about it for several months, I decided to pass on the nose job and instead took the money Baba had put aside and used it for a trip to study abroad in my senior year of high school. I was aware that I was making a choice—an intellectual and what now seems a feminist choice—that would set me apart from my sisters and some of my other female relatives. I was both proud and a little ambivalent about the choice I had made. I had decided that I would resist the trend and hoped that my other attributes would compensate for my nose's largesse.

Years later, I met and married a man who possessed a very large nose. Although he was Jewish and not Iranian, I felt a strange affinity for him. We both laughed at the idea that we came from cultures that sought to diminish the size of the noses we were born with and that marked our geographic origins. Perhaps I even had a little subconscious appreciation for how my own father had jokingly commented that large noses in men are a sign of both their sexual virility and character (a bit like Cyrano de Bergerac). As I grew older I came to appreciate how my nose *belongs* on my face—it works with my big eyes and pronounced chin, and I stopped fretting about it.

Some years ago, I watched the entire *Star Trek: The Next Generation* series on DVD with my husband and then nine-year-old son, encountering in it the race of people in outer space called the Ferengi. I noted to the two of them how powerful the image of large noses in the Ferengi was and how it marked them as foreigners and outsiders (the Ferengi don't belong to the United Federation of Planets and are a bit rogue). The word *farangi* in Persian means literally "foreigner." The Ferengi in *Star Treck* are associated with being greedy and solely motivated by profit—a characteristic that has long been an anti-Semitic stereotype and more recently has become associated with both Arabs and Iranians. It was an especially prominent depiction of Arabs and Saudis during the oil crisis of 1973—and became emblematic of a kind of avarice, profiteering, and greed. I told my son that the Ferengi were born from that time, when anti-Arab sentiment was at its height. I explained to my son that the Ferengi played to stereotypes about Middle Eastern people and, specifically, men from that part of the world. I told him, "Be proud of your nose, even if it gets big like your dad's and mine."

I came to appreciate my large nose again several years back when I learned from a CBS news story about Iran that it was the "nose job capital of the world." In a country where the celebration of physical beauty is limited by the efforts of the government to curb public displays of sexuality, both men and women seek to alter their appearance in response to the restrictive codes of dress and bodily presentation. While liposuction and breast and lip augmentation are the most prevalent subtraction/addition procedures in the United States, in Iran, the nose job, for both men and women, had become a standard appearance-altering practice (at a mere $1,500 there). This act of personal expression represents a rare opportunity for young Iranians who want to show resistance against their government's anti-Western sentiments by modeling the images of the European and American men and women they see in fashion magazines.

Mehrdad Oskouei captured the Iranian national obsession with nose jobs in a short documentary titled *Nose, Iranian Style* (whose title is a play on an earlier documentary called *Divorce, Iranian Style*, and both are plays on the title of the 1970s TV show titled *Love, American Style*). In his 2005 documentary, Oskouei considers the epidemic of nose jobs. The Italian photographer Fabio Bucciarelli documented the national obsession with rhinoplasty in his photo essay "Nose Job: Iran, 2009," which appears both on his website and in the US-based online newsmagazine *Tehran Bureau*. His series of photographs, shot in Tehran, are of young men and women wearing bandages across their noses in the postsurgical recovery stage. Each of his subjects (there is an equal number of men and women) is posing for the photo as if to say, "I own my body, I own my nose. And I can alter my nose myself if I please." Unlike the attitude of my sister, who hid her bandages and waited to reveal her new look to the world until she was completely healed, this series of photos documents the seeming defiance in getting plastic surgery to look more Western. The bandage itself is seen as a symbol of rebelliousness.

After many years, I've learned to own my nose just as it is. It's the legacy of my father and his teaching me to think differently about myself and about the ways others often do things without questioning their actions. I turn to poetry to praise my nose.

I am the only one of four sisters
who hasn't gone under the knife.
I resisted the pleas of my aunt and sisters
to become "more beautiful," "more you."
I've kept my stately proboscis
intact—choosing not to excise its grandeur.

It suits me, I suppose—evidence of my father,
those people who live in the dryer, hotter climes
of the Mediterranean, in high desert plateaus,
cooling themselves with naso-thermoregulation.
My old Jewish boyfriend used to say, "How do the goyim
breathe from those things anyway?"

On my wedding day, my husband (now ex), also Jewish
and rather plentiful in that region of his face,
completed his vows by saying, "There is no guarantee in love,
but of this, I am certain: if we have a child he or she
will have a really big nose." When I nuzzle him
with mine, he pulls back his face, jumps
at the coldness of its tip. Contrary to popular belief,
the nose is not merely cosmetic—it can gauge
temperature beyond the body.

And that's another thing I've realized
about the nose, that smell is an underrated
sense, perhaps a gift. Imagine
the possibilities for amplification: aromas
of jasmine, apple pie, saffron, lemon, rose

might grow more intense, depending on the height
and angle of that fleshy mound. I admit to having no
scientific evidence for this, but I do wonder
what happens when a person alters
the things they were born with.

Whole industries were born from Iranian women
watching blonde, petite-nosed movie stars
who made them forget that their own striking beauty
took thousands of years to evolve, only to be undone
by someone who decided that hairless, plucked, tucked,
sliced, nipped, and trimmed were the loveliest

of them all. I like to think of the nose as great art
waiting to be discovered. Like those large-nosed kings
depicted on sides of temples, on papyrus, on caves, in colorful
Mayan pictographs like Popul Vuh. Noses were signs
of nobility and prowess. Any king with a puny one
might have been thought of as small and impotent.

These days, I get a steady stream of emails offering penis
enlargement. But that's hidden, visible only
in bedroom interludes. The nose is the public display
of one's endowments—the relief map of a human face.
I study people's noses in order to read their origins—
to situate my gaze, to find how far out
in the world they really are.

Transmutations of/by Language

Raha Namy

Persian carpets and kilims are spread under their feet. The Persian food cooked by mothers and grandmothers is desired even by third generations. Framed Persian calligraphy hangs on their walls. Photographs from the good old days back home decorate their houses. Poetry nights are held to recite Hafez and teach Rumi. Persian pop songs make their bodies sway in Eastern moves. Blue plates and bowls filled with salted nuts sit atop their coffee tables.

On the blue walls of their Facebook pages, you have come to notice, however, that many Iranians living in the diaspora write in English. They live not only with their own people but also among others, speaking other languages, mainly English, and they need to communicate. But it is not just the posts aimed at different members of the new society, coming together in this shared new world and finding meaning in this shared language, that they write in English. They write in English even in posts directed to Iranian friends, in comments on Iranian friends' updates and feeds. Or sometimes they write in Pingilish, but they rarely use the Persian alphabet. Many know Persian. Many, though, have not learned how to type in Persian or do not even have the option of Persian language on their laptops and other devices. You notice that you, too, have a hard time thinking about and writing some statements in Persian. You make a conscious effort to keep the language present on your page, in your communications, in your life.

In an American city, an Iranian man expresses love to his American girlfriend by beginning an email with, in Pingilish, the words *ashegh-et am*, which means "I love you" in Persian. Othering the language of love, he is making it exotic and arousing, taking her into this other, unknown land; but he is also bringing the Other into his first language, into this previous other world of his, making it accessible to her, creating a bond, an intimacy.

In an Iranian city, an Iranian woman texts her Iranian boyfriend, addressing him as بیبی , which is "baby" written in the Persian alphabet. In bed with him, too, her language for the demands of the body is English. She cannot articulate the equivalent words in Persian. She finds them vulgar, unacceptable, unladylike. The English creates distance, as if it is not she who is speaking them but another, making the words OK to be uttered out loud. She does not even have the Persian words to mouth. Her knowledge of sex and eroticism is in the language of the Other. She has learned it from movies, mostly American, in English. Persian has been desexualized through cultural and official censorship.

You, an Iranian woman living in an American city. Your lover, an Iranian man living in an Iranian city. He and you speak in Persian, email in Persian, make love over Viber in Persian. You, the translator who constantly moves between English and Persian, the writer who writes in English, do not want any translations in this intimate space.

It was in your relationship with an American lover a few years ago that you came face to face, for the first time ever, with the failures of translation/migration on a deeply personal level.

Once, on a drive from Washington to Baltimore with him, the two of you listen for a while to the Iranian singer Googoosh and then for a while to Bruce Springsteen, switching back and forth. Listening to Googoosh's songs, which you have grown up with since early childhood, you get goose bumps and he gets restless and irritated. You try to translate the words of her songs and the memories revived by them, and you fail; and even when you succeed, everything sounds stupid and banal and you come to hate this partial sharing. You are not unfamiliar with Bruce Springsteen, but he does not touch you the way he does your lover. On that winding road connecting the two foreign cities, listening to the two singers' voices, you suddenly come to the realization that parts of you will forever remain untranslatable to this man from the other language, from the other country, both of which are nonetheless also yours, but forever only partially; and parts of him to you.

Once, he reprimands you for not wanting to accompany him to a stadium to watch a baseball game with him and his coworkers, for not being open enough to learn about his culture. You reply in anger that you are living his culture, every aspect of it, every day, every night, every damn second. And he . . . ? He has a choice for the what and when and how of his exposures and adoptions.

It is in that lover's simultaneous desire for and impatience with your foreignness, and in your own desire for and resistance to his, that you realize that, no matter what, your culture and your country will be the one always remaining in the margins, in the distance, an intellectual concept, a faraway reality, and that you will forever have a limit on how far you can—or want to—go into and settle in his. With your failure to navigate this personal in-between, you begin to fall into a deepening void. You try to force yourself to find home in this new land and language, but you keep failing, and the gap continues to grow inside you.

It was in your relationship with an Iranian lover in Tehran a few years ago that you came to realize for the first time that a lack of sufficient knowledge of English on his part could also be a hindrance in your togetherness with the men from your first country and language.

Your lover is a culturally savvy, well-read, movie-enthusiast architect, and the two of you have much to talk about, to think about, to share; but one night in bed, in the calmness and long hours of the dreamy wakefulness after lovemaking, while the two of you talk about work, you suddenly notice that you need to paraphrase and summarize for him the stories that you write in English. The fact that his English is not good enough means that reading your work demands an extra effort, and it won't just happen as another natural part of your shared experience. It hurts to think that he is a foreigner to a significant part of your being, a world you inhabit even when you are not typing the words.

You split your life between the States and Iran, moving across the borders, and you have lovers speaking this or that language. You keep losing your bearings more and more every day. You grow obsessed with belonging and longing, become consumed by wanderlust, trying to rebuild or rediscover home. It takes a long while and a lot of tearing your past and present and future apart and digging continuously deeper and deeper into your identities to finally come to the realization that you are not going to find a home anymore in one place or person or language.

You came to writing through learning English as a second language while growing up as a kid in Iran because writing was one of the main tools your English tutor used for teaching. The first essay you were asked to write, when you were ten or eleven, was in answer to the question "What would you like a ship to bring you?" You have kept that piece. Its paper is yellowing and the corners are disintegrating. The pencil-written words are fading, from black to gray to less and less visibility, disappearing into the many drawers the paper has been placed in, into the seconds of time piling up in between its original moment and its continuous existence, into the transfigurations of the girl who wrote it and the woman who keeps holding on to it.

You write for your English classes: book reviews and summaries, movie criticism, essays, etc. You watch bootleg English movies, pronounced illegal by the government, rented out weekly by movie men delivering them door to door in briefcases and bags. Later on, when illegal satellite channels become accessible, your main source of news becomes the English news outlets. You grow up reading world literature in translation and Persian literature influenced by world literature in translation. In a book market where, because of the lack of copyright laws, you find dozens of translations published for many of the world masterpieces, where the name of the translator is published next to the author's on the book cover, where translators create ways around the official censorship to give you versions of the original works (believing that something is better than nothing), you come to understand the significance of the translator's role, appreciating his/ her labor of love.

You continue your English class, writing and reading regularly, until you are eighteen and your tutor retires. You choose English<>Persian translation as your BA major, and from that first year, you begin to freelance as a translator, translating into your mother tongue. You begin learning French, again having a teacher who has you memorize stories, watch cultural documentaries and feature films, and write essays regularly. You continue your studies and get an MA in translation studies. At some point you begin translating into your second tongue.

Despite the translations and the French writing, a while after graduation you find yourself yearning to write in English again. You begin to ask around for teachers who offer advanced classes specifically for writing.

A coworker who hears of that yearning sends you an email, suggesting a writing challenge. What he really wants is to get you in bed. You are naïve and don't read between the lines, or you do and think you are beyond that, in control, and you accept the challenge. But then life explodes. Not that he is the reason; many other things happen and he is just there in the right moment (or in the most wrong one, based on which perspective you choose). You go from a woman happily married to the love of her life to a woman still in love with her husband but not in love with marriage and the life she is having; a woman who, lost and confused, does not want to let go of the thrill of new stories being written and of writing them.

The lover holds your hand and takes you into the madness of the world of words. The two of you meander through unknown neighborhoods of the city, making love in friends' houses, in the brackets of time stolen from your virtuous realities. And then you go back to the arms of your husband, finding yourself capable of giving him even more love now that you are feeling revived, now that you do not need him to give you what you need to survive. And yet you find yourself hating yourself, hurting deeply from the secret duality, from moving between one and the other.

You are lost and confused about the meanings and capacities of love, its challenges and responsibilities, are sure about only one thing: you wish to live with words and stories, both in the reality of the world and on the page. You reveal your truths to both men. You apply to a creative writing program. You try to cling to both men. You and your husband do not really work out. You and your lover do not really work out. You wish to hold on to both the old and the new, but the more you try, the more you fail. You finish the master's degree in creative writing. A few years after, you apply to a PhD program. You keep writing.

You wrote your first-ever real story in English in your fiction techniques class. About a girl growing up during the Iran-Iraq War who becomes a journalist. Worried about the imminent threat of another war, irritated by a brother who has built a home elsewhere, she does not want to leave her city under any circumstance.

That it was your first-ever real story is perhaps not totally true. You have writings before it that are stories. You just did not know that what you were writing were considered stories.

You never wrote in Persian, and it is only recently, years after writing in English, that you begin to write in your first language, not yet stories, but drafts, notes, and essays. But that too is not totally true.

You diligently kept diaries as a teenager. And in your undergraduate program, you wrote for a Persian literature class. You wrote a collection of vignettes, one of which was a scene from a weekend visit to a cemetery. Working as a translator, you also wrote some original short pieces in Persian for journals here and there. In retrospect, you see them as mediocre and insignificant, but they have familiar threads of your writing today. Perhaps they were the first steps you were taking in the world of words without knowing you were taking them.

The interesting thing is that in elementary and middle school, you hated writing your composition homework. You begged your great-uncle to write the essays for you, and he would help you with generating ideas and doing research but refused to write them—except that one night, when you left his room almost in tears, angry with him because he was making you sit into the late hours of the night and do it all alone, only to find in the morning that he had a complete essay ready for you on your desk.

People keep asking you about the choice of language. You know but do not really know. You write in English because you have practiced writing in English more systematically and more regularly. Because you have had great teachers in your non-native languages who have made you read and write and watch, a lot, who have corrected you, who have helped you grow one step at a time. You write in English because the already existing canon of Persian authors terrified, and still terrifies, you. You never had that concern about English because whatever you did was good enough for you, this being the foreign, faraway realm. Because you enjoyed the learning, the dictionary and grammar challenges, seeing your improvement little by little. Because it was through the necessity of learning this other language that reading and writing became inseparable parts of you.

For many writers, especially for expatriates and exiles, the first language is/becomes home. But if language is home, then what happens to you and others who work with several languages, finding it exhilarating to move from one to another, not getting settled in one or the other? Do you find several homes? Or do you lose all homes, living in dualities, becoming a wanderer in the space of borders, finding life only in disparate patches, some on this side, a few on the other, some beyond, a few close by? If language is home, do homes come in different accents? If language is home, is that home in the meaning or in the transcript? If one of your languages is written from right to left and the other from left to right, then are the homes you inhabit mirrors of one another? Clashing with one another? Or simply different from one another? If language is home and home is identity, does that mean you are forever torn between the multiple "yous" in multiple languages?

You want to believe there is home beyond language, beyond thought, beyond representation. You want to believe there is home somewhere regardless, somewhere without. You keep questioning and writing more and more about the meanings of home, the sources of identity, the consequences of language.

You leave the United States for months to go back to Iran, because you need to feel, breathe, smell, touch the first land, live the stories in the first language. You leave Iran for months to go back to the United States, because you learn and build in the second land, write the stories in the second language. While in the States, you surround yourself with Iran and the Persian language and arts. While in Iran, you surround yourself with the English and French languages and foreign arts.

Recently, you are becoming aware of a growing new sensation: wanting to move to a new land that will surround you with neither this nor that language, with yet another language. A place that will force you to face once again the challenge of coding and decoding, building language consciously and with effort, understanding it and not understanding it, simply trusting the still inaccessible sounds and forms to take you away into new mysterious territories. You are feeling the urge for yet another unknown, a place whose foreign oral environment will mirror your inner turmoil of constantly feeling like an outsider, a foreigner, no matter where, not fully belonging in the first or the second land, in the first or the second language, forever needing to flow.

Bodies flowing from one place to another for not-good-enough reasons are looked at suspiciously by governments, entities, and individuals who want the world in clear-cut borders and definitions. They have a problem with nomads. People who move with the seasons, following the rhythms of nature, permanently setting up temporary homes. People who do not believe in possessing and demarcating land but in coexisting with it. People who believe in more elastic definitions. They force nomads to settle in place. They appreciate them but only as part of a past, exotic and historic, celebrating them in glass boxes, like objects in a museum. They turn their lives into tourist attractions, the material for festivals and souvenirs. Civil men draw lines, finding identity in nationalism and patriotism, attaching themselves to land and place. That is how they learn and teach history, how they create memories. That is how they become the "we" against the "others" on the other sides of those arbitrary lines. That is how they exist.

But even nomads who do not belong to land and borders define themselves with belonging to tribes and clans. There has always been "we" vs. "others." Identity has always been closely tied to belonging, to being one of a definite whole. The trans-dwellers have always been trespassers. And trespassers are betrayers; they are not of this group, not of that group, always to be watched, always to be kept distant.

And trespassers who move in between countries/groups whose leaders come to identify one another as enemies are regarded as more of a threat. Being from a country of the "Axis of Evil" makes you more suspicious than the rest of the citizens in the land of the United States. Being from the land of the "Great Satan" makes you more suspicious than the rest of the citizens in the land of the Islamic Republic. The governments of both the host country and the motherland want you to belong either to this or to that, not to be constantly in motion between the two. It does not matter whether you are a physicist or a journalist, an artist or a doctor, a businessman or a student, or simply a tourist; it is politics that defines and decides the limits and the righteousness of your transitions between borders.

In the transborder extensions of your body and mind, you keep losing established relationships and you keep finding new ones. Some men tell you that at some point you need to choose, to settle. Others understand the wandering but find it a concern regardless, a problem for developing deeper relationships. And then he happens. He who seems to know, to understand, without your needing to delve into language to explain. He is from the first land and speaks the first language and the second, but more importantly he speaks your language of life that you keep carrying with you from one set of alphabets to another, from one geography to another.

As you try to gradually prepare yourself, mentally and emotionally, for the possibility of becoming an exile if you get to publish your books (because of their sexual, political content), you begin to develop an urgent desire to have a man by your side in the new lands and languages who is of your first land, sharing your collective past, knowing your culture, feeling (and not just understanding on an intellectual level) your concerns, speaking your language. You want him to keep you connected to the language and to the place. You want to hang on to him and to home through him.

You want to believe that he himself can be home, is home. But . . . but then, why do you not want to settle in him? Why do you want the two of you to be always one step away from one another, your bodies remaining borders of your beings? Can he be home in the moments he is inside you and you are around him, when his being is taking your being toward coming, toward becoming . . . ? Or can he be home even when away, far away?

You want him. You want him and still you cannot bring yourself to settle down, in one world or another, in one language or another, in one man or another. You want him, and you are afraid because you do not want to lose another man to this constant longing to leave. You know it and he knows it too: even in him you will not find a home. You will forever remain a wanderer, a woman in constant trans who knows the moment she finds a home she will die and the home will die, a woman who constantly needs to fly away, but only to be able to come back.

You have a complicated relationship with airports.

Tehran airport is the threshold of belonging vs. non-belonging for you, the last stop before departing the only home you have ever known, the only city you felt whole in for many years, until you did not anymore. The airport is also the space that offers you one last immersion in the mother tongue, the official, all-embracing oral and written alphabet that you are constantly exposed to unconsciously in the homeland, before you fly into the authority of other languages and need to make an effort to abstractly and consciously surround yourself with it. The Tehran airport is for you a marker of forced separations, a structure for the accumulation of all burdens of goodbyes.

You hate both the Tehran airport and the US airports when they are your points of arrival/departure from the other land. You can never get used to the weight of official uniforms, the coldness of their voices and gazes. You can never be sure what kind of welcome or adieu you will get. They are the space of governments, not of people and the open embraces that await you beyond them.

It is in the Tehran airport that he kisses you goodbye after only four days and nights of being lovers, and it is then and there that you feel there is something different about him. Only a week or so later, sitting in your Denver apartment, the sun and the blue skies wrapped around your nakedness, you ask him, lying in bed in the darkness of the night in his Tehran apartment, whether he would accompany you to unknown worlds. He says he would. No pauses. No hesitations. The two of you plan to meet in a few months in a third city.

Airports of third countries are soothing spaces to you. In them you can feel the outside world and your inner one consolidating. They are the true representation of translation and transition. It is in these spaces of in-betweens and non-belonging and temporariness, where everyone is a stranger, heading one way or another, speaking one language or another, that you can simply be. Out of place. Out of time.

It is in one such airport, in a city that is not yours or his, where both of you, in the course of a two-week sojourn, begin to learn new, unfamiliar words while you try to find your way around the right turns and the wrong turns of the alleys, around the curves and touches of each other's bodies, that you try to break away from him before you each fly back to your city, you to the West, he to the East. The two of you have, from the first moment, promised each other polyamory, a relationship without set borders, a commitment to continuous expansive organic translations and retranslations of togetherness. And even with that, fearing a solid presence and a structure, you try to break up all ties with him before it is too late to go back to your now familiar writerly self.

But he is not having any of it. He sits on the other side of the table as the two of you drink your cups of Turkish coffee, turning them around to wait and read your divinations, and he tells you he is not going anywhere, that he will be staying by your side, that he wants to be the man of yours to whom you keep returning, not the man who wants you for himself, who wants you to stay. As you hear the name of the city you are flying to amidst the words of the language you do not understand coming through the loudspeakers, followed by the announcement's English translation, you decide to trust those words spoken in Persian by this still-unraveled man in the mother tongue and set off on yet another wandering, wishing to rediscover more of the unknown, in the world, in him, and in yourself.

Gilad, My Enemy

Salar Abdoh

An endless escalator ascended to one of the entrances to the Imam Ali
shrine complex in Najaf, Iraq. Down below, Shia refugees from the
Tel Afar region in the far north, near Mosul, were temporarily being
sheltered. Majed Neisi, my working partner, and I stood around the
complex that late-June midday with a young Iraqi film crew on assignment for an Iranian television channel. The heat, 118 degrees in the
shade, seemed to turn everything into an abstraction, removed and
unapproachable. Naturally, I thought about American soldiers—the
battles that were fought here in the past decade, in 2003, 2004, 2007;
I thought about their uniforms and all the gear they had to carry in
this furnace. And perhaps one reason that I thought about them is
that even on my Iranian passport it says that I am a resident of the
United States; place of issue: Washington, DC. This is just another
typical dual frame of reference, of course. Nothing new about it. Yet
in a time of war, sometimes you long for more clarity and a definite
sense of belonging *somewhere.*

Looking at Majed, who is an Arab Iranian documentarian of
war from southwestern Iran, I knew that this was something he had
wrestled with all his life. Iran and Iraq had fought a bitter eight-year
war long before American boots ever tramped across these grounds.
To be an Arab then, and for a long time afterward, meant having your
loyalty questioned at every turn. Another Arab Iranian, a writer, told
me that during his army service they would often lock him away—
essentially hide him—during visits from commanders who had lost
men at the front lines and who would have been spooked to see the
"enemy" among the troops.

Identity, however, is channeled through a multiplicity of platforms, and race happens to be just one of them. When in southern Iraq now, in Najaf and Kufa (both staunch Shia cities) during a civil war when Shia and Sunni Muslims, not to mention Kurds, are essentially fighting an endgame over this land, one feels a certain relief at being with one's own coreligionists. This relief comes with a price, though. You ask yourself: So this is what it has come down to? Can I really be this glad to be safely tucked inside Najaf and Kufa with fellow Shia instead of being forty miles out in that inhospitable desert where bullets and knives await whomever happens to have the wrong first name?

Yes, is the answer.

On that long escalator ride at Imam Ali, there had been plenty of time to give oneself over to such thoughts. I had looked at Majed's pensive face again looking back at me from a few steps up and I knew he was thinking the same thing; we were thankful to be here among our own and to be safe. And yet, for those of us who occupy two worlds, at least on paper, there's always that sense that things could fall apart any minute, even here. One of the two passports that you own could be taken away. Or maybe both passports. Somebody might see through your fraudulence, your lack of commitment, your unconscious bad faith.

We were there to film the volunteer Shia fighters organizing to defend their homes and families against ISIS. There are, of course, absurdities that usually accompany such endeavors. That morning, for instance, in our semi-decrepit hotel room, it had dawned on Majed that if we managed to go north with the men, we might be asked, as their Iranian guests, to lead one of the prayers. We both know how to pray in private and quietly, but we are certainly no experts. What if I recited something incorrectly? What if I misplaced a word or forgot a segment? This pushed me to frantically Google the Shia prayer to make sure I had it down cold before I went anywhere.

There is also this: I didn't find my Googling of the Shia prayer something hilarious to laugh at afterward with friends and readers.

This isn't one of those humorous travel accounts. Way too many people have died on these battlefields in the past several decades, and I myself am too close to the subject; I'm not some unattached traveler slumming it in the Middle East. Rather, precisely because I am an Iranian, I felt the need to get things right, show respect, cover all the bases.

Ten days after riding up those everlasting escalators at Imam Ali's shrine (Imam Ali was the first imam of the Shia and the namesake of my father, one of my brothers, a nephew, an uncle, and any number of cousins and second cousins), I found myself at a place of worship again, this time inside a synagogue in the Iranian capital, Tehran, on a late Saturday morning listening to one of the community leaders giving a brief talk against, of all things, palm readers and fortune-tellers. When the congregation got ready to pray, I was politely asked to leave because they didn't want the authorities to wrongly assume there was any proselytizing going on in there. I had only to walk across the street from the synagogue to be inside my own apartment. Chance had it that the research I had been doing for a few years with a colleague at the City College of New York, about a group of Polish Jews who were saved in Tehran during World War II, had brought me to the very synagogue that happened to be directly across from my home in the heart of Tehran. The locals had just shown me where the Poles used to sleep in the basement of the synagogue and where they built their own annex for prayer next to the main building.

For a writer and researcher, it's an incredible stroke of good fortune to find what they've been looking for right under their nose. It's also a bit discombobulating. Because as a constant traveler in the world, as someone who must frequently negotiate more than one place and identity, you also learn that accidents can happen, and those accidents are not always so fortunate.

A mere few days after my synagogue visit in Tehran, I was again in the air, this time going back to New York, where a backlog of work and people to see was waiting. On a bus to Boston to visit another writer friend from Iran who had been given a much-deserved, and appreciated, residency at Harvard-Radcliffe, I received a text from my research colleague, Mikhal Dekel. We had not communicated much through the summer, a time when we're both usually in the Middle East, she in Tel Aviv and I in Tehran. I had been eager to tell her more about the synagogue visit and its association with the Jewish refugees of World War II. Mikhal's father and aunt happened to have been two of those Polish Jewish children who had been saved in Iran before being sent on to Mandatory Palestine.

But her text stopped me cold. In the latest war between Israel and Hamas, which had been going on for a while now, a close relative of Mikhal's, a young soldier named Gilad, had been shot and killed. I knew quite a bit about this Gilad. After years of working together on a book project, Mikhal and I were more than just colleagues. We knew close details about each other's lives and families. And, ironically, since both of us are Middle Easterners and spend major portions of each year in our respective cities, we have a distinct understanding and experience of the world that is hard, if not impossible, to share with most of our American associates in academia. I had seen Gilad's photograph and had met other members of his family. Mikhal wrote in her follow-up text message, "My family is in ruins. Things will never be the same after this."

In that Greyhound bus to Boston, the numbness I felt from this news slowly turned into a feeling of hopelessness. Iranian friends had been posting increasingly graphic images of death and destruction in Gaza in the past days. Sometimes these postings seemed more like a game of one-upmanship to show who can post the most terrible images to convey the suffering of Palestinians. One particular image of a young boy with his brains spilled out from the back of his head had kept me from revisiting Facebook for some time. And now Mikhal had written to me about Gilad. In this strange, topsy-turvy world of writers and academics and immigrants, where a man from Tehran and a woman from Tel Aviv might end up teaching in the same English department at a university in New York, I now felt that I actually knew an Israeli boy who had been killed in this latest war over there.

What, if anything, to do with this information? I couldn't share it with my sea of Iranian friends back in Tehran because, one, it would mean little to them and, two, they would confront me with the usual question—had I seen the latest body counts from Gaza? Needless to say, over the years Mikhal and I had had our share of discussions, sometimes heated, about all of this. But knowing a person who gets killed, a person who is not just a number and a statistic to you, changes a lot of things. Or maybe it changes just one thing: perspective.

I called Majed, back in Tehran. He was set to go back into Iraq for a long stretch of filming at the front lines. "Don't get killed," I said, sounding ridiculous to myself, and also melodramatic. But I had to say it, and he laughed his sleepy laugh eight and a half hours ahead in Tehran and told me not to worry. "I've been doing this a long time. Long before you and I started working together, Salar."

In Boston, on the peaceful and immaculately kept Harvard-Radcliffe lawn, I asked my Iranian writer friend Hossein Abkenar what he thought about living there in Cambridge. "Paradise," he said. "These people are living in paradise. They are lucky that way. The universe has been good to them."

Here was a man who had had to fight in the Iran-Iraq War. Later on he'd written an award-winning novel about it, *Scorpion on the Steps of Andimeshk Train Station*; the short antiwar novel had gotten him in some trouble back home and he'd been barred from publishing another novel for the last decade. So this one year of peaceful residency in Cambridge was nothing less than a lifeline for him, as, I suppose, teaching in New York is for me and Mikhal. Still, often I get asked how it feels to return to New York from the places I've been. "Is it a culture shock?" people ask. It's more than that, I think. One's investments are simply too deep for it to be just a culture shock— mine in Tehran, Mikhal's in Tel Aviv, and Majed's in the Khuzestan Province, where he was born during an Iraqi bombing raid.

So whenever I'm asked how it feels to be back, I return to details, to exact moments and emotions in particular places—to Najaf and that warm sense of shelter and security on the Imam Ali escalators, to Tehran, where, as late as 2014, the lights at the local synagogue burn brightly several times a week, or to that feeling of dread and powerlessness while riding a bus to Boston. I think of individuals. I think of their names, faces, and photographs. Of telling Majed to watch his back as he prepares to reenter the front lines in Iraq. And I think of Gilad.

Two Countries, One Divided Self

Roger Sedarat

My conflicted story as an Iranian-American best begins with the ancient Persians' greatest enemy, the Greeks. In Plato's myth of the divided self, Zeus splits the original two-faced, four-legged, and four-armed humans in two, which sends the respective halves in search of each other, longing to become one. For most of my life the hyphen between East and West has led me toward some illusive unity, even while keeping me separated, as a kind of minus sign.

My father, who came to the United States from Iran to attend college in the Midwest, became the most American man I've ever known. Sure, my mother, a midwestern farm girl majoring in home economics, learned to cook a few of his favorite dishes, such as *gheimeh*, a stew of split peas and cubed meat, and *ghormeh sabzi*, a stew made with green vegetables, herbs, and kidney beans, but he really fell in love with her meatloaf and coleslaw. Seeing his adopted country's expansive landscape with the exuberance of Walt Whitman, he'd take the woman who would become his wife on long road trips in his big Buick, exploring small towns along the highway as well as big cities such as New York and Chicago. Equally obsessed with America's booming economy, when a sociology professor took his class on a field trip to a new-concept fast-food chain restaurant in Illinois called McDonald's, he decided to buy into the American dream. Living frugally with his new family, which meant I'd get at best one pair of shoes three sizes too big that I could grow into over a few years, he invested whatever money he could set aside in the McDonald's company throughout his lifetime. When as children my older sister, Mary, and I took those same cross-country road trips with our old man as he'd done alone with our mother, he made us salute the golden arches each time we passed them on the road.

Yet despite his attempts to assimilate into American culture through its cuisine and free enterprise system, my father's Persian background continued to catch up to him in the West. I can't help but perform a kind of psychoanalytic reading of his biography, considering his obsession with Freud and his chosen profession of child psychology. For better or worse, Iran kept coming back to him like the return of the repressed. Living in San Antonio, Texas, as a kid, when I'd approach him in yet another one of his Buicks after my football practice, I'd find him listening to devastatingly sad Persian songs, to women emoting so much pain that the high, drawn-out notes kept me from opening the passenger-side door. It sounded like cats slowly dying in vats of hot water. As he listened intensely to the music, my old man would be sneaking a rare cigarette. Even at a time in America when smoking was totally acceptable, for some reason he never wanted to be seen doing it, as if it belonged to a secret part of him, back somewhere in his country of origin. He'd take a drag from his Winston and hold it in like the smoke from a joint, seemingly in time with the minor notes of the *tar*. As soon as I'd make my presence known, he'd frantically throw out the butt and hit Stop on the Sony tape recorder plugged into his cigarette lighter.

Randomly throughout our far-from-normal suburban life in the United States, the Iranian clan would appear, flying in from Tehran and Shiraz and taking over our home for weeks, sometimes months, at a time. During these visits I would go from having almost forgotten my Iranian origins to complete immersion in the Persian language and culture. Giving up my room to Grandma Taj, I'd sleep on the living room floor with a pack of aunts, uncles, and cousins, many of whom I'd never met before. My mother, a high school teacher at this point, would lose all control of her kitchen and most of her sanity, caught up in endless extended family drama while trying to meet the rather sudden and impossible expectations of her increasingly Iranian husband. Don't get me wrong. There was much to love about all of the changes, including the amazing warmth and intimacy of these relatives. But moving from complete American assimilation to instant Iranian acculturation became really unsettling. This disrupting pattern has continued throughout most of my adult life.

To show how hard it was for me to fully fit in with the Persian culture, I can simply start with my name: Roger Ted Sedarat. Do you know any Iranians named Roger Ted? To this day, my sister will call and leave a message on my voice mail, laughing about what our father named me. I adored my cousins, Ali Reza, Babbak, Mohammad, etc., but even nominally I didn't seem to belong with them. I understood some Persian, but I didn't grow up fluent (learning the language on my own much later), so there was always some communication breakdown. Needless to say, I missed a lot of cultural references, inside jokes, etc. You'd think I could at least have taken some kind of refuge in mainstream American society, but none of my friends had a house full of women with their heads covered and a tribe of foreign-speaking eternal visitors praying toward Mecca at certain points throughout the day. Despite my best efforts, I never felt like I quite fit in among my friends, either.

Then, as so often tragically happens in America among many ethnicities and races, I came to learn who I was by way of a much greater sense of exclusion. The Iranian Revolution in 1979 radically changed my father's country of origin, of course, but it also transformed my identity. This meant I'd quickly realize I was my father's son, far beyond his performance of Americanness. Around this time, I first started to see the kind of fissure in my old man's personality that Freud shows most reveals a damaged psyche. He'd try way too hard to fit in, a 5'2" foreigner with a thick accent wearing rattlesnake boots and a giant belt buckle shaped like the state of Texas with his suit like some of his native-born Texan colleagues who grew up with more authentic cowboy sensibilities. He'd even listen to Hank Williams in his Buick on that portable tape recorder.

One night he lay drunk in front of images of the burning American flag and blindfolded American hostages on Ted Koppel's *Nightline*. I was playing Monopoly near him on our shag-carpeted living room floor with my best friend, Benjamin Martinez. Ever my father's son, I was cleaning up, on the verge of making my opponent declare bankruptcy. Suddenly, the old man managed to get to his feet but then fell sideways onto our game board. Turning his head and moaning in pain, he had the race car, my chosen piece, stuck into his cheek. So much for his American dream. My friend went home, and eventually, when my dad stood up, I helped him down the hall to his bed. He leaned his full weight on me, making us both stumble along the way. After this night he kept falling down. He started driving drunk with me in his car; he drank himself out of jobs and eventually his marriage. I grew up terrified of the next big crash. His life came to feel so heavy to me. For better and worse I know we all end up carrying the burden of our parents.

For months after that night, as images of burning American flags and ferocious-looking bearded Iranians chanting "Death to America" kept appearing on TV, my father obsessively made and took calls from Iran. Considering that this man's extreme frugality would keep him from turning the AC on even during the 100-degree Texas summers, spending big money on phone bills seemed really strange. I understood enough Persian to know there was a family crisis involving his older brother who worked directly for the shah, but I couldn't grasp the details. I'm not sure he was even sharing much personal information on the phone back then. He'd never utter a word to his family about the personal crisis he experienced during that period (which I found out decades later involved his brother's execution). After 1979, my father would never really be OK again.

One late night I picked up the phone, expecting it would be the usual: his sister calling in unexplained tears. "Um, uh, hello?" I said feebly (at eight years old, I had little confidence, and even less phone etiquette). "Hey boy!" yelled a man in a strong Texas accent. "Um, yeah?" I replied. "You go tell your *I-ran-ian* daddy he has twenty-four hours to get his family out of the neighborhood, or we're going to burn his fuckin' house down. You hear me, boy?" I hung the phone up and screamed for my mom. I rightly figured she could handle the news a little better. But she basically just told me to ignore it, trying to dismiss it like they were just teasing us. Wishful thinking on her part, for sure. Two nights later, they smashed all the windows of my father's Buick. A week after that, they threw a brick through my sister's bedroom window.

My father finally sat me down for a big talk about what was happening. I felt relieved, assuming he'd help me make sense of it all. As a child psychologist, he most likely would give me some much-needed courage to keep going to school. (More and more kids were saying stupid things to me about the ayatollah.) "Look here, Rogie boy, when anyone asks where your family is from, tell them we're Greek." That's it, the culmination of what a PhD in psychology from the University of Wisconsin can do for your kid. "But Dad?" I asked. "We don't speak Greek." I thought I had him, but then he hit me with, "OK, then . . . tell them we're French. Just say *'Bonjour*,' and, you know . . . walk away. But be nice. Smile a lot."

As a kind of reaction formation, seeing him drink himself out of a job and then hide at home in fear, I instantly became the most radical third grader at Thousand Oaks Elementary School. My homeroom teacher, Mrs. Asher, confiscated a sticker from a classmate of mine of Mickey Mouse shooting the middle finger, with the caption "Hey Iran." I saw her show it to her teacher friend, whose class was right next to ours, separated by a divider. As they both snickered, I yelled out, "Hey, that's not funny! My Grandma lives there. Is it OK to give her the finger? Can I give your grandma the finger?" Mrs. Asher just dismissed my rant, telling me I needed to be working on my assignment. Even so, I stood ready to fight. Soon I actually did start to get physical, with other kids before and after school.

The revolution inadvertently awoke in me a desire to know the Iran my father was repressing. I grew up reading books and talking to relatives about its history. Summers, I got to go to stay with my uncle Nasser, who also had once worked for the shah's government and now lived as an exile in Bordeaux, France. We'd play backgammon and talk about the history of US intervention in Iran, how prior to the revolution the CIA had removed a legitimate prime minister, Mohammad Mossadegh, from power. He'd also tell me personal stories about growing up in Shiraz with my father. Most importantly, he'd recite the poetry of Hafez and Rumi, which I'd eventually learn how to read.

My search for the other half of my divided self extended into college, where in addition to studying philosophy and sociology I continued to learn about the literature of Iran. I even started gravitating to Islam for a while. Even so, I never let go of my father's appreciation for America. I think that's what so many stuck in this "us vs. them" mentality can't understand. It is entirely possible to simultaneously love and identify with different cultures, peoples, languages, etc. while still respecting, even loving, America. I'm proof of it. I eventually ended up pursuing a PhD in American literature, writing a dissertation on my favorite American poets, including Emily Dickinson, Robert Frost, and Wallace Stevens. All the while, though, I kept reading, and soon began translating, Persian poetry. I also started writing my own verse, which emerged out of America but also went into the Persian tradition.

The rest of my hybrid story has a ridiculously happy ending, something out of a Persian Sufi mystic's poem. I tell it repeatedly to all Iranians I know, and they almost can't believe it. I don't think I would either, if it hadn't happened to me. Before enrolling in graduate school, when I first graduated from the University of Texas, I played in punk bands while working in a mailroom (what else does one do with a degree in sociology and philosophy?). One day, as I was taking a smoke break outside this big office building in downtown Austin, an amazingly attractive woman with dark eyes and long dark hair came up to me and said hello. I tried my best to look cool, but I was terrified. "So, you don't seem like a typical Texas girl," I said, pretending to be casual, like I had game. "Where are you from?" She looked at me a little too long without responding, as if trying to decide whether or not to tell me. Then she replied, "My father's Iranian." What are the odds? "Mine too!" I said, a little too excitedly. "Yeah, right." She thought it must be a line I use, claiming to be from wherever the hot girl said she was from. To prove it, I showed her this gold Allah medallion my aunt Ezzat had given me; it had my name inscribed on the back, in Persian. "Oh man," she said, "you really are Iranian."

On our first date she told me that after having trouble for some time meeting a nice guy, she'd put an ad in the *Austin Chronicle* (this was pre-internet, when you had to actually go to print for such hook-ups). I had also for some time given up on dating, just like her. Tired of meaningless flings, I swore I'd hold out and then one day, God, the ultimate matchmaker, would present the woman I'd marry. It's like I felt it as a kind of premonition. Of course I started wanting her to be Iranian. The same aunt who gave me that medallion had also given me a small painted portrait of a beautiful Persian woman with long dark hair. I had put it over my writing desk in college and fantasized about her being my wife. Well, one day when going through personal ads in that local paper, for the first time in my life I felt compelled to actually cut one out. It felt like "the one." I swore to myself I'd respond to the woman who posted it, but then I couldn't summon the courage to follow through. It turns out that the ad I'd almost answered was hers: "Pretty Persian lady looking to meet nice gentleman, twenty-five years or older." Twenty-three at the time, I figured I didn't make the cut.

Returning to Plato's divided people, as corny and unbelievable as it may sound, I met that other side of myself in her. To fully convey our Persian connection, I don't think the Greek philosophy can do it justice. I need an allusion from our origins. For the classical Persian poets especially, one concept that originated in the Islamic tradition informed by Sufism is that the beloved becomes the object of intense affection, ultimately leading one to the divine. I suddenly wasn't studying the lines of another Persian ghazal, I was living them. Like me, Janette (also given a non-Iranian name by her father) had an American mother. Much as I grew up an Iranian-American in San Antonio, she'd grown up mostly in Lubbock, Texas, of all places, after moving there from Iran as a child. We discovered that we both had an older sister, Mary and Maria. We also shared the same kind of sarcastic humor common in our Persian families, *ba-namak*, or "salty," humor, as they say. All our friends and family commented about how we looked a lot alike. We even drove the same make of car: Nissan (I'd long abandoned my father's love of Buicks; they kept breaking down on me). Growing closer together and ultimately getting married and having kids, we've competed for years as to who is more Iranian. Recently we ended up taking one of those blood tests to discover our deep ancestry. It turns out mine came up completely surrounding the southern region of Iran, where it all got started, while she was diagnosed as more Tunisian. "*Man inja irani hastam,*" I tell her, pointing to the veins in my arm to show her where it counts.

Early on in our marriage I got to know much more about Iran from Janette's experiences with the country and culture. I actually became an Iranian citizen through my father, and we planned my very first trip there with our then two-year-old son. My old man almost had a heart attack when I told him I was going. Of course we had a perfectly safe time. We made it to Shiraz, and we discovered that back in the day when the city was much smaller my family had lived less than half a mile away from hers. It turns out that her eldest uncle, a poet and critic so acclaimed they put him on a postage stamp, had gone to elementary school with my uncle Nasser.

Despite more than twenty years with the Iranian-American woman of my dreams, I can't entirely say I've reached some fantasy of wholeness, at least not when it comes to my divided ethnicities and cultures. We sometimes struggle, in our personal life, to negotiate a place among relatives and the greater Persian community. We have such busy lives and demanding careers that we tend to just stay in our own private sphere. However, I do think we've retained the best of what we inherited, placing a strong importance on family and going out of our way to keep making delicious Persian food. As a poet and translator, I've also remained in political conflict, having helped render into English the verse of fellow poets who must remain anonymous or even go into hiding. This has been a source of real tension between my wife and me and has made it possibly unsafe for us to travel to and from Iran.

In addition to this political problem in my marriage, I've had to deal with criticism by Iranians for my calling out the Iranian government on some real injustices. What I've written in the past in no way means I absolve America of its much more unjust interventions throughout the world, which I vehemently attacked in my poetry collection *Haji as Puppet: An Orientalist Burlesque.* Aesthetically, I'm a little mystified by someone else's claiming the right to assess my critiques. I mean, Hafez, our go-to poet in the Persian tradition, made the calling out of hypocrisy his predominant theme, and writers I know and love have really suffered unjustly in Iran, so they deserve my support and even my speaking out. Aside from my own political beliefs and my argument about expressing them, my greater point here is that for better and for worse, the division between the two nationalities and cultures I've inherited has followed me into yet another conflict.

The gift through all of this has been that rather than resenting the tension between Iran and America, which I inherited from my father, I've come to create poetry with it. One critic called *Ghazal Games*, my second collection, which makes postmodern play of the great Persian form, "Rumi meets Wallace Stevens." I got to work my love and desire for Janette into these poems too, inserting her into the role of the beloved, even while qualifying the historically misogynist implications of such an act. To bring just a little literary criticism as well as Sufi mysticism into my conclusion, I sometimes wonder if I'd really even want to be just one thing or the other. The classical masters, after all, seem to inhabit the space between the material and spiritual worlds. Even more, they objectify and figuratively play with the constructs of their own ego-identities. Reflecting over my own life story, I see now how all that separation I felt has been an illusion. Through writing and connection to my beloved Iranian-American wife (my "better half"), I found a complete life where I most felt divided: between my two countries.

Mothering across the Cultural Divide

Katherine Whitney

"We're still going to Chaharshanbe Soori tonight, right?" my nine-year-old daughter, Leyla, asked as we trudged up the steps to our San Francisco apartment. We'd just completed our walk home from school, and she was already plotting our next move, expressing her desire to take part in the annual Iranian New Year tradition.

"Of course we are, love," I replied, half wishing she hadn't remembered. I fumbled with the key in the fading light.

"I'm hungry," whined her four-year-old brother, Kian.

It was the witching hour between school/work and dinner. I was also one week into a two-week stint of single parenting, as my husband, Farhad, was away in Ireland on a business trip. So frozen mac and cheese and a glass of wine sounded just about the right speed—not a long slog in rush-hour traffic across the Bay Bridge to Berkeley, where Iranians were gathering to mark their annual rite of spring: jumping over fire to clear out the cobwebs of winter and renew themselves for the year ahead. But I'd promised Leyla we'd go, and it was my job to get her and her brother there.

"We'll just grab some snacks and get in the car, OK?" I told my children.

Kian shrugged off his backpack just inside the front door and plopped down beside it. "I'm not getting in the car. I'm not going anywhere," he declared.

"Kian," my daughter implored, "we *have* to go. It's *really* important." After a pause, she added, "You'll get to jump over *fire*!" This was a brazen attempt to appeal to his known pyromaniac tendencies. I appreciated the strategy of my fiery redheaded girl. She was eager to embrace her culture and wasn't going to let her brother's resistance stand in her way.

Kian quietly considered his big sister's enticement for a moment, then decided that stubborn refusal was likely to give him more leverage. He crossed his arms over his chest and stayed put.

"*Puh-leeze*, Kian," Leyla pleaded. "We *have* to go. We're Iranian, and this is what Iranians do."

"I'm not Iranian," Kian replied.

"What are you?" I asked, curious about what he'd say, even at the risk of derailing Leyla's efforts to get him into the car.

"I'm American, like Mommy," Kian declared with confidence. "Besides, what kind of Iranian doesn't even speak Farsi?"

This was an echo of conversations Leyla had been having for years with her father. She desperately wanted him to teach her Farsi, but for reasons he couldn't really explain to her, he resisted. The sole card-carrying, 100 percent Iranian in the family didn't seem all that interested in transmitting his culture to his kids, at least not overtly. Along the way it had become my job.

Farhad came to the United States from Iran in 1979 just as the Islamic Revolution was coming to a head. His father dropped him off at a boarding school in Connecticut and returned home to Shiraz. Farhad was fifteen years old. He wouldn't see his parents again for seven years. He wouldn't see his homeland again for two decades.

It wasn't a great time to be Iranian in America. Back home in Tehran, revolutionary students seized fifty-two American diplomats and held them hostage for 444 days. In the United States, Americans tied yellow ribbons around mailboxes and trees in support of the hostages and expressed open hostility toward Iran and Iranians. Like many young Iranians at that time, Farhad just tried to fit in. And he did a pretty good job. His parents had sent him to the American School in Shiraz, so he spoke fluent English almost without an accent. By the time I met him a few years later, in college, he was a smart, funny, basketball-loving physics major with only a vaguely international flair.

Farhad's parents, who'd remained in Iran, were initially skeptical of the idea of their son's marrying an American. His mother, Giti, once told him, after he described how I'd repainted all his black furniture when we moved in together in San Francisco, "You know, a wife isn't like furniture. You can't just paint her a different color if you decide you don't like her." That said, once she and I got to know each other we became each other's biggest fans. To this day, I look forward to her annual visits to the United States, which are punctuated by long, lively games of canasta. Farhad's father, Tamadon, also gave his warm consent, after traveling to Massachusetts from Iran to meet my parents at their home.

For our wedding, on a bluff overlooking Tomales Bay, California, we created an untraditional ceremony "from whole cloth," as the saying goes, writing our own vows and commissioning, from my musical sister and her husband, an adaptation of *The Owl and the Pussycat* for violin and double bass. We turned the Iranian portion of the wedding over to Giti. She and her friends prepared the *sofreh aghd*, a satin cloth laid out with candles, eggs, flowers, and sweets. During the ceremony they held a silk canopy over our heads while our guests rubbed pillars of sugar above it to ensure sweetness in our marriage.

But in our early married life together, there was scant evidence of Iranian culture. There were little touches, such as Farhad's signature pomegranate margarita, invented years before it was chic to serve crafted cocktails at dinner parties. And his personal take on the traditional Iranian *naan panir sabzi* appetizer, which he made his own by adding roasted walnuts, olives, and dates to the customary flatbread, feta, and greens.

When the kids were born we gave them Iranian first names. We weren't making a statement; we just thought Iranian first names would sound better with their dad's Iranian last name. But I wondered what else they would glean of their Iranian heritage. Would they speak Farsi and be familiar with Iranian folktales? If so, who would teach them? I knew what I would pass on from my New England childhood. I'd take Leyla and Kian to the library before they could read, as my dad had with me, and make up long, elaborate stories to amuse them. In the summertime I'd take them swimming in the Atlantic Ocean and sailing on Buzzard's Bay. My dad had grown up in the same small coastal Massachusetts town where he and my mom raised my sisters and me. My hometown had embraced me, my father's daughter, with open arms. I'd do what I could to help Leyla and Kian feel that in San Francisco. But how would my New England Yankee traditions mix with Farhad's Iranian heritage? Neither Farhad nor I had spent much time thinking about our backgrounds and how different they were. I realized that roots don't really become relevant until children arrive and parents face the task of figuring out how to raise them.

"Are you going to speak Farsi to her?" our French-, English-, and Hebrew-speaking French-Israeli friend asked Farhad just after Leyla was born. When we became parents in the mid-1990s, San Francisco was full of multicultural families essentially competing to be the most ethnic in a city where diversity was prized. Many Bay Area children grow up speaking multiple languages at home and then go on to bilingual schools designed to prepare them for a global society.

"My Farsi's so rusty," Farhad replied, shaking his head. "It doesn't feel natural. And anyway, it seems weird to speak to the baby in a language Katherine can't understand."

It wasn't until years later that I learned what it takes to raise a bilingual child, how each parent must speak to the child exclusively in their mother tongue in order for a second language to take hold. It requires more discipline than our family would ever have. And when Leyla was a baby, I didn't even know what questions to ask about how to teach her a second language.

It wasn't until Leyla turned three and started preschool that Iranian culture became more than cocktails and appetizers in our family life. The change was initiated by a flyer that came home from school in her backpack one day, inviting families to sign up for "Family Share Day."

"What's special about your family?" the flyer read. "What traditions or stories can you share with our Teddy Bear class?" Hmmm, I thought. What *is* special about our family? We didn't really have any family traditions yet. We still felt pretty new at this. But we *were* half

Iranian. In the context of multicultural San Francisco, Farhad's Iranian half seemed "special," though we hadn't really worked out what that meant yet.

I walked into the kitchen with the Teddy Bear summons in my hand.

"What special things do Iranian families do?" I asked Farhad. He shrugged. A consummate and ever-experimenting chef, he was preparing tamarind for pad thai, separating the thick paste from the tough fibers by pushing it with his fingers through a strainer.

"What about holidays?"

He thought for a minute. "Well, there's Nowruz," he replied finally. "Persian New Year. First day of spring."

Nowruz? I'd never heard of it. We'd never observed it. And Farhad, up to his elbows in tamarind paste, was too preoccupied to provide me with details. So I turned to the internet to research it myself.

I learned that Nowruz is pretty much the most important holiday in Iran. The word *nowruz* literally means "new year," and it marks the first day of spring in the Persian solar calendar. It's an ancient festival predating Islam, with roots in Zoroastrian traditions.

In Iran, preparations for Nowruz begin weeks before the actual day. People clean their houses, bake sweets, choose gifts, and buy new clothes. On the Tuesday evening before Nowruz—called Chaharshanbe Soori—people light bonfires in the middle of the street. Some are large, others small, depending on the neighborhood and the zeal of the fire builders. Then everybody, old and young alike, jumps over the fires. They symbolically cast into the fire all the bad things that have happened during the year and take from the fire its invigorating red glow. It's a purification rite.

In every house a special Nowruz table is set, called the *haft sin*. The *haft sin*—which means "seven *s*'s" in Farsi—consists of seven objects starting with the letter *s*, each symbolizing growth and renewal. In the center is the *sabzi*, green grass sprouted from wheat or lentils. Around the *sabzi* are garlic (*sir*), apples (*sib*), jujube fruit (*senjed*), vinegar (*serke*), a custard made from walnuts (*samanu*), and the spice sumac (*somaq*). A mirror, a Koran, a book of poems by Hafez, a goldfish, an orange in a bowl of water representing the Earth in space, coins, colored hard-boiled eggs, and various sweets are often added to the arrangement, along with framed photographs of absent family members.

Nowruz is observed at the moment the sun enters the northern hemisphere on the vernal equinox. Thirteen days later, on Sizdah Bedar, which means "thirteenth outside," Iranian families pack large picnics and head to a park to spend the day outside. They take the *sabzi* that has been growing as part of the *haft sin* and cast the sprouted greens into running water—a river or a stream—to symbolize renewal and rebirth.

This was so rich! I didn't stop to wonder why we hadn't been observing this wonderful holiday all these years. Even if Farhad hadn't felt compelled to celebrate Nowruz, he had opened the door. I could take it from here.

For family share that first year of preschool, I printed out a picture of a *haft sin* from the internet for the kids to color. I helped them plant grass seed for *sabzi* in little plastic cups. And I made a little "fire" from bunched up red and yellow tissue paper for them to jump over. In the classroom, I told the kids, "This is what our family does for Nowruz," even though we'd never done any of it at home.

Throughout Leyla's preschool and early elementary school years, Nowruz was our go-to family share activity. Every March, Leyla and I strode into her classroom with a kit of supplies to make take-home *haft sins* along with our engraved silver plate for serving delicate chickpea flour cookies that we picked up at the Persian grocery store. And after a few years of sharing Nowruz with her classmates, Leyla demanded that we start celebrating it at home.

Leyla had been passionate and focused from the time she was a tiny baby. Whatever possessed her possessed her fully. And starting when she was just a little girl, Leyla began piecing together her mosaic identity by collecting and assembling whatever diverse fragments of her Iranian life she could track down. There was Nowruz, of course. And the beautiful hand-knit dresses that arrived by mail from her grandmother in Iran. And the cousins on Farhad's side of the family, two girls close to her age who lived nearby, whose parents were both Iranian and who spoke two languages—one of which Leyla didn't understand. Now Leyla wanted Nowruz to be more than something we just trotted out for her classmates and teachers at school.

At six, Leyla put her Japanese fighting fish in its bowl on the sideboard of the dining room—her substitute for a goldfish—and enlisted me to help her assemble a *haft sin* around it. Unlike a good Iranian woman, who knows to pack a bowl full of wheatgrass seeds in early March, then cover it with a damp towel until it starts to grow, I'd forgotten to sprout the *sabzi*. So I ran out to Safeway to buy a little plastic pot of wheatgrass. *Thank god we live in California, land of wheatgrass-juicing health nuts*, I thought, walking home with my precious package. As I transplanted the grass into a filigreed silver bowl under the critical gaze of my daughter, Farhad came home from work and took note of what we were doing.

"You bought the *sabzi*?" he observed.

"Yes!" I responded enthusiastically, running my fingers through the tightly packed, bright green blades. "Isn't it beautiful?"

"That's cheating," was his response.

Wait a minute, I thought. *I'm cheating*? I was pretty proud of my last-minute solution to the *sabzi* problem. Leyla ignored him and I followed her lead. She asked me to take a picture of her as she held each individual item—*sabzi*, apple, garlic, sumac, jujubes, vinegar, and a chia-seed porridge, as I hadn't been able to track down any real *samanu*. She posed and I snapped pictures. Then she carefully placed the items around the fishbowl centerpiece. Farhad watched us for a bit, then turned toward the kitchen to put down his backpack and make a cup of tea. "We'll send these pictures to your grandmother," I said to Leyla once we'd finished. I knew Giti would appreciate her granddaughter's cultural enthusiasm.

Leyla found and peeled a banana for her brother. Kian was still sitting before the front door, his preschool backpack beside him, refusing to budge. She knew feeding him would facilitate getting him into the car.

"Here you go, Kian," she said in the singsong of forced cheerfulness that I knew would turn to irritation if he continued to resist. Kian begrudgingly accepted the banana, but the sit-down strike wasn't over. I had to pick him up and carry him down to the car. Once we were all buckled in and headed toward Berkeley, we hit the rush-hour bridge traffic backing up to leave the city. Then it started to rain. I sighed.

"It's OK, Mama," Leyla sang out from the back seat. "We have umbrellas in the trunk!"

In Berkeley I drove in circles, feeling my way toward the Persian Cultural Center. I finally spotted bright klieg lights and heard the thumping beat of Persian music.

"Looks like it stopped raining," Leyla said hopefully as we parked.

Against my better judgment, we left the umbrellas behind and made our way toward the street party. The whole block was closed off for the celebration and crowds of people swirled around under the lights. In the middle of the street in front of the Persian Center was a line of three Duraflame logs, spaced about ten feet apart, each nestled inside a disposable aluminum roasting pan that was, in the interest of fire safety, carefully placed on a sheet of tin. The line of logs was cordoned off on either side by a row of orange traffic stanchions looped together with yards of yellow caution tape. People were already queuing up at one end, preparing to run the gauntlet, even though the logs had just been lit and there was still more smoke than fire.

Stomachs rumbling, we followed our noses toward the savory aroma of meat being grilled behind the cultural center. The long line for food snaked along the driveway next to the building. We took our place at the end, hoping the line would move quickly. It didn't, thanks to the fact that people kept cutting in front of us. Each time someone slipped ahead of us, Leyla flashed me a look of utter dismay. "This isn't fair," she telegraphed to me with her eyes. "Why are they doing this?" I had no idea what to do. I looked back at her and shrugged my shoulders.

Leyla sidled up closer to me. "I don't look Iranian," she whispered despairingly. "Because of my hair." I noticed she had pulled up the hood of her pink-and-brown striped sweater and tucked all her curly red hair up inside it. It had started to rain, but that wasn't why she'd pulled her hood up. I looked around. We definitely stood out, especially me, with my pale complexion, blue-green eyes, and light brown hair. How ironic, I thought, that a year earlier, on a family trip to Iran, Leyla's strawberry mane had drawn warmth and affection toward her. People had reached out to touch it and commented to Farhad about how beautiful it was. There her hair had made her feel more a part of the place, while here it was making her feel like a fish out of water.

"Honey, everyone knows you're half Iranian. Why else would we be here?"

She shot me a look of great skepticism. My reasoning was not persuasive.

"I wish Daddy was here," Leyla said mournfully as another young couple drifted into the line in front of us. Did she think his authentic Iranian presence would have prevented them from cutting in line? Or was there more to it than that?

Kian grew restless and wandered off to rearrange the large rocks that lined the edge of the driveway. "Kian, come," I called out from time to time, as we inched forward toward the food. Calling out his Persian name became my way of saying, however faintly, "We're legitimate, we're Persian, we belong here." I didn't feel it inside, though, and neither did my daughter.

When we finally got to the head of the line, we were famished. A woman stood on the other side of a long table and smiled at us. Attached to the pole of the pop-up pavilion sheltering her from the rain was a menu scribbled on a piece of cardboard. I could read the prices—familiar numbers and dollar signs. But the menu offerings, written in Farsi script, were completely opaque. I smiled back.

"What would you like?" she asked. I went out on a limb and asked for a lamb kebab. We'd been to Iran and had eaten at Persian restaurants, and I knew my way around a kebab menu. Besides, I could see them cooking on the grills behind her.

"We're all out of lamb," she replied. I looked at her, looked at the meat grilling behind her, and then met her eyes again.

"What *do* you have?" I asked.

She nodded her head toward the posted menu, and when I didn't reply she offered, "We have *jujeh* kebab."

I wasn't sure what that was, but I confidently replied, "I'll take three." She handed over three paper plates piled high with rice and saffron-tinted chicken kebabs. I handed her twenty dollars.

We ate our dinner squatting on the blacktop, huddled under another pop-up pavilion to stay out of the rain. I wasn't sure how much of that transaction Leyla had taken in, or whether she realized we'd been denied the lamb. And I wasn't even sure if we *had* been. Maybe those kebabs on the grill weren't done yet. Maybe they weren't even lamb! There was no one willing to translate for our straggly trio of two half Iranians and their American mom. No matter, we'd do our jumping and go home.

Once we'd cleaned our paper plates, we headed for the fire-jumping line, which had grown considerably since our arrival. The logs were burning now, and the flames were dancing. Leyla was excited to jump, and as we got closer to the head of the line, she was like a horse before a race, wriggling her shoulders and hopping, first on one foot, then on the other. She turned to me and whispered, "What are you supposed to say when you jump?"

"My yellow sickness to you, your red glow to me," I replied, having mastered my script from our years of Nowruz family sharings.

"No, in Farsi! What do you say in Farsi?" she pleaded anxiously. We were almost at the front of the line and she wanted to get it right.

I held up my index finger and turned to tap the shoulder of the woman in front of us. Leyla pulled my hand down and gave me a dark glare. Shaking her head violently, she silently mouthed, "*No!*" I'd almost made a fatal mistake. Asking someone for the correct Farsi saying would out us as interlopers, frauds, tourists. If we didn't know what to say, we didn't belong here.

When the man directing traffic at the head of the line said, "Go," Leyla took off, quickly putting as much distance between herself and her family as she could. Meanwhile, now at the head of the line, Kian froze. Behind us, a boy of about ten grew impatient. Muttering "Come *on*," he skirted around us and charged ahead. Finally, I grabbed Kian under his armpits and walked the gauntlet, lifting my boy, stiff with fright, up and over each of the three small fires.

At the end of the line, we looked around for Leyla. It was dark now and raining harder. She'd been upset, and I wondered whether she'd run off somewhere. Then I noticed that she'd circled around to jump again. Kian and I waited on the sidelines and watched Leyla make her second run. She saw us and came up afterward, announcing breathlessly, "I said my chant this time. Let's go home."

As we walked back to the car, Kian asked me, "How come *you* didn't jump over the fires, Mama?"

He was right. I'd been so focused on getting him over the flames, I hadn't figured out how to jump myself. "It's OK," I told him. And I thought, *I'll have to last another year with my yellow sickness.*

A year later, on the morning of Chaharshanbe Soori, Farhad called from Tehran, where he'd gone to nurse his mother through recovery from surgery. Eleven and a half time zones ahead, they had already done their jumping in Iran. He regaled me with stories of how people had set off homemade fireworks in the streets, how his cab had had to slow down and wait for all the explosions to go off before continuing on through an intersection, and how, from his aunt's sixth-floor apartment, it had sounded as though there were a war going on outside. The bonfires were huge, he said, three feet across, with flames leaping even higher than that up into the air.

I was planning to take Leyla and Kian, now ten and five, to Berkeley again that evening. This year the weather was clear, and daylight savings had come two weeks earlier, so it wouldn't be so dark.

But after school, Leyla announced that she wanted to stay home.

"Are you sure you don't want to go?" I asked her. "It's your heritage."

"I'm not even Iranian," was her reply. Followed by, "I wish Daddy was here. He's *always* away for Chaharshanbe Soori."

"He's not always gone," I said. "Just last year. And, well, this year too."

She looked at me with a mix of irritation and triumph and marched off to her room. Later, after jumping rope outside and clearing her head, she came around. She was in a better mood, but she still didn't want to go to Berkeley.

"I'm just too tired. Not tired physically, but . . ."

"Emotionally?"

"Yeah, emotionally."

After dinner, we lined up four votive candles along the concrete path in the garden outside. Earlier, Leyla had turned to the internet to research and print out the Farsi words she was supposed to say. Holding the paper in her hand, she cautiously stepped over the small flames, reading aloud, "*Sorxi-ye to az man; zardi-ye man az to.*"

Then she said it in English, leaping with more abandon. Kian came outside in his jammies and did his own enthusiastic jumping. Then Leyla disappeared into the house, yelling for me not to extinguish the flames—not yet. She reemerged wearing the bright red skirt and the shawl with dangly mirrors that her grandmother had sent from Iran. There, in the privacy of our backyard, with little touches of authenticity, we made the ritual our own.

As Leyla grew older, she became more and more captivated by Iran and what it meant to be Iranian. We moved to Berkeley when she was eleven, and there we stumbled across Golestan, a Persian-language preschool that, despite all odds, opened its heart to us. Even though Leyla was well past preschool age and didn't speak Farsi—a criterion for enrollment—the school's director took Leyla under her wing. For several summers, Yalda took on my young daughter as an "intern," letting her observe teachers and straighten up the classrooms when the kids went outside to play. Later, when Leyla was in high school, a Golestan teacher came to our house to instruct her in Farsi. Steeped in the language-immersion pedagogy of the school, Azam spoke no

English to Leyla. Instead, one evening a week, she and Leyla sat at our dining room table, their heads together in concentration, working out pronunciation, grammar, and the squiggly lines of Farsi script with the help of illustrated workbooks.

One evening when Leyla and Azam were working, Farhad bounced into the house fresh from a game of tennis.

"*Salaaaam!*" he enthusiastically greeted Azam, who rose up from the table.

"*Salam,*" Azam replied.

I stood there wondering whether this was the first time he'd seen them working together like this. Never breaking her policy of speaking only Farsi, Azam went on to tell Farhad what they were working on, pointing to Leyla's handwriting notebook. Farhad was engaged and smiling. Leyla remained seated, listening intently to Azam, then Farhad, turning her head from one speaker to the other as if she were watching a tennis match. I wondered how much of the conversation she understood.

Observing from a slight distance, I found the whole scene surreal. *It's not like Azam is her SAT tutor*, I thought, *or coming over to help Leyla with her math homework. We're paying her to teach your daughter your own native language. Why don't you think this is weird?* Farhad didn't seem to register the dissonance that I saw in the situation.

Later it struck me: my Iranian-American husband just didn't struggle with his identity. As a child in Iran, he didn't have to think about it, he was an Iranian in Iran. Then, after he was brought to the United States as a teenager, he became thoroughly Americanized. At first, this was a way to fit in and survive. Eventually, after getting a green card and then US citizenship through work, American became his new identity. "You're more American than Iranian," his mother said to him once, before we were married.

But in truth, the issue of identity is more nuanced, even for someone who doesn't really think about it that much. Over the decades we've lived together, I've seen him pull seamlessly from both sides: warm hospitality and lavish Persian cooking on the one hand, competitive American sportsmanship and technological prowess on the other. Farhad's dual identities are so entwined that it is hard for him to separate one thread from the other. But his daughter, growing up in the United States, wanted more access to the Iranian thread. And so did I.

While, like Farhad, I didn't think much about my own identity before having kids, things changed when I took on the job of raising two Iranian-American children. Once I became their mother, I inherited the woman's work common in so many cultures: that of interpreting and creating family traditions—some that were not mine to start with. My task was to come to an understanding of Iranian culture and weave it into my family's life, and into mine as a mother and a wife. It's something that's come slowly, over time, from an accumulation of details. So it wasn't at all weird to Farhad that Azam was teaching Leyla Farsi in our dining room. Leyla wanted to learn, Azam was a good teacher, and I made it happen. That's what moms do.

This spring, 2018, Nowruz creeps up on me without warning. It's been a rough year, between fallout from the Trump presidency, my double hip-replacement surgery, and the death of my dear father just a few weeks before the holiday.

When I confess to Leyla, now away at college, that I forgot to set out the *haft sin* this year, she texts me a photo of hers. She's watercolored each element of the *haft sin*—vinegar, garlic, custard, apple, jujubes, *sabzi*, and sumac—on its own piece of thick paper and identified each item in English as well as in a lacy Farsi script. They look like Persian miniatures. It's a portable, traveling *haft sin*, taped up on the wall of her apartment, and I covet it.

Chaharshanbe Soori falls exactly a month to the day after my dad died. Because of this and all the stress of the past year, I feel pulled, compelled, by some force greater than myself to go jump over the fire. Of all years, this is one when I feel the need to shed my yellow sickness and collect a little red vigor from the fire's flames.

Despite having moved to Berkeley from San Francisco ten years earlier, we've only gone to the Persian Center for Chaharshanbe Soori as a family a few times. We went in the early years, when the kids were still preteens and didn't mind being seen with their parents. But by the time Leyla hit high school, she was more interested in going with friends than with family. And Farhad never really liked the scene there. "Too crowded," he complained.

I try to coax Kian, now sixteen, to get off the couch and come with me. But he's nursing a sprained ankle, the result of a skateboarding mishap. Kian's Iranian identity is more low key than his sister's, limited to exchanging knowing nods—like secret handshakes—with the handful of Iranian-American boys who go to his high school.

"Nah, I'll pass," he says.

"I'll buy you kebabs," I say, a blatant attempt at bribery.

"Bring me back some?" he counters hopefully.

Absent any company, I drive downtown alone and back myself into an impossibly small parking space. As I'd done so many years before, I make my way toward the thumping beat of music in front of the Persian Cultural Center. As always, the street is blocked off. There are now two lanes of flaming logs—still Duraflame and still sitting in aluminum pans on sheets of tin—to accommodate the increased crowds that come in from all over the East Bay. I get in line and text Leyla.

"I'm at the Persian Center," I write her. "I can't remember how to say the chant in Farsi."

Behind me, a woman says something in Farsi to her neighbor. I hear the English word *tourist*, and I wonder if she's talking about me. I still don't speak the language, but I've learned enough vocabulary to get the gist of what people are talking about. And it's especially helpful when they slip in an English word here and there. I look around. I still stand out as much as I did that night twelve years ago. Everything I've internalized about Iranian culture, every word or phrase I've learned, everything I've taught my kids is invisible to the people around me as I stand here in line.

I turn and smile at her, pretending to have understood what she said. She smiles sheepishly in response. *You have no idea*, I think.

In front of me, a family fans out across the two parallel runways. Two sisters hold hands and jump together on one side. In the next lane over, their older brother races to beat them to the finish. Then it's my turn. I haven't heard back from Leyla. So I run and jump on my new hips, chanting in English, "My yellow sickness to you, your red glow to me."

As I walk back to the car, I feel better for having jumped. But maybe it's not so much a deep connection to Iranian culture that's changed my mood. Maybe it's more that I needed some ritual, any ritual, to channel my grief. In recent years, my work as an ambassador to this culture has diminished. My children have grown more fully into their Iranian-American selves and are deciding what that means on their own. I consider the possibility that I've excavated as much as I can from this culture that isn't mine and that's never completely let me in. Long ago, after our first of three family trips to Iran, when the kids were very young, I imagined our family life as a tapestry I was weaving, one with an Iranian warp and an American weft. And I imagined that one day, I would hand over the unfinished weaving, with all its complicated threads, to my children for them to interpret, pick apart, reweave, and embroider with details of their own. *Perhaps*, I tell myself, *that time has come.*

I'm almost to the car when I get a text back from Leyla.

"*Sorxi-ye to az man, zardi-ye man az to*," she writes. "[Let] your ruddiness [be] mine, my paleness yours."

"Thank you," I write back.

My Mom Killed Michael Jackson

Shokoofeh Rajabzadeh

In June 2002, in Tehran, an entourage of cars carrying my aunts, uncles, and cousins drove my sister, Reyhaneh, and me from Meh- rabad Airport to my grandmother's house in Narmak. The windows were down. My aunt's cigarette smoke knotted the scent of fresh smog. Billboards adorned with Farsi script and displaying photos of smiling women in hijabs peppered the freeway. Our five-car pha- lanx drove in one horizontal line across the three-lane highway. And Michael Jackson sang for us the whole drive home. First, "Beat It." Then, "Dirty Diana." Then, "Thriller." Each of my cousins asked us, "So what's your favorite Michael Jackson song? I'm sure we have it. We can play it for you. They probably listen to Michael Jackson every- where in America."

Neither my sister nor I knew a single track by name. "Oh, we love all of them. How could you go wrong with Michael Jackson, right?" we said.

We were introduced to Michael Jackson that summer in Tehran. It was the first time we had traveled to Iran after having immigrated to the United States twelve years earlier, when we first landed at San Francisco International Airport for what we expected would be my father's two-year MBA study abroad. We might have heard Michael Jackson blaring from the headphones of the occasional Walkman in high school, or seen his music videos on the TV screens at the Fud- druckers in Hacienda Plaza, but at that point, we couldn't and didn't want to distinguish his voice from the melting pot of alienating Amer- ican pop culture. If it wasn't rap or hip-hop, we just assumed it was another white artist who sang for all the white parents, children, and citizens who surrounded me and Reyhaneh, the only Middle Eastern girls in the Pleasanton Unified School District, distinguished by our unibrows, mustaches, and hijabs. In our social map of the campus, the white people who listened to pop music were the same people who, on good days, threw pizza at us in the quad, and on bad days, like those that followed 9/11, followed us everywhere but into the girl's bathroom yelling, "Go back to your fucking country, you terrorists. Fuck you!" So, it's possible that we may have heard Michael Jackson's music, but we had not sought it out.

In Tehran that summer, there was no escaping Michael Jackson. He sang at every family gathering. The older cousins taught the younger cousins how to execute his moonwalk, his twists and turns, and his crotch-grab. We tried to learn the moves too, but mostly we just watched our cousins dance while we cracked open sunflower seeds and put salt on sour plums. Michael Jackson led us on long night drives up to "Tehran's Rooftop," one of the mountains that surround Tehran, and stayed with us during large family dinners in our grandma's backyard.

In fact, there were only two times during the day when Michael Jackson had to be silenced. The first was after midnight, when my grandma and aunts were asleep, when we stayed up until dawn playing hands of Shelem, smoking hookah, drinking tea, and eating feta cheese, toasted *sangak* flatbread, and walnuts. The second time was when my grandma, Aziz, smoked her hookah—always on her favorite leather chair in the living room, always the orange flavor, always while watching TV shows that were the equivalent of *The Oprah Winfrey Show* or *The Dr. Oz Show* on government-sponsored TV. On both shows, citizens called in and were counseled by the hosts about intercourse timing, relationships, childbearing, and working outside the home.

Michael Jackson was the background music for that summer of accomplishments and firsts. That summer was the first time a stranger hung on to my eyes and wouldn't let go—not because he had never seen "one of them Muslims" before, but because he thought I was absolutely beautiful. It was the first time a boy asked me for my number. The first time I rejected a boy and told him to get lost. The first time a boy followed me and slipped me his number anyway. It was while listening to Michael Jackson from the speakers of a flip-phone in the forests of Northern Iran with my two chain-smoking cousins at the foot of a misting waterfall that my sister and I smoked our first cigarette—a Dunhill. "Smoke it," my cousin said. "You can feel the music vibrating in your body when you breathe out smoke with his words."

We went to Iran every summer after that, and while we were there we experienced what our white American classmates enjoyed every day in the United States: the privilege of just being teenagers. In Iran, we weren't resident experts of the Muslim American experience, nor were we expected to have some insight into Ahmadinejad's madness. We were just teenage girls. In Iran, where the standard height for women is five feet, we were comfortable in our bodies. No one considered thick body hair a sign of hormonal imbalance. In Iran, boys found us attractive. We relished applying makeup as we got ready to eat out. We felt fashionable while observing hijab, enjoyed the privilege of fitting in without standing out, of being seen without being gawked at. In Iran, with Michael Jackson as our soundtrack, we tested the limits of authority, selfishly imagined ourselves at the center of everyone's world, and made bad choices with boys and our bodies. In Iran, we were free.

We left that freedom whenever we left Iran and came back to a California that repressed us as Other. But in the States at least we still had Michael Jackson. He sounded the same played from speakers here as he did from speakers there. So Michael Jackson became the anthem to the nine-month stretch that we spent in California every year before we returned to Iran. Though Reyhaneh and I never spoke about it, in a place with people who constantly reminded us that nothing was ours and no one was like us, we felt like Michael Jackson empowered us to be who we really were. In Iran, his voice and face and movements absorbed our newfound understandings of courage, belonging, and confidence. When we were in California, we drew on him whenever we felt estranged, depleted, or defeated. Michael Jackson taught us how to stand taller. Now, when we were at Starbucks and someone stared at our hijab for too long, we gave them the "beat it" stare. In my mind, I condescendingly told the white barista wearing a wifebeater—the one who spoke to me very slowly, accentuating every word, and who wrote "Shock your face" on my coffee cup when he heard my name—that change starts with the man in the mirror. And during the nights when everyone else was at a football game, a homecoming dance, or a block party, I'd tell myself, "You are not alone."

My mother was also different during those months we spent in California. In Iran we cherished her resonant laugh that emerged from the corner where she huddled with her sisters, losing track of meals and prayer times. In the States we noticed our mother turning more and more to prayer. She prayed more often and for longer hours in California than she ever did in Iran. The prayer itself took only minutes, but my mother stayed, either kneeling or prostrated on the prayer rug, with her airy, dark blue, paisley-printed chador over her head, for an hour or two afterward. She gently rocked back and forth while whispering. All we could hear were the occasional *s* sounds that made it past the uneven space between her top and bottom rows of teeth.

When we were little, we dashed in and out of her chador whenever she stood at prayer. If we timed it right and had all our toys at hand, we could slip under the light fabric draped over her body, play a few seconds of house—pour each other a cup of invisible tea from our plastic teapot—and then run back out before she bent over in prayer and knocked her butt on our heads. We would poke her butt when she had her forehead to the ground and try to tickle the bottoms of her feet, and when none of that distracted her enough, we'd say the word *fart* because that was guaranteed to make her laugh in the middle of recitation. Some nights, though, she would turn off the lights and close her bedroom door and lock it. On those nights, we knew she was having a serious discussion, one that could not be disrupted.

In our teenage years, the number of these silent, dark nights of prayer increased. Looking back, I suppose my mother had a lot to pray about. One summer, I returned from Iran wearing jeans, without back pockets. I got myself a "boyfriend," whom I never actually saw because he lived hours away. We just talked on the phone about how hot he thought my ass looked in pocketless jeans the one and only time he'd seen me. Another year, I lied to my parents and told them I was going to the football game with girlfriends, but instead I went with our family friend's son, who happened to be a hot basketball player with a six-pack. My parents couldn't understand that I needed kids at school to see that I could score a hot guy even though I had a unibrow that looked like a river gorge across my forehead. That same year, my sister started dating a boy from community college who was taller than all of us, wore baggy pants, cackled too much in front of my parents, and interrupted Reyhaneh every time she spoke. When my parents tried to explain that our boyfriends were disrespectful and showed signs of being emotionally abusive, we shut them out.

Sometimes it seemed like those prayer sessions gave my mother insight into what we were doing behind our parents' backs. For example, one time, during my final year of undergrad at UC Berkeley, I was spending the night at my fiancé Mehdi's apartment instead of my dorm room. We were both supposed to be studying for exams. After we had made out for a few hours, and crossed every base but the last, my mother called.

"*Salam, azizam.*"

"*Salam, Maman.*"

"*Khoobi?* What are you up to? How is finals studying going?"

"I'm good. It's going well. You know, just busy."

"Good. Are you studying right now? Is it a bad time?"

"No, it's not a bad time. I'm just studying with Mehdi out at a café." I was lying on my stomach on the floor, typing a draft of a paper.

"Oh, it's so quiet."

"Is it?"

"Is it a holiday on campus or something? Are all the students gone?"

"A holiday? No. Why?"

"It's just that, usually when I call and you're at a café or out with Mehdi I hear a lot of cars and sirens and police cars and all the rest of the city."

"Oh. Yeah. It's a quiet night around here for some reason. I guess everyone's in the library," I said as I shot up and ran to the window of his bedroom, bent over as much of my body as I could out over the ledge, and desperately tried to suck as much of the street noise into my cellphone as possible.

"Well, OK. Have fun! I'll see you this weekend. I didn't want to disturb. I just called to see how you're doing."

"Thanks, *Maman*. I love you," I said, still hanging my body out of his fourth-floor window.

"*Khodafez, jigar.*"

The following Saturday, after she prayed, my mother came into my bedroom and asked me to sit down. We sat cross-legged on the thick, red Persian rug in my room, facing each other. "I'm worried about you," she said, as she stretched out her fingers, her hand like a starfish, and pulled them together, dragging her nails along the carpet, a movement that when repeated four or five times managed to bring all the bits and pieces of trash and crumbs out from the rug into a small pile right at her palm. "Don't do anything you'll regret. You're so close to being married."

"I know, *Maman*. I'm not doing anything. Don't worry."

"It can just feel so right sometimes, but still be at the wrong time."

"OK. I know," I said in a tone much sharper and snappier than hers.

"I'm only saying this for you. This isn't my body or my life. It's yours. But it's a decision you won't regret."

That incident only shortly followed one where my mother and father spontaneously decided that we should stop at Peet's Coffee & Tea, where my sister worked the opening and weekend shifts, to say hi to Reyhaneh on a Saturday morning before going on a hike at Sunol Regional Wilderness. A few days earlier my dad had found her cigarette butts in a wad of aluminum foil at the bottom of a trash bin in the yard, and he'd had a long conversation with her. He'd calculated how much of her paycheck she would end up spending every month if she let herself get properly addicted to the poison. My sister was left with no choice but to swear she would quit. And yet, that morning, when we pulled up to Peet's and my mom and I jumped out of the car to go in and say hi, hug her, and return to the car, we found Reyhaneh squatting outside of Peet's with her back against the wall, wearing her black leather jacket and thick, black eyeliner in her water lines. She had a cup of coffee in one hand and a cigarette in the other.

Later, Reyhaneh asked me whether I asked them to stop by, and I repeatedly said no. "I swear to you, Rey, I didn't say a word."

"Well, then, why the hell did it cross their minds to stop by *that* day of all days? It was my only cigarette in a month."

"I don't know. I really don't. I'm telling you, it's creepy."

The older we got, and the more secrets Reyhaneh and I concocted and kept from our mother, the more we felt threatened by her evening stretches of solitary prayer in search of clarity. Every night when she closed the door, we felt vulnerable, as if our minds and hearts and souls were subject to a search. As if even the deepest corners of our minds were no longer ours alone. We anxiously waited her out, wondering what she had learned about us this time, what suspicions her antenna had picked up.

Then, in 2009, my sister decided to make a pilgrimage to London to see Michael Jackson's *This Is It* concert. Reyhaneh was nineteen. Nineteen is the age an American child backpacks through Europe or a string of developing countries to "find herself," with little interference from her parents. But by Iranian standards, nineteen is no more grown up than fourteen. And by the Iranian standards of my family, the idea of a nineteen-year-old girl traveling to London, a bustling city, was unbearably frightening.

When Reyhaneh got up at 3:00 a.m. to sign up for the Michael Jackson ticket lottery, my mother and father neither objected nor showed interest. I imagine they assumed the idea would deflate on its own when her name wasn't drawn. But Reyhaneh's idea very quickly transformed from ethereal to material when her name was drawn within days. She won the opportunity to purchase a ticket to the 2010 concert.

"I'm going to go to a Michael Jackson concert in London," Reyhaneh announced to our parents one afternoon while we were having tea.

My mother and father both looked at their tea glasses, brought them up to their lips, and took a sip before setting them back down.

"It's just a concert," Reyhaneh continued in the silence that followed her announcement. "Everyone our age has been to a concert."

"Why don't you wait until he moves his concert here?" my mother asked.

"Because I don't know that he will! You don't understand. I can't miss this opportunity to see him. Besides, I signed up for a lottery. I won a ticket."

"You didn't *win* a ticket," my father said. "You won the chance to *spend money* on a ticket, yes?"

"Yeah. But I still won."

"Only in America," my father shook his head and mumbled.

"Wait, isn't that how hajj tickets work in Iran?" I asked. I was also at the table, but was mostly remaining silent. "Doesn't your name get drawn and then you can register and buy tickets?"

"Yes. But we don't call that winning," my father replied.

"You've never left the country except to visit my sisters, and now you expect us to just be comfortable letting you get on a plane and go?" my mother continued.

"Why don't you all just come with me then?" Reyhaneh suggested.

"You know why. Because one, we are not citizens. The visa process is difficult. And two, because your sister's wedding is in two months!"

At this point, the average US-born-and-raised child would slam her fist on the table, push back her chair, stand up, and yell, "Well, I'm nineteen! I don't even need your permission to buy a ticket and go! And I already have money raised from working at Peet's. Hopefully you'll all come around." So it came as a surprise when Reyhaneh *did* raise her voice and say all of those words, in that order.

The following day my mother leaned against the doorway of my room and looked at me while I lay on my bed, texting my fiancé.

"Just let it go, *Maman*. She's just going to a concert and coming back," I sighed.

"But she's never been anywhere like that. A big city, alone. It's too much."

"It's a city, *Maman*. There are millions of people there. She's not alone."

"We are not like the millions. She stands out, Shokoofeh. We all stand out. It's not safe."

"I mean, you and Daddy left Iran and came to the United States when you were only a little older than her."

"Exactly. I know what it's like to leave home, to leave family."

"Mom, she's not emigrating! She's going to a concert."

"We weren't emigrating either, Shokoofeh. We were leaving for an MBA. I was supposed to be back home with my sisters two years later," she said, tearing up.

I rolled my eyes. "You're so dramatic."

"You don't understand."

"No, clearly I don't understand how a concert is related to your immigration story." I paused before adding, "Well, what are you going to do?"

"What can I do? I just won't give her any money for the trip, if she asks. I won't sign any of her papers if she needs signatures."

"Yeah, she probably doesn't. And she already has Peet's paychecks saved up. You know her, she barely spends."

"Well, there's nothing we can do if she isn't going to wait for permission. I will just pray that what is best for her happens."

Over the next few weeks, Reyhaneh printed and filled out her visa forms. She purchased plane tickets and found a hotel and figured out what she should eat while she was there. She also listened to Michael Jackson nonstop, every day, every minute, in her car, in the shower, in her bedroom. She was memorizing every song before the concert. In the meantime, my mom and I had the same conversation over and over again. It always started with "I don't know what to do" and ended with "There's nothing I can do but pray."

And every night, just past sunset, she closed her door, turned off the lights, and kneeled at her prayer rug with her forehead to the stone. Sometimes for an hour, sometimes for two.

The day Michael Jackson died, Reyhaneh, Mehdi, and I were sitting at a Thai restaurant waiting on pad thai, pad see ew, and coconut curry. I was complaining about the flowers for the wedding and asking Reyhaneh about the dance she was planning to perform with our two best friends. Then she looked at her phone, brought her left hand up to her mouth, and said, "Oh my god. Oh my god." She was tearing up. Her lips were quivering. "Michael Jackson just died."

Mehdi asked for the food to go. Reyhaneh and I went out to the car and sat with our hands fisted under our chins, feeling tears fall one by one. At home, Mehdi was the only one who ate. Reyhaneh and I sat on the living room sofa and stared at the backyard. After a few hours, we called everyone in Iran, all the cousins and aunts and my grandma, one by one. When my grandma picked up the phone, she said, "It's very upsetting. But man, is it something. The most important religious figure in Iran could die and you wouldn't see so many young people so upset. These singers, they really are loved." We knew we had lost more than our favorite singer, but we didn't know what it was then. "What are we going to do?" we both just kept saying. That afternoon, our living room and our life in California felt so far away, so separate, from Iran. What we didn't know then was that Iran would never feel close again.

A few days later, the concert producers sent an email to all the people with *This Is It* tickets that said "given the circumstances," they could either get a refund or receive a hologram ticket for the price they paid. Reyhaneh asked for the hologram ticket, a choice my dad shook his head at when he found out and mumbled, "Only in America."

Days before my wedding, my mom leaned against the frame of my bedroom door with a smirk splayed across her face. She said, "Isn't this weird?"

"What is? That twenty people still haven't RSVP'd?"

"No. I mean, I prayed for her, and then this happened." Her smirk was now a full-blown smile.

"What? Did you pray for him to die?" I said, raising my voice.

"Of course I didn't. What kind of thing is that to say?"

"Well, what did you pray for?"

"I don't pray for any specific thing. I pray in generalities. I don't assume I know best. I prayed for Reyhaneh's summer to be safe and productive, for your relationship to be healthy and fun."

"But that's what you asked for. What did you really want?"

"I didn't want her to go, that's true. But I didn't want this to happen."

"I don't know, *Maman*. From where I stand, it seems like you had a hand to play in all of this."

"Don't be silly," she said, laughing.

"I'm serious. I mean, there wasn't any other way for her not to go, was there? You know your daughter better than anyone else. When her mind is set, it's set. And Michael Jackson wasn't going to just cancel *all* of his shows at once. You should have thought about that when you prayed," I snapped.

"We left our family for a short trip and we never went back."

"What does that have to do with it?"

"Never mind."

"You never understood Michael Jackson, *Maman*. You were never a teenager in America."

"What does that have to do with it?"

"Never mind."

"May he rest in peace," she mumbled as she left.

Am I an Immigrant?

Roxanne Varzi

This year my son will turn eight, the age I was at the time of the Iranian Revolution, when my American mother brought me to the United States, leaving my Iranian father in Tehran. When Donald Trump was elected president, my son asked if we would have to move to Tehran. My Iranian husband and I did what my parents did during the revolution: we lied, saying that he had nothing to worry about.

For years after I moved to Michigan as a child, I hid in the shadows, scared to death every time Iran was in the news because it meant I would be bullied at school. Parents picked up their children in cars with bumper stickers that read "Bomb bomb bomb, bomb bomb Iran" (a takeoff on the song "Barbara Ann," by the Beach Boys). I hid my identity, to the degree that I could: I didn't exactly fit into my midwestern surroundings. People were always asking where I was from. "Here," I'd tell them. "What about your parents?" they'd follow up. I'd think of the humiliation my father suffered at the Detroit airport every time he flew to the States to visit us. We would wait and wait and wait at Arrivals and he'd come out last, despite his green card, having had every inch of his possessions searched and, often, every piece of Persian writing he had with him photocopied.

My grandmother told me to take my *Mayflower* descendant certificate to school, but she never seemed to understand that I wanted to be accepted for who I was—and even if half of me was *Mayflower*, it wasn't the half that really defined me. For the first eight years of my life I lived among Iranians, Americans, and Europeans without a thought to politics. As an Iranian-American child in Tehran in the 1970s, I never felt alien the way I did in the United States.

It wasn't until I went to college in Washington, DC, that I came out of the shadows. I was sitting in my dorm lounge watching American families being evacuated from Iraq during the first Gulf War. The children leaving their Middle Eastern fathers behind at a Middle Eastern airport in the middle of the night reminded me of myself. The next day I began planning a teach-in. When the day came and I stood up in front of hundreds of people and spoke, the comment I heard most was: "I had no idea you were Middle Eastern." It was time to recover the identity I'd spent years trying to hide. After college, I lived for a year in Cairo, then a year in Tehran before returning to the United States for a PhD in anthropology and Iranian studies.

When 9/11 came, I was writing my dissertation in New York. I'd spent a decade in the city feeling at home in the world for the first time since I was eight. But that changed. I was told nasty things about "those Muslims" while waiting in line at the grocery store or the doctor's. I was scared to fly, not just because of the possibility that a bomb would go off but because traveling was hell with an American passport that says, "Place of birth: Iran." I had to be careful not to carry anything with Persian writing onto a plane; I had to avoid speaking Persian at airports.

I kept quiet while incidents that seemed innocuous to most continued to occur. In the spring of 2016 women wearing hijabs were asked to leave a café I liked: one more place to boycott. Trump's win in the Republican primaries was taken by many as a call to racism and hate.

But then, on the morning after the election, something magical happened: people began posting on Facebook and writing texts and emails declaring solidarity with Muslims for the first time since 9/11. Gloria Steinem promised that if any of us have to register as Muslim, we will all register as Muslim—making identity a political choice rather than something you're born into.

I have both an Iranian and an American birth certificate. Issued by the US Embassy in Tehran, my American birth certificate states, "Birth of an American citizen abroad." I was baptized and raised Catholic in a community of Irish missionaries and Americans in Tehran, but by Islamic law I'm Muslim because my father was Muslim.

Am I an immigrant? My mother is American, born and raised in the United States. Her ancestors came over on the *Mayflower*, and one of her great-grandfathers came from Germany. We visited the States every summer in the 1970s. When we moved here after the revolution we lived in her childhood home with my American grandmother. I grew up watching *Sesame Street* and *Little House on the Prairie* and eating Kentucky Fried Chicken. I am an American, an Iranian, an immigrant, a citizen, a Catholic-Muslim agnostic anthropologist.

My father waited years before applying, reluctantly, for American citizenship. He feared the day would come when he would have to choose, and in that choice something would be lost. He died before Trump announced his "Muslim ban." I was at the LA Opera that night, listening to Mozart's *Abduction from the Seraglio*, staged on the infamous Orient Express, which moved seamlessly from East to West. Meanwhile, just a few miles away, at LAX, an even more impassioned, angry drama was beginning to play out as protesters arrived to take the stage and to remind us that if we didn't act, then something would indeed be lost.

1,916 Days

Mandana Chaffa

I remember sleeping on a fur coat in a cloakroom.

I remember a roulette wheel spinning spinning spinning, but maybe I imagined that.

I remember the restaurant on the bridge.

I remember Baba bringing home scarce bananas because I loved them so.

I remember Maman and Baba listening to the cassette player in the living room, drinking and laughing while I danced for them.

I remember—in exact detail—the layout of our apartment.

I remember being sick and standing in my crib until Maman came to get me.

I remember Baba blowing cigarette smoke in my ear because it ached.

I remember being forced to lie still for the mask that smothered my face, before they removed my tonsils.

I remember being held close on Baba's lap, unseatbelted yet perfectly protected, as he drove with one hand.

I remember sitting on the kitchen counter while Maman ground beef for *kotlet*.

I remember the nimbus of half-asleep in the car, listening to muted Mahasti and the murmured lullaby of my parents talking, as young couples do.

I don't remember Isfahan, Shemran, Shiraz, Ramsar. I don't remember my mother's mother. I don't remember the smell of fresh *naan sangak*, straight from the baker's oven. I don't remember so many precious experiences except through the filters of others' memories. I am my own unreliable narrator.

I remember the day we left, on a visit that turned into a stay that turned into a lifetime. I remember the pound of Swiss chocolates I ate as we went from plane to plane to plane. I remember the terrifying clamor of JFK. I remember holding hands very tightly. I remember meeting strangers who were family. I remember being silent, bereft of language. I remember the end. I remember the beginning. I am five.

I am further in five.

It is September 13, 1971. It is the first day of school and I am accidentally in first grade, unexpectedly in the United States, unprepared for what may come.

All I know is, I am five. It is the most you can count on one hand: *yek, doh, seh, chahar, panj.* I am alone in a room full of children who are all bigger than I am, moving in fast orbits around a center to which I am not affixed. A maypole of six-year-olds, diving, leaping, laughing, and connecting, while I stand ribbonless, an unsheathed nerve. I have not yet learned to conceal the quiver that will give me away like that of the young gazelle on the Serengeti on Mutual of Omaha's *Wild Kingdom*, where Marlin Perkins waits safely in a hut with a mai tai, right before *The Wonderful World of Disney* on channel 4 every Sunday night, on the television with rabbit-ear antennas. But I don't know Disney yet, I don't know of any Magic Kingdom, and it is not a small world after all.

I am in a classroom, but I don't have a word for classroom. I don't have a concept of classroom. I am from the old world, tentatively in a new world, but not in a Christopher Columbus kind of way; more shanghaied than settler.

I am just five. I do not speak English. Around me, they babble. They are loud. They expend energy. I curl up like a baby hedgehog and retreat further into myself.

It is September 13, and somewhere not too far away, someone is yelling, "Attica! Attica!" And me, I am encaged in a scarred wooden seat-and-table contraption in the back of the classroom, lost. Lost is not knowing. Lost is having no imperfectly folded Rand McNally map as guidance. Lost is seeing no reflection in a room of blondes, blue eyes, clotted-cream skin. Even the brunettes look different from me. It is the time of Marcia Brady, and I am not, nor will I ever be, cool hip far out groovy.

Immigrant. I-mmigrant. I am migrant.

But you're not a migrant. You're not a refugee who escaped, but an unexpected pioneer who has come for a stay and is planting roots into the soft, loamy soil of New York in the early seventies. There is scant recognition of your birthplace connections slipping away like the tide on a moonless night, no compound fracture of permanent dislocation breaking through the skin. It won't be until a fall day eight years later, as others demonstrate oceans away, that a door slams shut—still unclear whether it was a clang of release or of exile?—but until then you are as yet unaware that your personal geography has been lobotomized, earthquaked, with a *there* you will never physically touch again.

You live in a dual existence of an irrevocably transformed former country—crystallized in your mind after 1,916 days, kept alive by the umbilical cord of familial rituals—alongside this melting pot that you have adopted and that has transformed you in turn. You want to ask Einstein: is it possible to have a parallel existence in a different present? Have you left enough of your DNA there, 1,916 days of it, so that it lives on, walking through streets you will never see as an adult, eating pale orange cantaloupe that intoxicates with its perfume before it reaches your mouth, feeling both insignificant and eternal at Takht-eh Jamshid, and scribbling your stories in the garden shrines of the great masters? And what of your shadowy existence that stayed behind? Does she yearn to be where you are? Do you and your spiritual wombmate meet in dreams, in a *chai-khaneh*, with your mother's brewed tea in warmed, delicate, curved *kamar-barik* glasses and the smell of cardamom cookies in the air, or in a cloned Starbucks, a sleeved, disposable white-and-green cup in hand while Macs tap disjointedly around you? You talk through a veil that obscures yet romanticizes, and dream of a taste of the Other's life, not bifurcated by a foot in two worlds. What language will you speak?

What will you say to one another that you can't express to any other living soul? Who else can understand the complicated topography of your unmapped road? Though your life is an ode to words, to connection, you live in the shadowed hollows, in the Without Country, lacking satellite guidance, no Sacajawea at your side. You carry your tangled roots with you in a backpack that both weighs you down and gives you wings.

It is now decades after the year of fivehood. I have spent the better part of a life here in New York, in Whitman's Brooklyn, in Fitzgerald's West Egg, later walking the streets of my beloved Frank O'Hara and Langston Hughes, down to where O'Neill, Beckett, and Wilson proclaimed their own migration stories. And ever beside me, Rumi and Hafez accompany my meandering rambles whispering devotions, the *Shahnameh* reminds me of my royal lineage, and Hayedeh sings to me of drunkenness that cannot soothe the pain of remembrance and loneliness. I will always be of many, and of none. Time hasn't eroded my essential Persianness. Instead, it has distilled it to a deep garnet glaze that drips an indelible pomegranate stain, with a trace of rose water that emanates from my pores, marked by the steady tone of the *zarb* played by the grandfather I never knew that tracks my sometimes stuttering heartbeat.

Even as part of me will eternally be tethered and ancient, like the Sarv-e Abarqu in Yazd, each repotting has subtly altered my foliage, my perfume, my thorns. Perhaps I am like the Pando of my adopted country instead, my roots unimaginably wide now, sprouting limbs in unexpected locations that seemingly have nothing in common, other than myself, and this narrative I have created, interwoven with cunningly hidden flaws to ward off the evil eye, through which I am protected and propelled by equal measure.

Like Billy Pilgrim unstuck in time, I am still five, again five, never not five. Then, I hadn't yet encountered Hansel and Gretel who were lost or Dorothy who was lost or Dante who was lost. In their stories are the wordcrumbs through which I shall find my way toward the home I will build, a house of nouns and verbs in Persian, in English, in other languages, in unlanguages, in whirling dervish thoughts, and shards of heart shrapnel, in truth and illusion; in solitude and full-throated aria. Outside, there is no number or street name, no borders, no state, no other sovereign than I, and the words.

Culture beyond Language

Leyla Farzaneh

At family reunions on my father's side of the family, my relatives jabber away in Farsi like exotic birds, their hands spinning and twirling like Persian dancers. I grew up without any training in the language, so it has always been hard for me to get involved in these conversations. After the obligatory "*Chitoreen*, how are you?" I have to switch back to English. When I was young I would just hang around the outside of the crowd, sneaking the chocolates and other candies that my aunt left out in glass dishes around the house.

The feeling of being left out is only exacerbated by the fact that I don't in any way resemble a typical Persian. Born to an Iranian father and an American mother, I am fair skinned and always on the verge of anemia. My hair ranges from auburn to strawberry blonde depending on the season, and I lack the dark body hair that characterizes most Persians. My closest cousins on my dad's side have strong, dark features, and they used to have dark body hair until their father, a plastic surgeon, laser removed it. Unlike me, they grew up in a dual Iranian household, where they learned to speak Farsi and got a taste of Iran's culture through Persian dance classes.

My dad tells me that when I was younger he tried to teach me Farsi, but I was entirely uninterested. Although I applaud his attempts, telling me to repeat words back to him while I was preoccupied with playing with my dolls didn't cut it. The real problem, for me, was there was no structure to the way he taught me the language and no reason to learn it. My dad came to the United States from Iran when he was only fifteen, an impressionable age when you are still figuring out who you are and when all anyone wants is to fit in with the majority. Although I doubt he will admit it, I don't think he really wanted me to learn Farsi.

To him, being Iranian was just his nationality and not his identity. He ended up on the East Coast, where he finished high school and then went to North Carolina for college. He never found a community of fellow Iranians who were also displaced by the revolution. As a nerdy, vaguely Middle Eastern—but not specifically Iranian-looking—teenager, he assimilated well to the American lifestyle. In the middle of the hostage crisis, he was forced to disassociate from the country where he was born and raised. I used to blame my father for not making his culture a part of our family until I realized that he identifies as American more than Iranian. Ironically, it has been my American mother who has incorporated Iranian culture into my upbringing.

Ever since I can remember, my mother has been the one setting up the *haft sin* for Persian New Year, helping my younger brother and me jump over the fire during Chaharshanbe Soori, and bringing us to the beach to throw the *sabzi* into the bay. That my dad has had little involvement with these traditions speaks more to his approach to holidays in general and less to his lack of celebration of Iranian culture. What astounds me now, when I look back, is the amount of effort my mother put into teaching her children about Iran. If not for her, we would have grown up in a completely American household, learning about Iran only as a country somewhere around Iraq, as most American children do. I used to be embarrassed that my mother didn't speak Farsi. When we would go to my aunt's house with Persian friends and my mother would need Farsi translated into English so she could understand and contribute to the conversation, I felt the discomfort that she herself may not have even felt. Now I realize that my mom connects to Iranian culture in a way that my dad doesn't. She writes about her experiences during trips to Iran, plans and carries out our celebrations of Iranian holidays, and even serves on the board of a Persian cultural-immersion preschool. Maybe one day she will learn the language, but she has found a way to make Persian culture her own without it.

After obsessing for many years over my inability to speak Farsi, I finally realized that being Iranian is about more than just speaking the language. Because I couldn't speak Farsi, I labeled myself an outsider from my own heritage. I focused on the ways I stood out from typical Persians rather than on what I have in common with all Iranians. I have learned that culture is more than just language, and culture means different things to different people. Recently I was talking to my father about what being Iranian means to him. He told me that the parts that he relates to most are the ways Iranians place emphasis on helping people, especially family, and on being kind to strangers. For my dad, being Iranian means practicing the forced politeness of *taroff* with Iranians and non-Iranians alike. It means cooking way too much food just in case someone unexpectedly stops by for a meal. It is sharing conversation and laughter with his mom or his aunt or his sister and being generous and kind to his extended family and friends. My father didn't teach me Farsi or emphasize celebrating Iranian traditions because that is not what being Iranian means to him. Instead, he instilled these Iranian ideals in me. I can learn Farsi, but these virtues are harder to learn. Culture isn't one-size-fits-all. We keep the parts of culture we like and relate to.

To me, being Iranian means going out of my way to appreciate how important my grandparents and extended family are to me, whether talking on the phone with my grandmother in Iran or spending time with her when she visits the United States. Being Iranian means being proud of my ancestry and advocating for Iran in a time when many in the States are afraid of Iranians. It means drinking chai and eating *fesenjoon* and other Iranian dishes, dishes whose recipes I hope eventually to learn and pass down. And for me, learning Farsi is also part of accessing my culture. I am taking classes in Farsi because I want to learn, not because I feel that I have anything to prove. It is different to be learning what the words mean rather than merely repeating back what I have been told to say when I greet someone. I am learning Farsi because I like understanding my father's conversations with my grandma, and one day I want to be able to speak with her completely in Farsi. I am learning Farsi so that my cousins and I can whisper about people in our own language without anyone else understanding and because with modern technology, and an Arabic keyboard, I can text my extended family in Farsi. I am learning because although culture is more than just language, knowing Farsi helps me better understand and connect with my Iranian culture.

MEMORY/LONGING

Forget Me Not

Shideh Etaat

Sometimes I think my grandmother's dead, and then I remember she's not. When I visit my family in LA, I go and see her at the rehabilitation center where she's been rehabilitating for twelve years. They've stopped coloring her hair. It's all white now, but thicker than ever before. Beautiful and also frightening. Before, her hair was always dyed, blown out every Friday at 10 a.m.—a steady appointment. When I go see her, she says only a few words, mostly to my mom, who enthusiastically asks her questions as though she were a newborn. She smiles at my mom, her Farsi words for "I'm OK, I'm good, are you good" loose in her mouth. It's good to hear her voice and to know there's enough will inside of her to still want to speak.

I don't know what to say to her, so I rub lotion into her hands. The lotion smells like nothing. Her nails are now blank where there was always some version of red polish before. My mom feeds her, and I'm amazed how she treats my grandmother as if she has a long way to go, as if bringing her slushed-up watermelon to drink and buying her cute pajamas will make her happy. And who knows? Maybe they do. She's smiling, for a second, and it feels like enough. I rub the lotion in slowly, massaging her soft skin, trying to pass my love through my touch. My mom repeats over and over again who I am, that I'm married now, that I live in San Francisco, how I came all the way here just to see my grandmother.

Everyone has a different version of my grandmother. Mine goes like this: She loves me deeply, but she's also jealous of me. She holds me in her lap when I'm a child, lets me pull on her pearls, and, when I'm thirteen, tells me the most important thing in life is love. She also becomes anxious and depressed easily and wants all my mom's attention, and so for a little while, I hate her for that. I watch her take too many pills, and dramatically beat on her own chest when she's upset with my grandfather, but I also watch her start her life over in a new country and grow curious about my life, wanting to know whether I have a boyfriend, whether I've ever loved someone, making sure I know that she didn't really love my grandfather like that, as they were first cousins. That she missed out on a romantic kind of love. A person is never one thing, and my grandmother is many, but I doubt anyone sees her the way I see her—equal love, equal pain.

My mom got sick my last year of college. A couple of months before that, my grandmother started forgetting things. First she forgot where her keys were, words slipping on her tongue, and then she forgot to turn the stove off. It became dangerous for her to live alone, so she had to move into the rehabilitation center. My mom didn't tell her about the cancer. What was the point? It would upset her, and she'd forget about it soon after. At first I hated going to see my grandmother. The hallways reeked of piss and microwavable dinners. Visiting her was another thing I was burdened with. My mom, the dutiful daughter, out of love or guilt, I'm not sure which, tried to make things as normal as possible for her. We'll be right back, she'd tell her, so she wouldn't lose it when we left. My grandmother despised my dead grandfather for not coming to visit her, and no one ever told her the truth. When she could still walk, we'd take her to restaurants and family gatherings, and things didn't seem all that different, but the truth was that everything was.

I don't know when things changed, exactly, mostly because I wasn't expecting anything to. Maybe the summer I graduated from college and moved back to LA, she reached a certain stage of Alzheimer's that transformed her into, not a different person, but the truest form of herself. Or maybe I was the one who changed. In college, I started dealing with my own anxiety and depression. I felt like I was drowning. It became difficult to breathe, to hear myself, that part of me that was on my side and could calm me down. No one could help me, not even me. I started taking medication just like my grandmother had, and nine months into it, when I was feeling more like myself, decided to taper off. I didn't want to depend on anything outside of myself to be OK, but also I didn't want to be like her. Maybe experiencing what she'd suffered from for so many years made me understand her and not believe it had just been a cry for attention. That summer, I didn't feel like carrying my resentment toward her around anymore.

My mom, my aunt, and I would wheel her to the corner café, where the owners knew us and would help us lift her wheelchair over the incline of the entrance. She would sit there looking comfortable, wrapped in blankets, wearing her PJ's with the ducks on them. She asked me one day why I was showing my breasts to everyone.

"How else am I supposed to find a husband?" I said, and we laughed about it. It felt like a very long time since I'd laughed with her. She asked me why my jeans had so many holes in them. I said, "I bought them that way," and she couldn't believe me, but every time she looked at me, it was if she were seeing me for the first time.

Her eyes lit up, she smiled, and then she looked at my mom and said, "She's beautiful. More beautiful than you," and we laughed again. And yes, she couldn't tell you my name or what year it was, or why she was sitting in a wheelchair, but there was an ease to her I had never witnessed before—the ability to just sit and be, not worried about all that had gone wrong, not dreading life and all its uncertainties. I started to see her as a child, a teenager—a young woman filled with hope and the desire to be free despite a culture and a country telling her that what she wanted didn't matter. My mom asked her if she wanted ice cream, but it was a pointless question because it was her favorite thing in the world. The vanilla ice cream came, and I fed it to her. She slowly tilted her head from side to side in approval and said, "Bah, bah." It was the ultimate sign of bliss.

There are certain things that take me by surprise. Like when my mom tells me about my grandmother and the dentist. How when my mom was little, my grandmother would get dressed up and go to the dentist on a weekly basis. As a child, my mom thought her mother's teeth were seriously damaged, but it's clear she just wanted his attention. I'm also surprised when my mom tells me she was a *santoor* player and even played songs on public radio in Iran or when my older cousin tells me that when he was twenty-four and he first moved into his own place, my grandmother would call him a couple of times a week—that this was their secret ritual no one knew about, that my grandmother would talk to him about girls and relationships and tell him to make sure he was using condoms. I don't expect to feel jealous of this, but I do.

The letters surprise me even more. How, when we clean out her closet, we find letters written on the inside of book covers to my grandfather after he died. I ask my aunt to read them to me because I can't read Farsi, and the voice is poetic and desperately in love. "All I want is for God to take me too so I can be with you again," she writes. I was unaware of this poetry that lived inside of her, and of this apparently deep and passionate love for my grandfather that I never witnessed a day in my life. But like I said, there are so many different versions of any one person, so I don't know why I'm so surprised. I shouldn't be surprised by the white hair, or her heavy breathing that made me think of death the last time I saw her, or how she kept scratching herself obsessively. I asked my mom about it and she said it was like a phantom itch—that she'd grown accustomed to scratching herself to find relief when the wound had been there, and now that the wound had healed, the very act of scratching helped her feel some sort of ease. I shouldn't be surprised by how I wanted to cry when my mom looked at her as if she were her baby and my grandmother looked at my mom as if she were the mom. I shouldn't be surprised that this disease took her from us but also gave some of her back to us. I shouldn't be surprised that when the fortune-teller who tells the future from coffee grounds tells my mom that my grandmother will die by the end of the year, it's not sadness I feel for her, but relief. I can feel how tired she is, how time is pressing on her body, how close she is to being free. What doesn't surprise me, though, is how imperfect she is, how imperfect we all are, and that she tried her best to do the only thing she ever really wanted to do—to love and be loved.

Errand

Babak Elahi

May 19, 2014, afternoon

I sit in the hallway outside intensive care. My mother has been moved from her private room at Shahid Bahonar Hospital in Niavaran in north Tehran. It's the fourth day of my visit to Iran after a forty-year absence. I stare at the wall, trying to read an informational poster flanked by spare oxygen tanks. I grew up illiterate, an orphan of this mother tongue, speaking just enough household Persian to get my needs met but inept in the formal nuances of polite conversation. I once told dinner guests that they'd been tiresome bores when I meant to say what a pleasure it'd been to be at their service. I've been teaching myself to read Persian in middle age, but when it comes to complex legalese in my estranged language, my reading slows to a crawl. I need a dictionary. Still, I understand that this is a patient's bill of rights. Here I sit, feeling helpless and frustrated. I read the writing on the wall.

I begin to think that there is something I can do. I try to analyze these words, to build an argument around them. I will prepare a legal brief. I will be Perry Mason. I will try to ease my mother's death, and console my family. I copy words in my broken script into a small notebook: *hoquq*: rights; *bimar*: patient; *ehteram-e kamel*: complete respect.

My aunt Shamsi calls me back into the ICU for a few moments more with my mother. She can no longer articulate words. The cancer has crawled its way into her liver and is eating her alive. I say "I love you" in English, and "My life is good. I am happy. Don't worry about me" in Persian. This is what I think she needs to hear. My brothers and I represent her life's work, and I want her to feel that it has been worth it.

The attending nurse becomes anxious, and ushers us out of the room. The medical staff is still trying to sustain life rather than ease death.

Christmas, 2013

We're in Carmel Valley, California, at Shamsi's house, where she and my mother live together when they're in the United States. It's also where my wife, our two daughters, and I stay when we visit from Rochester. Two of my brothers, Farshid and Homayun, live nearby with their families. My other brother, Farhad, the only childless bachelor among us, has been living with my mother and Shamsi for some time now, traveling back and forth with them between Iran and Southern California. He has taken to referring to himself as the butler.

My mother tells us she's going back to Iran this spring, to save us the trouble and expense of a funeral. "If I get better I'll come back. If not, it'll all be so much easier in Iran than here." This is not entirely a practical act, but part of a script we've all been reading from for decades: the themes are my mother's self-sacrifice, her sons' guilt, and subterranean anger that occasionally erupts into direct conflict. Despite the prognosis, or perhaps because of it—three to eighteen months—we all pretend that she'll be coming back in six months, and stick to the script.

For all my life, my mother's lines in this family drama have been punctuated with the phrase *fada't sham*: "oh, that I be sacrificed for you." In a sense, it's a stand-in for "I love you," which my mother and aunt utter only in English. *Duset daram*, literally, "I like you," sounds too shallow, and *ashegh-et am*, "I'm in love with you," or, even, "I'm your lover," too romantic. But *fada't sham* is short and sweet, and even tells a story: one life lived for another.

In common speech, phrases like this, or *chaker-et-am* (I'm your servant), are not to be taken literally. They are, like signing a letter with the meaningless words "Your humble servant," a formal flourish. But in my family, and especially for my mother, the words seem real, more like a promise than mere politeness. We account for ourselves on the ledger of emotional debt.

Circa 1948

I met your father at a big party, and Aziz didn't like him. She was my older sister, after all, and had promised our mother to take care of us. When I saw how handsome he was—like Clark Gable—I imagined how beautiful our children would be. Well, see, you are beautiful sons, aren't you?

Nowruz 1393 (March 21, 2014)

I call to wish everyone a happy Nowruz. In Iran, Shamsi and my mother have more or less adopted a young immigrant Afghan family. Shamsi hired Habib as a housekeeper, caregiver, and odd-job man when her husband broke his hip. When Habib's wife, Bibi Gol, came from Afghanistan, the two of them moved into the ground-floor apartment of Shamsi's three-story house in Niavaran. Bibi Gol and Habib now have two children—Parisa, nine, and Omid, twelve. My mother tells me she named Omid, and sometimes she calls him "Babak" by mistake.

April 4, 2014

Abbas Kiarostami is artist in residence at Syracuse University, a day trip from Rochester. My wife, Jenny, and I go up to see my favorite of Kiarostami's films: *Taste of Cherry*. I'm eager for her to love it as much as I do. Afterward, we talk about the scene in which Mr. Bagheri tries to dissuade Mr. Badii from taking his own life by telling the story of the mulberry tree. Bagheri tells Badii that he, too, once tried to kill himself. Unable to toss the rope around the branch of a mulberry tree, Bagheri climbed up to tie it round a limb. But after tasting a ripe mulberry, he couldn't stop eating them. Then some schoolchildren happened by and asked him to shake the branch and send down the sweet fruit. The taste of mulberries and the laughter of children reminded him that life's simple joys outweigh its problems. Badii cynically asks whether his troubles miraculously vanished after this. Bagheri says, "Of course not, but my mind changed." Jenny likes this Zen Buddhist message.

The following week, the head of Middle Eastern Studies at

Syracuse invites me back out for a dinner party honoring Kiarostami. I drive up alone this time, and soon find myself trying to hold up my end of a conversation in Persian with the cinematic genius. But—as I should've guessed from his films and poetry—he speaks directly, simply, without pretense. He tells me that, after having made films in Italy and Japan, he plans to shoot his next film in America, the subject to be the lives of seminarians, young men in the process of joining the priesthood. He asks, "Can you recommend a short piece that shines a light on this issue? I'd love the piece to be very short, a page if possible. Simple and brief." I'm stumped.

Later, Abbas's (it's now first names with us) translator gives me his phone number, and I tell him that I will try to find something and get in touch. I've been given an assignment from one of Iran's greatest contemporary artists.

May 9, 2014

I've booked my flight for June, but when I find out that my mother has stopped eating, I know I have to go sooner. Luckily, I recently renewed my Iranian passport after years of working through a bureaucratic maze to replace a lost Iranian birth certificate. The reissued birth certificate, with its brown cover, the photograph of me as an adult inside, and the date of my birth, Ordibehesht 16, 1344, according to the Iranian calendar, and the maroon-covered passport, with the date of my final departure from Iran forty years before, these documents give me courage for the journey.

I also pack another document. In researching the question of the lives of seminarians, I mostly came up short, but I did find Randy-Michael Testa's article "St. Sebastian in Boston." It's far too long, but I think Abbas will appreciate Testa's powerful personal observations about the dark passion he felt for Saint Sebastian's martyrdom. I make a copy and bring it with me, hoping to deliver it to Abbas.

May 13, 2014

I call Shamsi's house from Dubai and learn from Farhad that while I was not falling asleep somewhere over the Atlantic, my mother was rushed from the house to the hospital. I board a flight around midnight for a 3 a.m. arrival at Khomeini International Airport.

May 14, 2014

From Shamsi's house—almost kitty-corner from where Aziz used to live, and where I visited forty years ago—we walk down Feyziyeh Street, past a school, where I glance enviously at the boldness and aggression in the speech and gestures of the adolescent boys. I remember these streets of Niavaran from my last visit, when I was nine, a return after leaving five years earlier, in 1969, when we moved to England. Now we turn left onto Manzariyeh Street, and when we get to Bahonar Hospital, I learn that visiting hours are limited according to gender: men are allowed into the women's ward only between 2 and 4 p.m. It's now 11 a.m. Shamsi and Bibi Gol make a fuss, and the security guard and nurses relent.

After the initial hassle, the mood in my mother's room is almost festive. She's awake and alert, and happy to see me. We hug and I kiss her. She thanks me for coming. The darkness inside her body is seeping out into the drainage bag next to her bed. Her movements are drawn out. But the bright leaves of the tree just outside her window almost reach into the room to embrace us with their green vigor. The sunny mid-spring day, her white gown with its floral print, and her still-bright face turn my jetlag-weighted sorrow into giddy unrealistic hope. My mother asks Bibi Gol whether I've brought any gifts for Pari and Omid. Bibi Gol says I have. My mother beams.

May 17, 2014

On the third day of my visit, my mother is becoming less coherent, sleeping more, and requiring more drugs for the pain. She's bloated. Her face has lost its wrinkles as the cancer blooms in her body, making her skin balloon out. She flits in and out of consciousness; I hold her. I know that she hears me, and I try to say things that I think will bring peace. I try to complete this errand of love.

We leave her room. I'm becoming more despondent, increasingly worried that she's suffering needlessly. Ms. Ghasemi, the head nurse, sees us all crying in the hallway and comes to us. She's open in her manner and direct in her speech. In a culture of formal courtesy with a host of unwritten and unspoken rules, she's completely free and easy, making her kinder and more generous than even the most formally polite friends and acquaintances I meet.

She says that it's only a matter of days now and that the best we can do is ease the suffering. I ask her why visiting time is even more curtailed. I ask why my mother should continue to have feeding tubes. "Isn't it time we start to simply ease her pain?" I think back to when Jenny's stepfather died lying on a medical recliner, sedated with morphine, in his own living room with his wife holding him. I want something like this for my mother. But Ms. Ghasemi says that it's not so simple. The ethical, moral, and religious expectations are always to preserve life. I realize, too, that my stepfather-in-law's death was unusual. As for visiting hours, she says my mother is excitable when we're in the room. It only causes her to suffer more.

That evening, Ms. Ghasemi stops at our house briefly, and during this visit she tells me that her mother and my mother were friends and playmates in their childhood, and that they played and walked through the gardens of Vanak when they were young, reminding me of a story my mother told me once.

Circa 1939

I was not even nine, and my mother was sick, and we went out to Vanak for holiday and rest. We camped there in the orchards. Aziz made aprons for us, with pouches. We would walk far into the rose gardens; it was so beautiful. We picked petals and stuffed them into our aprons. We came back to my mother lying down on the kilim and told her we were pregnant with rose petals.

May 18, 2014

I think of her body now, pregnant with her own death, and try to conjure the girl I never knew, pregnant with the scent of roses.

May 19, 2014

After reading the patient's bill of rights again, and worrying that we have little time left, I present my legal brief to Farhad, but he's not buying it. The patient's charter gives doctors ultimate say over diagnosis and treatment. Then I realize: this isn't a right-to-die document; it's a pro-life manifesto. But out of a sense of desperation I uncharacteristically argue with my brother. As the youngest of four sons, I'm perpetually deferential. Except occasionally. Except now.

Farhad doesn't look at me. He continues to work on a drawing in a large sketchpad. As a trained graphic artist and designer, he turns to the visual for solace just as I try to find courage in words. His patience is fraying. "She insisted that we take her to the hospital." When I say something about dignity, he asks, "What dignity? She didn't want to lose control of her bladder and bowels in Shamsi's house in front of everyone." I press my case: "She needs to be at home, with us, with plenty of drugs to ease her dying." I continue pointing to the language in the patient's bill of rights—respect, access, dignity. I've even looked up a scholarly article on the subject online. I quote this at Farhad, until finally he asks me, "What are you trying to prove?"

I'm trying to prove that I am a good son. I'm trying to prove how smart I am. I'm trying to prove that I am enlightened about death. I'm trying to prove how stupid I find Iran's policies on gender and hospitalization. I'm trying to prove my love—to him, to myself.

November 20, 2006

At an academic conference in Montreal I tell a prominent Iranian historian that I'm thinking of writing a book about metaphors of illness in Iranian literature and film. He tells me that in the early twentieth century, Iran was sometimes depicted as an ailing mother who needed the aid of her sons to regain her health. I still haven't written the book.

May 20, 2014, morning

Shamsi answers the phone and begins to cry.

May 20, 2014, afternoon

When someone dies, it's essential to buy sweets. We go to three different confectioners and bakers. We buy much *zulbia, bamieh*, rice-flour cookies, halva, candy, and almond cookies for family, friends, mourners, grave diggers, taxi drivers.

May 21, 2014

Two taxis take us all to Behesht-e Zahra Cemetery, well south of downtown Tehran—a long journey on a hot day. Shortly after we pass the massive construction site for Khomeini's shrine, we reach the cemetery, a clean, well-organized, sprawling place. The deceased are taken into a central hall, where wide screens display their names, indicating that their bodies can now be taken in and prepared for burial. In the center of an expansive atrium sits a person-sized vase filled with rose petals. Next to it stand uniformed men. I look at the screen, waiting for her name. Farah al-Molouk Arbab Amin.

Bibi Gol and another female friend of the family go back to wash my mother's body as part of the ritual. Soon my mother's shrouded form emerges from a low communicating window. Her body is placed on a plastic stretcher, and we carry her to an altar, where a mullah recites from the Qoran. We mourners repeat Arabic phrases from the recitation. We lift her again and take her to a van. The cemetery stretches to the horizon, and the body must be taken a few kilometers out. We follow in taxis.

The ritual calls for the eldest son to enter the grave, receive the body, and lay his mother on her side, to face the *qibla*, the direction of Mecca, as if the dead are perpetually praying. Farhad climbs down into the grave, and the pallbearers, all men, hand my mother's shrouded form down to him, avoiding contact with her body. Farhad's face is a frozen mask; later he will tell me, "It was only when I was down there that I felt any peace through the whole damned ritual." During this process, a second mullah begins reciting, this time through a loudspeaker saturated with reverb, his voice echoing through the sun-drenched heat of concrete, dirt, and squat trees. My mother is buried not far from her older sister—Aziz of the rose petals.

She raised my mother and Shamsi after their mother died. Also buried nearby is my uncle—Shamsi's husband, whom she called simply "Doctor," as if it were his only name. Bibi Gol and Shamsi sprinkle rose water around the grave. We all throw petals into and around the grave from the massive bouquets we have brought. I walk away from the gravesite to a narrow path nearby, shaded by trees just big enough to provide cover from the sun. I walk toward a bench. I sit, desolated.

May 23, 2014

In the period between the burial and the *hafteh*, time opens up. Farhad and I take a long walk up to the mountains just north of Niavaran. We talk about the past, about regrets, about brokenness. I apologize for my harangue about the patient's bill of rights. He says he's glad we had the argument. It was necessary. The air has turned clearer than it's been for days, and we can't help ascribing a magical cause to the change in the weather, something about our mother's spirit.

We've hiked this mountain several times during my visit. This time, we pass a troop of soldiers—regular army, not Revolutionary Guard. Their easy camaraderie reminds me of the post-credits sequence in *Taste of Cherry* when a platoon stumbles onto the shooting location. I think guiltily of my cinematic homework, and when we get back to the house I call the number for Abbas's translator and send him the pdf of Testa's essay through Facebook.

May 25, 2014

On what would have been my mother's eighty-fourth birthday, we again hire two taxis and drive to Behesht-e Zahra. The wide boulevard leading to the cemetery is lined with florists and stone carvers. Business has been good for decades. We spend another afternoon at the gravesite. Bibi Gol brings out plastic bottles of rose water, which we pour liberally over the grave.

May 26, 2014

I grieve for Shamsi the most. I sit on my mother's bed in the room they shared, and she tells me, "She was my everything. My friend, my sister, my mother, my daughter." Their mother died young, and neither of them had a daughter, so I see the logic of the mother-and-daughter kinship loop she makes for them. "What will I do without her?" she asks. Each bed is flanked by a nightstand with pictures of their children and grandchildren, and Omid and Pari. I try to imagine how she will spend the coming nights now, without my mother to talk to at bedtime and morning. She tells me again she has lost everything, catching her breath as the tears come.

May 27, 2014

Habib runs out for fresh bread for breakfast. I sit with Shamsi, and she starts telling me a story, part of which I have heard and part that is new to me.

My mother had been trying for years to get back the deed to property she once owned up north, on the Caspian Sea. Vague memories bubble up from my toddlerhood of standing at the water's edge, thinking that low tide stretched to the horizon, as if the water were endless but shallow. In the confusion after the revolution, it was difficult for many people to hold on to property like this. My mother had entrusted this land by the sea to an old neighbor, a good friend. This, it turns out, was a grave error. In a series of bad deals and broken promises that I still don't quite understand, the property was coopted by this neighbor, who now refuses to hand over the deed.

Shamsi tells me that my mother tried even in her last weeks to regain ownership of this land. Another friend of the family, an engineer, like my father, had promised to intervene. He kept promising that he'd get the deed and hand it over to my mother, but delay led to delay, broken promise to broken promise, and nothing came of it. She had little else left, and this, in retrospect, would have been her last errand, a last gift—to leave a piece of Iran to her sons.

May 28, 2014

The day before my flight our neighbor Mamad Taghi walks across from his realty office and calls Farhad and me down to help him. He wants to gather mulberries. Sunshine seems to glow through the green-white translucence of the fruit on the tree in front of our house.

Bibi Gol brings out a large sheet with a simple floral print. Parisa, Omid, and I hold the sheet open as Mamad Taghi and Farhad shake the tree's trunk, rattling its limbs. The mulberries rain down, making muffled plops on the light cotton. Shivering leaves, bright clear sun, crisp air, soft fabric, laughter of man, woman, and child. Here, on a short street off Niavaran Avenue, in the middle of the road, I catch mulberries in a sheet. The touch of the cloth links me to Pari and Omid, the air and sun connect me to Bibi Gol, Farhad, and Mamad Taghi. We gather fruit, and we place some in a bowl on the kitchen counter. "Mulberry" in Persian is the simplest button of a word: *toot*. Maybe this is why I have come back to Iran after forty years. Not to bury my mother, not to kiss her goodbye, not to console my aunt and my brother, but to reap this crop, to shake this tree.

May 19, 2014

Her final attempts to communicate were wordless, a language neither written nor spoken, neither Persian nor English, only her fight to be heard, to be held in this world, to exist. None of us understand this language of the dying, but we will learn it quickly enough when the time comes. In the meantime, I guess at a translation: she wanted to walk the earth again, taste mulberries, hear the sweet sound of children's laughter.

July 5, 2016

When I read Abbas's obituary, I remember that I'm not sure whether I completed my errand for him or not. I was never able to find him. I know he never made a film in the United States. I did send the Testa piece to his translator, who tells me now that he read and enjoyed the piece. Still, somehow I feel that I might have failed him. Perhaps if I'd sent him something sooner, shorter, more apropos, we would now have a Kiarostami film made in America. I now ask you all for absolution. I console myself with the thought that my life imitated his art in the gleaning of mulberries, that posthumous gift from my mother, reminding me of small harvests, of imperfect loves, and of incomplete errands. We have no choice but to learn to live between wish and fulfillment, in that place of elusive but deepest joys.

The Color of the Bricks

Farnaz Fatemi

I am in my aunt Simin's kitchen in Mashhad and we are cooking *lavoshac*, the original, Persian version of fruit roll-ups. We pull the stems off kilos of fresh sour cherries, pull out their pits, and drop them into a large pot on the stove. She teaches me the sounds of common talk. I listen with my rough Farsi, often sure I'm mistaken about everything I hear. When her cleaning lady arrives, Simin claims that she is late, tells her she is lazy, mocks her for complaining about something going on in her family. I understand what she says. I'm silent, but not because I don't have anything to say. I knew Simin felt walled in. The world she had thrived in for the first thirty-five years of her life shrank suddenly in the late seventies. I can almost imagine that meanness to another human is simply her ramming up against those walls. Maybe she would have been mean no matter what had happened to her country. We stir the big kettle of cherries cooking down to what will become a paste, then a dried fruit sheet. The fruit needs to cook slowly, sugars diffusing, flavor deepening.

In Iran, a taxi driver taught me what to look at.

I see the woman at the end of the off-ramp in north Tehran. One plastic grocery sack hanging on each wrist and hair tucked into an amber headscarf. She stands on her island of sidewalk, as if expecting someone. Gazes in to each driver, then lets go. Taxi driver says, "She is working." No one can accuse her of doing anything wrong. She is alone and she is standing and she is holding her shopping. Her body leans discreetly toward the road. I twist to look as long as I can. I want to see a slowdown, conversation, how she gets in carefully.

I had never been in a cherry orchard. When my uncle Reza hears this, he arranges for him, Simin, and me to drive to a friend's, outside the city. We spend the morning moving from tree to tree, free to be haphazard about the harvest, to pull whole handfuls at once into our baskets and cardboard boxes, nestle them into the trunk of Reza's old Peykan, to imagine that the weight of all of them brings us down closer to the earth as we idle home. I take video on my camera of our stained hands, Simin on a ladder, the lush treetops, the sounds of my lips smacking when I sample the cherries. Later, I make a short film to send to friends and family, with "In My Life" by the Beatles as the soundtrack.

I stop believing I know why I'm here.

My cousin Mahnaz was sixteen when I visited her in Isfahan. I was thirty-four. She was born shortly after the Islamic Revolution. While she talked about her country, she began to cry. "I can criticize it, but I love Iran so much and I wish all of us younger people could put it on our shoulders to make it better." After her university entrance exams, she left for several years to go to school in England, and she has recently returned to make a professional life in Iran. Mahnaz's parents taught their children to be proud of where they came from. And how to be angry when the country changed in ways they couldn't accept.

Foreigners write Wikipedia entries shrinking the place. They list current despots and convince themselves there is little left to know. I—we—Iranians—know better. The borders won't hold the people. A bursting could happen. They want more and are public relations wizards at heart. They can't shut off their impulse to tell stories about themselves.

I am trying to explain what it feels like to have not come from a place and to have come from the very same place.

I returned to Iran as an adult in 2001. I visited the mosque in Nain, the town where my parents' grandparents were born. How can I help you see the mosque made of bricks in this town I've only seen once, this town from which both my parents descend? If you can't see the color of the bricks, I'll be lying. You'll get to a place you think you know, not the one I know. It's the tide of your already imagined ideas that I resist. For over a decade, I have tried to explain by describing the bricks as butter yellow. Butter yellow: great-aunts and -uncles in the dust of the courtyard. Surely you notice? A mosque, yellow cream, earthy, rooted and rooting me into it. Nain, town of my ancestors. I could take you back two hundred years. A breeze in the courtyard carries the voices of people with my name.

It's a balmy spring weekday, and I'm walking with a new friend on the grass-lined path next to the Zayandeh River in Isfahan. Hundreds of people on either side of this urban river are doing the same. In front of us, two men lock arms and clasp their hands as they cross the Si-o-se Pol bridge, disappearing into the line of people and thirty-three stone arches. I think of fatwas. I think of the rules this breaks back home. Two men, fond of each other, announcing: *We're friends.*

None of my relatives would confess to unbelief. Do I shame them when I claim it for myself? They instructed their children how to pray, which direction to face, how the body changes, as it kneels and curves over itself. How soothing to try to get closer to god, or just to be outside near the mosque's walls with other people. I eavesdropped, and it happened to me, chronically faithless, standing there listening for them: I felt their elbows brush mine, heard the blood moving even under all those clothes.

Isfahan is where my father was born and where I turn thirty-five. I surrender to a compulsion to call him, tell him where I am. I was a toddler the last time he went to Iran. He is a shy person, someone who doesn't tell stories of his childhood. For the first time in my life, I can ask him questions about that time, and he sometimes has something to say. I ask about the scores of cats I hear my grandfather cared for—his tender heart, the way he took in strays. My father mocks him—stupid tendency toward feline friends. Another story he tells just once: he is a teenager, school honors, a prize in his hand, they stroll home together. His father is mute.

Ghormeh sabzi tastes different in Iran, and so does lamb. I realize that lamb has terroir, like wine. The flavors last long in the mouth, burnished and tender. Eating in Iran is as familiar as my mother's kitchen. So it isn't *that* travel experience. It's this other one: The smell of that working-class *obgushteri* in Isfahan etches its memory on the meal. Joy can come from a bowl of soup. Sitting in the courtyard café of the Abbasi Hotel on a tart spring evening makes the noodles in the *ash-e reshteh* a rediscovery, soaked through with lemon and parsley.

Alone for a month in a relative's Tehran apartment, I am determined to navigate a capital city of seventeen million, hoping not to stick out, unsure it really matters if I do. I find my way to the women-only Metro car when the train pulls into the station. I'm as nervous as I've ever been traveling, sure I'll attract attention. Whatever I do, I'll always be the American-Iranian who has arranged myself into a long manteau, sleeves pushed down to the wrist for modesty, the top button buttoned over my chestbone, and my head wrapped in a pashmina-like hijab—the one thing I wear that I think is pretty. I carry something to read, a book that's not in Farsi, as much as I wish it were. I also hold a map, try to keep it hidden. Track the stations as we pass through them. I don't want to miss the one near the Jom'eh market, where I'm aimed. I stand for the whole ride. I make way for the older women with their full-length chadors, who drag carts for shopping into our car. Out the window I see young men in short sleeves waiting in a huddle at their stop. I'm trying to really reside here, take up the things I've explored before, without depending on family to get me around. I feel like I'm holding my breath. I check the map each time the train slows down to stop, and strain to understand the names as they are called on the PA.

I try for several months to write a poem. Instead, I write an op-ed that I never publish (but read to audiences) called "You Should Go to Iran." I want to introduce Americans to the young women I meet who say they are comfortable with headscarves, to the strangers who invite Americans into their homes and feed them sweets and tea. All of this takes place in the months immediately following 9/11. I feel funneled to the center of a much bigger storm than an individual could ever quell. It feels as if I'm saying the same thing over and over—Don't ruin my country—except that I stumble on the word *my*. It isn't a lie. Iran will continue to stake out space in my internal life. But it isn't accurate. I have the choice to defend Iran, and I suspect I could get away with not doing so. But that's probably not true. In my heart, I know Iran owns me.

Renounce and Abjure All Allegiance

Renata Khoshroo Louwers

> Illness is the night side of life, a more onerous citizenship.
> Everyone who is born holds dual citizenship, in the king-
> dom of the well and in the kingdom of the sick. Although
> we all prefer to use the good passport, sooner or later each
> of us is obliged, at least for a spell, to identify ourselves as
> citizens of that other place.
>
> Susan Sontag, *Illness as Metaphor*

Unsure what to do after we learned that my husband Ahmad was likely to die within three years, we went out for Persian food.

The eggplant in the *kashke bademjan* melted across my tongue as saffron wafted from the rice at a nearby table. Foods and spices unrecognizable to my American palate ten years earlier had evolved into staples. My taste buds savored the flavors as my brain churned in overdrive to process the news. The crimson and cerulean carpet, laying its three thousand years of Persian history at my feet, counseled perspective. As I finished the eggplant, a slice of sky outside shifted to lavender and the couple at the next table started arguing in Farsi.

How could this news coexist with such a sky?

With clickety-clacking heels and a delivery more transactional than empathetic, the oncologist had told us a few hours earlier that Ahmad's bladder cancer was not curable. It could be pushed away for a while, but it would come back. We were looking at anywhere from eight months to two or three years, she said.

Well, is it eight months or three years?

It will depend, she said, on his response to the chemo intended to quell the ever-increasing pain in his hip.

"I'll finish the citizenship paperwork when we get home," Ahmad said to me as he took his first bite of eggplant.

Cancer imposed an urgency on our every action. Within weeks, our life morphed into something unrecognizable. An avid jogger, Ahmad was running on San Francisco's Embarcadero in April 2013 when he noticed swelling in one leg. It was the initial clue of a stealth metastasis. By July, he needed a walker. And I needed to take an extended leave from my job as his pain accelerated and his medical appointments proliferated faster than we could manage.

Long before the diagnosis, Ahmad enjoyed pontificating about the "art of life," of keeping perspective and balance. To him, it was about the idea that life is meant to be enjoyed—with people and fun and meaningful activities—and that the grind of work and toil (especially American style) is not why we are here.

Cancer enhanced this sense that we must live well. We attended a German film festival despite the fact that it was on a chemo-treatment day. We took in the view of San Francisco after a lunch in Sausalito. When he wasn't too groggy from the narcotics that quickly became crucial for managing pain, we visited cafés and shops and watched sailboats on the bay. We attended a Persian comedian's show in Berkeley. Ahmad's goal, even more so than before the cancer, was to be out—out of the house, out in the city, out with friends, out visiting family, out soaking up all the good that life could offer.

But the greatest urgency the cancer inspired in him was a drive to become an American citizen. It seemed to have triggered his readiness to declare an allegiance to America that he hadn't previously been ready to affirm.

Despite having lived in America for more than thirty years, Ahmad still held only an Iranian passport. In the early 1980s, Iranians who returned to Iran with an American passport were sometimes harassed and treated like traitors. Since most of Ahmad's family remained in Tehran, he had long harbored the fear that an American passport could create problems for him or his family. For years, he lived with a physical presence in the United States but with a mindset that was neither entirely American nor still entirely Iranian. He straddled two countries, two cultures, two languages—as so many immigrants do—and wasn't fully at home in either.

His very rare visits to Tehran further exacerbated his outsider status. Familiar streets had been renamed, urban growth made childhood neighborhoods unrecognizable, the summer retreat "village" his family used to frequent (which had seemed so far from Tehran in his childhood) had become a suburb, and the currency was so devalued that he had to rely on merchants to help him count out the right amount even for small purchases. People had little patience for his lack of cultural savvy—he was Iranian, after all, and spoke Farsi, why didn't he know how much bread cost?

As a US resident, Ahmad cycled through periods of considering US citizenship. He would convince himself he needed to get it, print a flurry of forms, and talk about filling them out, but then the forms would be filed away in our cherry cabinet. A few months later, the cycle would repeat. Now, in the context of cancer, American citizenship felt like a tool of hope: as the American dream offered the attainment of prosperity and freedom, maybe citizenship could offer respite and options otherwise unavailable? Maybe American initiative could tackle this problem of intractable illness.

Ahmad first came to the United States in 1976 to attend an American university while his large family remained in Tehran. Like so many Iranians arriving in that era, he had intended it to be a short-term stint in a friendly country. But then the Iranian Revolution erupted like a lightning storm, scattering families and electrifying Americans.

Overnight, Iranians in America felt shameful and feared for their safety. They found themselves rejected from jobs for which they were well qualified. They faced anti-Iranian graffiti in the streets and hostile comments on the radio. Sheer exhaustion from discussing Iran and politics of any kind often led them to downplay their heritage.

"At a party in those days, a guy once asked me where I was from," Ahmad recalled. "I didn't want to talk about Iran, so I told him I was Greek. And he said, 'I thought so. I'm from Greece too,' and he started speaking Greek!'" Ahmad had to "confess," and they laughed about it. But those small, weighty choices about how to present oneself loomed often.

Americans' general view of Iran consisted of hostages and ayatollahs. Apparent good versus evil, innocence versus guilt. Few knew of the United States' involvement in overthrowing Iran's democratically elected leader in 1953 to install the corrupt but pro-Western shah. And so, as Americans tied yellow ribbons with good intentions, they languished unaware of the roots of Iranian resentment toward the country that relished lecturing the world on democracy.

I first met Ahmad in a small, now-defunct bar called Fuse in the North Beach neighborhood of San Francisco in January 2000. Through a mutual friend, we were both there as part of a large, loosely connected group that seemed to overtake the entire space. The cacophony of rising voices and an incessant beat of techno music made it nearly impossible to converse. Ahmad and I happened to be standing next to each other.

We were a strange match. He, a blue-eyed, sandy-haired Iranian in his fifties who had been in America since the mid-1970s. Me, a fair-skinned, redheaded American in my thirties who had just moved to San Francisco. When I told him I had grown up in Baton Rouge, Louisiana, and had just arrived from there, he recalled a New Year's Eve trip to New Orleans in the late 1970s. He had wandered the French Quarter and witnessed the festive ambiance.

"I thought, *Wow, the United States is good*," he laughed. But New Orleans, he said, was just a stop on the way to his destination of Jackson, Mississippi. To which I asked the obvious question: "Why Jackson?"

He explained that he had an Iranian friend who had attended college there and subsequently married a local woman.

"They welcomed me and drove me around to see the sights," he said. "I was in the back seat while his wife told me about the places we passed. I couldn't really understand her accent. I thought my English was good, but it got me worried when I didn't catch most of what she said."

He said his Iranian friend noticed via the rearview mirror that he seemed uncomfortable.

"You can't understand her, can you?" he asked in Farsi.

"No," Ahmad admitted reluctantly.

"Don't worry, I can't understand her either," his friend replied, and they laughed.

I yearned for the lightness of that story as I helped him complete the citizenship paperwork soon after the diagnosis in 2013. Over the years, he had sometimes reflected on the naïve curiosity that bubbled up during those first days in the United States. As is often the case upon one's arrival in a new country, simple activities evoke fascination and tend to remain lodged in the memory for years, though the novelty wears off. He would laugh about a meal he had had at McDonald's in Jackson—the first time he had ever encountered a McDonald's—when he believed it was something special. Yet somehow, that fascination with this place—America—and what it took to finally arrive and stay here had remained with him. It had never worn off.

From time to time over the years, it would strike him anew. A trip to Safeway to buy tea would render him reflecting on the overwhelming choices America presents at every turn.

"In Iran, there's one kind of tea," he explained, "black tea. There's one kind of ice cream, Akbar Mashti. Here, it's endless. You don't know how to decide. But it's all so organized that even though it's overwhelming, you're impressed by the efficiency."

It was that love of America's efficiency and organization—and work opportunities—that kept him tethered to the United States for so many years, despite being far from family. But for so long, he had hesitated to upgrade his status from permanent resident to citizen.

I had known little about obtaining American citizenship before I met Ahmad. As I learned more, I realized that the US government offers a murky, mixed message regarding citizenship: Americans can hold two passports, but they are recognized by the American government only as citizens of the United States. In addition, the US citizenship oath states,

> I absolutely and entirely renounce and abjure all allegiance and fidelity to any foreign prince, potentate, state, or sovereignty of whom or which I have heretofore been a subject

or citizen; . . . I will support and defend the Constitution
and laws of the United States of America against all enemies, foreign and domestic . . .

If America deems Iran an enemy country, what does this oath
mean for an Iranian whose family remains in Iran? For many, maybe
it is simply a perfunctory step in the process. But for others, how do
they rationalize and find peace with the idea that their families and
their birthplace are tagged as enemies and that they must agree to
defend their new country against *that* enemy? In Iran's eyes, an Iranian citizen is forever Iranian (as are his children, even if they are not
born in Iran). I started to better understand the emotional as well as
practical complexities of becoming a citizen.

I could understand how Iranians who were tied to the prior government, led by the shah, likely didn't blink at the suggestion that the
postrevolutionary government was an "enemy." But apolitical Ahmad
seemed concerned about feeling disloyal to his family and his childhood memories of his country. When he traveled to Tehran in 2007 to
see an ailing brother, the Iranian border official requested his American passport. The official seemed surprised that he didn't have one.

That encounter apparently convinced him it would finally be
"safe" to become an American. Still, he deferred for six more years.
On his return from that 2007 Tehran trip, I met him in Germany and
we flew back to the States together. It was the first time we had traveled overseas since 9/11. We had longed to travel but feared it too.

As our plane from Germany touched down in Atlanta, I braced
myself for a challenging reentry. We had once endured a very difficult
entry into Canada, with the border official harassing him about why
he hadn't become a US citizen despite living in America for so many
years. I had ended up nearly in tears, but Ahmad took it in stride. I
steeled myself for a similar confrontation in Atlanta. I expected it;
hours earlier, we had endured an extensive search and questioning
before boarding our flight in Dusseldorf.

We had arrived at the airport early, anticipating a leisurely breakfast. But the German officials took us to a back room and removed

every item from our luggage. A man and woman sifted through our clothing and random souvenirs. A novelty German license plate that said "Renate" (the German spelling of my name) was momentarily viewed with suspicion as a stolen license plate. The woman then X-rayed each empty suitcase.

They were relentlessly polite in conducting this search. "I am so sorry we have to do this," said the woman, who wore a brunette ponytail and a crisp navy blazer and skirt, in accent-free English. "You see, it is because you have passports from the two different countries and because he has been to Iran. The American carriers require this. If you were flying on a European carrier, we wouldn't have to do this."

Translation: "It's not our country doing this, it's yours."

It was a moment in which I felt we were being shamed both for being Iranian *and* for being American. There was a strange mix of shame and pride about place, with which we both were so familiar. Iran was so often viewed with suspicion among Americans and Europeans: if you're from Iran, does that mean you're a terrorist? America was so often viewed by Europeans with suspicion: if you're from America, does that mean you're an aggressive, loud person who is going to cause trouble? Additionally, my home state was a place viewed by many on the East and West Coasts of my own country with suspicion. I could often sense the unasked question: if you're white and you grew up in Louisiana, does that mean you're a racist?

Ahmad and I talked often of the unexpected similarities between Louisiana and Iran. Both were oil-rich terrains from which the lucrative black honey was slurped away by outsiders for great profit, most of which did not return to the exploited natives, many of whom were poor and lacking access to education and opportunity. Yet people from both cultures felt a great sense of pride about their home, and both cultures also shared richly textured histories, full of conquests and the great art that can come from hardship. Louisiana's Cajun food and jazz and Zydeco musical traditions are known worldwide. From Iran, it's the saffron-infused rice and kebabs as well as the poetry of writers such as Rumi and Hafez that are so well known.

Perhaps, too, it was a murky mix of shame and pride about

America that caused Ahmad so many false starts at US citizenship. America was a land of highly organized wonders in which efficiency reigned supreme in a manner unknown in other countries. But it was also a country of "rotten brothers," as Ahmad liked to say, a country in which democracy was for sale and money seemed to dictate so many decisions. It was a country that perpetuated stereotypes about 9/11 terrorists and Iran, even though none of the 9/11 terrorists held an Iranian passport.

Finally, in the Atlanta airport, we made our way to the passport control official—a large blonde woman who seemed many years older than she probably was. Her disheveled curls and utter lack of interest suggested that she had a calendar under her counter on which she was checking off the days until retirement.

We cheerfully handed over our passports. The aloe and alcohol scent of the hand sanitizer I use while traveling wafted a little too strongly around us. She didn't even blink upon seeing that one passport was Iranian and the other was American. She nonchalantly flipped through Ahmad's passport first and, without a word or any eye contact, bestowed the coveted *ka-chink!* of the stamp and slid the passport across to him with an unenthused "Welcome to the United States." She similarly gave mine a perfunctory review. With that, we were back in.

I felt simultaneously delighted and outraged.

"Not even a question?" I asked Ahmad, incredulous, as we ate hamburgers in the food court. "We haven't left the country for six years for fear of this moment, and she doesn't even ask a question?"

He reminded me that this was a good thing. And he was right. But uncertainty about border crossings with an Iranian passport continued to nudge Ahmad a bit closer to obtaining US citizenship. On any given day, in any given country, a border official could zip him right through or detain him for hours with questions. The contrast between the experiences in Dusseldorf and Atlanta, bookends of the same flight, reminded us of how much uncertainty traveled with us when we traveled with an Iranian passport. Although a US passport was not a guarantee against this, it certainly seemed to provoke fewer questions.

In 2013, as we sat at the kitchen table filling out the citizenship application, I remembered that day and hoped that he would survive the cancer long enough to have the luxury of another border crossing, whatever it might bring. The uncertainty of crossing a border actually sounded joyful relative to the uncertainty of the cancer.

The application required detailing the dates and destinations of every trip he had taken out of the country since obtaining his green card many years earlier. We needed his Iranian passports for this task, and I expected him to open the locked filing cabinet where he kept key documents to get them.

Instead, he went to his closet and rummaged through the pockets of a jacket I had never seen him wear. From the depths of an interior pocket, he pulled out a stack of burgundy Iranian passports, neatly encircled by six rubber bands like ribbon around a present. This incident precisely captures Ahmad's mystifying mix of vigilance and randomness in securing important documents. A chronic low-grade anxiety over and fascination with spies and conspiracy theories is common among Iranians. In the early days of knowing Ahmad, I had mistaken this trait as specific to him, but over time, I realized that while it was a personal trait, it was also part of a mind-set that permeates Iranian culture. For Ahmad, it manifested itself in this way: the important stuff went in the locked filing cabinet, but the really important stuff went into random pockets of old clothing, based on the rationale that it was a less likely hiding place. The CIA propaganda campaigns in Iran in the early 1950s to help overthrow Mohammad Mossadegh profoundly affected the Iranian view of the United States. For many Iranians, and for Ahmad in particular, this manifested over the years as suspicion and distrust of any government. The result was a vigilance somewhere on a spectrum between cynicism and paranoia. In the context of his illness, I found it strangely comforting that the passports were in the jacket pocket. Storing them there suggested that he was still himself, still cautious about his actions. Cancer hadn't taken that yet.

For several hours one Sunday afternoon, he flipped back and forth through pages of aging Islamic Republic passports so we could piece together the exact travel dates of his numerous trips abroad, mostly to Europe, since moving to the United States. As he read off the dates, I created a list that we could later transfer to the application. It felt like we were writing a memoir. We had momentum. Movement. Hope. It was a feeling we hadn't felt since before the devastating diagnosis a month earlier.

With travel details and biographical information filled in, the application was nearly complete. We talked about the American history test that was required, and I drilled him on a few practice questions. We needed to obtain one more legal document, and then the application would be ready to send.

But by the time the document arrived a month later, the cancer had distracted us from the application process yet again. While it was the cancer that had inspired Ahmad to apply for citizenship, it was also the cancer—with its pain and side effects and grogginess-inducing drugs—that kept derailing his efforts. We lingered in the muddled territory between life and death. It was a fixation on his citizenship in the "kingdom of the sick" rather than that in the United States that overtook our days. Just before that last document arrived, we had learned not only that the chemo was *not* helping but that the cancer had progressed rapidly during the treatment. His pain had escalated, as had the dosage of daily opioids to manage it. We continuously wondered how much time we had left together.

In the end, it wasn't spies or menacing border officials, nor talk radio or missing documents, that proved to be our problem. It was a copying error in a cell that multiplied itself into a vicious tumor. A "copying error" sounds like a mistake in the citizenship paperwork, a letter transposed, a clerical snafu. Instead, it was a letter disrupted in his DNA that determined Ahmad would remain in this physical realm more than eight months but not nearly three years.

Four years later, the bundle of burgundy passports remains bound with crumbling rubber bands, together with the citizenship application, in a plastic IKEA bin in the closet.

Learning Farsi

Darius Atefat-Peckham

When I was six years old, my grandparents, Papa and Bibi, took me to a Nowruz celebration at a beautifully decorated hall near their home in Saddle River, New Jersey. There, I watched them laugh and speak Farsi rapidly with men and women I'd never met before, men and women who offered me endless food and hospitality, complimented my "good looks" and manners, and spoke Farsi in my ear. Bibi whispered translations in my other ear, moving her hands.

Three years before, when we were living in Amman, Jordan, I was in a car accident that took the lives of my mother and brother. This New Year's celebration was my first exposure to a greater Iranian community since their deaths, a culture and tradition I had no idea I needed so badly. These men and women looked just like my grandparents, just like me, and in the betweenness of this night, we were all fast friends.

For the party's finale, we were funneled out of the hall, many people still clutching each other's hands, echoes of the dance still in their step. I was caught in a torrent of children rushing the small fire we'd soon jump over: a symbol of new beginnings, of renewal. But for a moment I pulled away, navigating my way through the crowd in search of Papa and Bibi. When I found them, they politely declined my request to jump as many families were doing, holding hands and leaping together. I stood with them for a moment, insistent that they should get in line with me.

Soon, though, I was jumping with the rest of the children, reentering the line again and again, Papa and Bibi forgotten and receding in the waves of now familiar faces. "*Dobareh?* Again? How many more beginnings can a small boy have?" an old man said to me, chuckling in line just behind me. I shrugged and smiled, searching for Papa and Bibi in the crowd once again. When I found them, I saw them speaking to one another worriedly, hushed. When Bibi saw me looking, she took a long drag of her cigarette, smiled, and motioned with her hands for me to move up in line. I grinned back at her. At the time, I thought little of her thin smile, of her worried eyes, of my grandfather's grave discernment. I was ecstatic. It was a good night. After all, this Nowruz was the only time I'd ever watched my grandparents dance together, dance at all.

The next day, weary from the night before, we drove to the park where my mother used to play, where she made her first friends. We wrote notes on little pieces of paper and taped them onto helium balloons, letting them go in memory of my mother and brother. "Remember Susie and Cyrus," Bibi used to tell me. "Remember them always, Dada." I remember Bibi beside me, holding the balloon between her knees, hunched over her note, muttering her thoughts with her pen pressed against her lips. I can't remember whether she wrote her note in Farsi or English, or how many seconds it took for the balloons to be enveloped by the clouds, for the colors to disappear, completely out of sight.

For a long time, I resisted Papa and Bibi's pride—their obsessive musing over our past, the comparisons they made between myself and my mother, the vision they had for my life, and their proud sense of Iranian nationalism. "I mean, God, we've done nothing! *Hichi!* Nothing!" Bibi often said, defending her entire country as if it had personally asked her to, as if all the years she'd spent in America had taught her better than to find fault in anything Iranian. I learned quickly that if something was Iranian—whether it be the food, the carpets, the intellect—then it was the best. No questions asked. And if somebody did try to argue with her on this matter, her face would twist into a confused grimace, her English becoming more broken, as if the Persian language and culture themselves were stumbling their way from her mouth, weaving themselves into her language. As she often said, she'd fight "like a hell" for her country, and she made sure everybody knew it.

Sometimes, though, tired of the yelling and anxiety in defense of her homeland, she'd become quiet. "Dada, it is so beautiful in Iran," she'd say, uttering her country's name softly, rolling her *r*, unlike the news reporters she hated so much. "It's E-ron, Dada," she'd tell me, and scrunch her face as if she smelled burning *tadig*. "Not I-ran. Always make sure to say it beautifully."

She showed me hundreds of pictures of Iran, of the markets and the parties in the streets, of her family, *my* family, my aunts and cousins dressed in hijabs, their faces bright and starlit beneath their scarves. She showed me pictures of my great-grandmother, small and standing in her kitchen, a woman who knew hardly any English, and who would die before I got the chance to meet her. However, she telephoned me at least once each time I visited Papa and Bibi in New Jersey, repeating the phrase *duset daram*, telling me she loved me, over the line. "That," Bibi always told me, "is the Iranian way."

When my great-grandma held parties, Bibi said, it was just as much about the food as the people. She described sprawling tables that held Iranian food of all colors—a mural of sorts—and the kitchen where she worked that overlooked her beautiful garden and the flowers she carefully tended. In the back of the garden, seen through the kitchen window, was a roomy shed where, several years after the accident, my great-grandma created a welcoming bedroom area for a small boy, placing my old clothes and stuffed animals on a skinny bed, awaiting Reza's arrival.

Reza's family was on the verge of living on the streets when Great-Grandma took them in. Reza's father was her gardener; when hard times hit his family, she insisted that they stay with her until they landed on their feet. And because of the love with which she must have asked them, I imagine there was no way he could have said no.

When Bibi shows me pictures of Reza, a two-year-old clad in my brother's rain boots and my old Thomas the Tank Engine T-shirt that we sent him, my heart aches for my brother, Cyrus. It's striking how similar the two boys look, and I understand immediately why my great-grandmother fell in love with Reza so quickly. "We call him *Agha* Reza," Bibi tells me, and I see it clearly—the serious face I know so well from pictures and videos, my brother's raindrop eyes.

Just after my fifteenth birthday, well into my high school years and with the frequency of my visits to my grandparents dwindling, Bibi and I ate chicken kebabs together one day. Afterward, as she often did, she praised the meal, which *I* had cooked (with a considerable amount of help from her, of course). "*Khaeyli khoob!*" she exclaimed, and wiped some saffron from the corner of her lips. "Very good!" I saw her eyes fill with pride, followed by a tinge of sadness. "Now I just hope that you still come back," she joked. We both laughed, but I sensed some truth in her voice, some uneasiness. I wondered if she thought of my great-grandma and how she was never able to meet me.

There did come a point when I felt the need to embrace my heritage—my mother and her past, the Iranian literature and history she so loved to study—in order to have more good times with Papa and Bibi. The arguments between us had become too intense, the launches into the past too unwieldy. There came times, too, when I felt disgusted with my own country's politics, and I had to fight the urge to all but reject my American heritage and embrace only my Iranian one. I found solace in learning Farsi but hated the self-consciousness I felt when I practiced it aloud. I read and studied some of my mother's favorite Sufi poets, including Rumi, Hafez, and Attar. I delved deeper into the things my mother left behind in search of the sense of tension that she felt in the world and the empathy she wanted to cultivate in everyone.

Each time I began this deep dive into my heritage, I remembered the way Bibi fed me pomegranates—the Iranian way. She'd knead the pomegranate's skin, strong knuckled, until it turned black and the pressure built up inside, a sea of red. She'd stand over the kitchen sink, a sewing needle poised above the fruit, while I waited for the moment when I'd bend forward and seal its skin with my lips, and the slosh of tart flavor would rush and fill my mouth. Bibi would smile. "*Shoma hazerid? Are you ready?*"

As a young girl, my mother collected wooden turtles. She'd ask Bibi to bring them home for her from Iran. They were simple at first, dozens of wooden toys with flat bobble heads that nodded an unchanging

"Yes" every time I picked them up, as if talking for my mother, intricate designs hand painted on their shells, colors that suggested whimsicality and magic. As my mother got older, Bibi brought home bigger and more complicated turtles, expensive ones laced with gold and silver and made of valuable stones. Bibi made this a tradition.

When I was nine years old, Bibi showed me the collection of wooden turtles and let me take one home with me. "Careful, its neck will break," she advised me as I shook one up and down gently. I took the turtle in my hands carefully, then, and felt bad for having been harsh with my mother's things. I let the turtle nod, keeping my hand rigidly still, and watched until it became motionless, pretending it had fallen asleep in my palm.

Later, when I was going home to Ohio with Dad and my stepmom, Rachie, we watched a truck in front of us run over a turtle, hidden in its shell on the highway. I saw a shard fly to the side of the road, and I heard Rachie cry out in the front seat. We stayed silent for a moment, the highway continuing to move past us. "Maybe he wasn't hurt," I suggested, and tried to look out the rear window, back the way we had come. In the back seat, I imagined this turtle, his armor-like shell shooting off the truck's tire and into the forest beside us, poking out his head when the spinning had stopped, shaken. I thought of the wooden turtle I'd brought home, my mother's name inscribed on one of its feet. When I took it out of my suitcase, unwrapping Bibi's careful packing job, I found the turtle's neck broken, its head lying still against its colorful shell.

Above the kitchen table in my grandparents' house is a wooden carving of a peacock. The tip of its beak points down in modesty, or maybe in self-admiration, its tail draped over its shoulders like the beaded wedding gown that Bibi made my mother—white pearls placed by tired hands. My mother made this carving for Papa and inscribed a note on its back: "In memory of the peacocks we chased together." When I asked, Papa told me that they used to chase peacocks in the botanical gardens after school in Switzerland when he was working there for the United Nations. I imagine him running after screeching birds, sweating beneath his suit and pulling his daughter along, the man who groans when he gets up from his chair, who wears a winter hat and overcoat to bed, swaddled in blankets, shivering. "She never intended to catch them," he told me, his eyes watering. His hands shook against the table. "She wanted to see them spread their wings—to see their color."

Recently this winter, while walking in town, I heard a woman behind me talk to her friend about why she didn't feel the need to attend the upcoming protest of the recent executive order banning immigrants from seven Middle Eastern countries. "I just feel like, as much as they talk, people in the Middle East aren't doing *their* part. They aren't standing up for what they believe in. They seem lazy."

I almost turned around and said something. This woman, her Starbucks coffee cup shaking in the cold, a ring of lipstick on its rim, made me fight to retain my empathy. I thought of women like her in Iran during the revolution, ones who wore their veils slightly askew and their lipstick too colorful, too prominently. Their bodies, from which color was banned, their curves and beauty banned, bodies that were beaten and abused, thrown in dark jail cells, dulled gray. I thought of my mother and the work she did to celebrate and nurture the beauty of Iranian culture while in America, risking her happiness, her relationships, and her family—a nurturing that I desperately want to continue myself. I wanted to tell this woman, with the faux-fur jacket and the diamond ring resting on her almost translucent finger, that it's courageous to take a stand in a place where you will be punished for it and that it is cowardly to stay quiet in a place where you can believe freely. But I didn't. I stood in front of her and I thought sadly of my mother's wood carving hanging in Bibi's kitchen above the waft of her food's sweet smell—its feathers missing the bright colors of the real bird's plumage, yet beautiful all the same.

Almost every year, Bibi set up a *haft sin*, a traditional Nowruz table adorned with the many Iranian symbols of renewal, love, and beauty. She told me stories about the beauty of my great-grandmother's table in Iran, all of the seven requirements accounted for, while we watered the *sabzi* and covered it with a wet cloth for the night. I was always amazed by how fast the *sabzi* grew, tall sprouts of wheatgrass shooting out of the seeds by the second day of nurture, full and thick like Iranian hair.

On the thirteenth day of growth, we'd drive out to the river in the woods where they used to throw the sprouts with my mother, Bibi turned in her seat and telling me stories of Amu Nowruz, or Uncle Nowruz, Santa's Iranian counterpart, my eyes wide with the fantasy. Papa would laugh along with her. When I was seven, Bibi was the first person to tell me that Amu Nowruz and Santa weren't real, a heartbreaking moment of truth for me; at first I refused to believe her. "Believe what you will," she said to me and shrugged. "It's reality." When she told me this, I thought of what had happened the last time we threw the *sabzi* in the river, the clump flying through the wind, settling on top of the water, and rushing away. She'd said, "Dada, quick, make a wish to Amu Nowruz!" And I had. When we got home, a present was sitting in the living room—a Wiggles CD and a boom box to go with it. I cried with joy. I believed.

Bibi once handed me a copy of *That Kind of Sleep*, my mother's collection of poetry—a stunning portrait of Iran and the people there. "Is it signed?" I asked tentatively, my fingers flipping through the pages (the first of many times). Bibi took it from me, and though I knew it was irrational, I expected her to give me a new copy, one that had been signed for me by my mother before she died, a profound note inside about life that would give me a sign of who she was, how I should proceed without her. "Of course," Bibi said, and left the room. When she returned, I noticed the way her hands shook when she gave the book back to me. She smiled, and for a moment my hopes rose. Quickly, I opened it up to the page with my mother's name. I found an inscription under the title, written in Bibi's sideways scrawl. I looked away without reading what she'd written and thanked her.

One night recently, while watching Donald Trump in a press conference, Papa slammed the remote control on the side table. "Stupid son of a bitch," he said, and struggled to get up from his chair. Sometimes, when he drives, Papa will mutter strung-together Farsi words under his breath. *"Zahremar pedar sag,"* he'll say, and blush after, as if embarrassed that he'd ever said such a thing. With some careful probing, I once got him to tell me what this particular curse meant: "Snake poison to your face, father of a dog!" We laughed hard while I said it over and over in Farsi, a young child cursing everything and nothing all at once.

Bibi has always been a storyteller. She's told me many stories about my mother, lacing poignancy into them to try and explain to me my mother's death. I listen to her, always, watch the way her arms sway emphatically as she speaks, jealous of her ability to relive these memories that I long for. At the same time, I wish that I could rid her of the weight these memories cause. It's always unsettled me, the way this grief has affected my grandmother: she's destined, now, to be the storyteller, never again the story. I understand her moves toward profundity. I do the same thing when I ruffle through my mother's things. Her emails, pens and pencils, to-do lists, and love letters to her high school boyfriend—everything was written for me, it seems. And to an extent, much of her life was profound and difficult to explain. She seemed to be aware of the brevity of her life in a way nobody else could be, and she lived it with that in mind. Still, I think that sometimes, grieving her loss, her short existence, we look for meaning that isn't there or that points back to us, not at what's lost.

Once, as I listened to Bibi's stories, it hit me that the only time I'd ever hear my mother's voice again would be spoken through another person's mouth. In that moment, like many other moments in my young life, I yearned to hear her voice, a sentence or word that I could hold by my ear, that could be played and replayed, lifelike. I yearned for something that would humanize her, something tangible like the nothings I read in her diaries, lines that I pored over, exhausted with trying to find profundity in every wondering or curiosity or swear word. I wanted a reminder that she was just a human being, somebody I could admire and learn from instead of the goddess she was made out to be. "Saint Susie," my father called her when people talked of her this way, and he was right. When people who knew my mother talk to me about her, they make my mother perfect in their memory—an impulse that is unbelievably frustrating because it leads me no closer to knowing who she really was. Yet I'm still just like all the other people who thought they knew her, in a way. I still imagine that her voice is perfect, beautiful, a pure chime just like the music of Bibi's golden bracelets sliding against one another on her wrist, again and again proving to me her point.

When I was little, Bibi used to bring home *gaz* from Iran. When I think of *gaz*, I remember Bibi softening the pearls of nougat candy in her palm, moving them around like marbles before she handed them to me, my mouth watering. I remember her hands coated white—in the flour that kept all the pieces separate.

My great-grandmother always sent for Isfahani *gaz* before Papa and Bibi arrived in Tehran, paying the extra postage for the best of the best from my grandfather's birthplace. When Bibi handed the *gaz* to me, she reminded me of my great-grandmother's love, that she would *die* to see me, that it was one of the only things she wanted because she missed my mother so much.

When I talked to my great-grandmother on the phone, her love for me was evident. I always started the conversations, yelling so she could hear, "*Salam*, Grandma *jan*!" And for many years of my childhood, knowing no better, I thought her name was Jan—but *jan* is a word meaning "dear" or "dearest" in Farsi. Bibi told me once that my great-grandmother only ever learned a few words of English, but that every one of those words had something to do with love, with me. And so, the only words and phrases I'll equate with my grandma *jan* will forever be "*Salam*, Darriush!," "*Duset daram!*," "*Azizam!*," "I love you!," and "I kiss you!" The name Jan would be fitting.

Although I've never been there, I yearn for Iran. After my great-grandmother passed away, I felt profound guilt for never having gone to visit her, for the times when I'd complained about talking to her on the phone, the language barrier being a problem I felt I would never conquer. When I was fourteen years old and Bibi called to tell me the news of her death, I was dumbstruck. The United States suddenly felt smaller to me. I felt trapped. I wished, silently, as I used to when I was little and we threw the *sabzi* in the river, that I could go to Iran, or somewhere else, and feel free. I thought of the balloons that we let go in memory of my mother and brother, that tossed about and flew in the air with ease, and wondered if they popped and fell back to earth, if someone found them and read the attached notes, wondering where they came from. I listened to Bibi's weeping, the phone digging into my cheek, her voice echoing in my head: "*Azizam*, I only wish you could have met her."

I think often of the many things that kept me from meeting my great-grandmother—the anger and misunderstandings between Iran and the United States, and the fear that people have of otherness, all stemming from a lack of empathy, from a choice. And, honestly, I *am* angry. I wish that I could wash my hands of it all, as I washed from my fingertips the flour that separates *gaz*. And always, when I taste its sweetness, the pearls of rose water running down my throat, I can hear my great-grandmother's words of love: "I love you, I kiss you, I love you."

Sometimes I think back to that night at the Iranian New Year party, wishing that I had left the line of people and grabbed Papa and Bibi by their coat sleeves. I wish I had pulled them, laughing as they gave themselves up to me, my fingers entwined with theirs like rope, to begin again—taking flight together, the fire nipping at our heels. And I imagine that when we touched Earth again, we'd look to each other and smile. Bibi would say something in Farsi and I'd translate her words perfectly, understanding that, *dobareh*, we can take as many turns as we like.

Delam Tang Shodeh

Shireen Day

I stood on the front patio of my home in Boulder, Colorado, and glanced toward the mountains, where rocky and forested ridges traced outlines of possibility against the sparkling blue sky. My three-year-old daughter sat near me, busily packing sand into a dark green bucket. Her spirals of brown curls danced in the sunlight. My six-week-old son stretched and then curled like a bug in the sling wrapped against my chest. His heart beat evenly, still linked as one to mine. I breathed deeply and savored the pleasure of being a new mother. It was a moment of bliss, suddenly shattered by the blare of the cordless telephone.

"Hello?"

"Shireen *jan*, you need to come to New York. Today."

My chest tightened against the suction of my uncle's hollow voice.

"*Amujan*, the baby is only six weeks old. I'll come in a few weeks."

"Your father needs you."

I gritted my teeth.

"Is he still in the hospital?"

In the seven years since my father's heart attack, when the contrast dye in the angioplasty damaged his kidneys, I had visited him often. I visited him at home, but almost never when he was in the hospital. He forbade it.

"Shireen *jan*, your father is dying." The words dragged with a somber tone of defeat. "Come. Today."

I knew my father had been dying, but to think that he could die today—that was unbearable. He was too large a presence to ever be dead. I hung up the phone, clutched my son's tiny body, and remembered everything I knew about my father. I thought about the world he was born into seventy-seven years before. It was the first of many family stories of how he beat the odds.

The Bakshandeh family lived in a large house fringed by two mud-brick synagogues on a small dirt road in a village between the Alborz Mountains and the Caspian Sea in Northern Iran. On a chilly winter day in 1919, hazy shafts of sunlight drifted into a small room in the home, where the midwife used an unsterilized knife to cut my father's umbilical cord. So many children died in childbirth and infancy that no one noted the date of his birth. He was ultimately the middle child of seven, but his childhood ended when he was five years old. It ended when his mother and her most recent newborn died not long after the child took its first breath.

I remembered that my father had told me how on his first day in medical school, his professors explained the concept of sterilization. Immediately after class, he sent a telegraph with instructions for his eldest sister, Gohar, to teach the midwives how to sterilize their instruments. I wondered if it was even possible to count how many babies' lives he had saved in his sixty years in pediatric medicine.

I knew my father had been waiting to see his new grandchild. He adored my daughter and he would soon adore my son, but if he was still in the hospital, I couldn't take both kids. I asked my mother-in-law to watch Chloe and booked a ticket for myself and Charlie.

The next day, with Charlie snuggled against my chest, I boarded United flight 482 for New York. This was the baby's first flight. As I took my seat by the window, I imagined the day when my father would tell Charlie about his own very first time in an airplane.

On a cold, clear morning in early February 1947, surrounded by his four tearful sisters, two brothers, and many other relatives who had flocked onto the tarmac, my father and three other passengers, all of them doctors, boarded a well-used, rusty-looking DC-4 for the flight from Tehran to New York.

They traveled for almost a week in an unpressurized cabin. There were no flight attendants, no comfortable seats, and no food service.

On the first day, the plane went as far as Cairo before stopping to refuel and to allow the crew and passengers to sleep. The second day, they flew to Dakar, Senegal, where they needed to land before one of the Gold Coast's infamous thunderstorms tossed them about like a leaf in a tornado.

As they began their descent, the men in the control tower demanded to know who was in the plane and what they wanted in Dakar. The DC-4's British pilot didn't speak French and sent the copilot back to see if anyone could help. Over the roar of the propellers, the copilot asked, "Does anyone speak French? *Parlez-vous français?*"

My father sat up straight and said in English, "I speak French."

"Come with me, sir, they will not let us land and none of us in the cabin speak enough French to get through to those idiots."

My father spoke Farsi, Russian, and French fluently and had begun learning English. He strode past the copilot and stepped into the scorching cockpit.

For an instant, the bright sunshine blinded him. He noticed the three crewmen swabbing the sweat as it poured from their foreheads. On the runway far below, he saw a variety of buildings protruding from the patch of green that lifted up out of the Atlantic. If the plane didn't land in Dakar, there was literally no other place to go.

"I will talk to them," he said in accented English. At six feet tall, he had to crouch as he grabbed the handset and spoke into the radio.

"*Allô? Allô?* This is Dr. Bakshandeh," he said in French. "Can you hear me?" A barrage of static filled the cabin. "*Allô?* Who is this?"

"This is ground control."

"Listen to me. I am a doctor. We need to land at your airport."

"Who are you?" demanded the voice, interrupted by waves of static.

The airplane crew exchanged nervous glances.

"What do you mean?" My father's face flushed. "I am Dr. Bakshandeh. This plane has four passengers. We're all doctors."

"You cannot land in Dakar," said the disembodied voice.

My father felt his heart stop. "This plane can't cross the ocean without fuel. We'll leave for Brazil in the morning, and then we are going to America. That is all you need to know." He spoke with an authority that was difficult to ignore.

"Are you truly medical doctors?"

"Of course we are!"

"Then we will talk to you in person when you land."

He turned toward the pilot. For the first time, he noticed that the entire crew wore only shirtsleeves. The heat in the cockpit had also drenched him in sweat, but he had no intention of loosening his necktie or removing his jacket. Smiling bemusedly, he said in English, "You can land now."

"What did you say to them?" asked the pilot.

"Nothing really. I just know how to convince them," he said with a grin before he turned abruptly and went back to the cabin. He was never one to share the details of his negotiations.

Once on the ground, the four doctors were asked to help take care of some sick soldiers stationed at the airport. Then, just before dawn, the weary travelers boarded the plane again and headed for Brazil, then Trinidad, and finally to Miami, the final stop on the way to New York.

Like all the other stops, Miami involved an overnight stay. The next morning, as the passengers prepared to board the plane for the final leg to New York, the pilot called them all together and said, "I've brought you where you wanted to go. I'm not flying any further."

My father turned toward him and said, "What do you mean? You must take us to New York."

"I said I would bring you to America," repeated the pilot. "This is America. My job is done." He spun on his heel and walked away. While the other three passengers began to panic, my father simply walked up to the Eastern Airlines ticket desk and purchased four tickets on the next flight to New York.

Each time I heard this story, I marveled at the authority my father and his identity as a doctor could command. He was like a king. He had saved his own life and the lives of everyone on that plane. And as I looked out the window and into the clouds below, I couldn't let myself imagine that this man who could talk a plane out of the sky was about to die.

I don't actually remember landing at LaGuardia or taking a cab to Tisch Hospital in Midtown Manhattan. I was worried about leaving Chloe at home. She had always traveled with me to see her *baba*, which is what she called her grandpa. But I reminded myself that her American grandparents would keep her safe. I inhaled deeply, kissed Charlie's head, and stepped into the elevator that would take me to my father.

I had expected him to be sitting up in bed reading the *Wall Street Journal*. I had expected him to tell me how delighted he was that I had come. I had expected him to be telling everyone what to do. I hadn't understood that he truly had been clinging to life for the last three months.

He lay in a private room on the ninth floor. A solitary window opened onto a concrete wall, and the filtered light cast a gray pallor over his swollen body. A bag of clear fluid for his peritoneal dialysis hung above him. It was connected to his abdomen by a long, clear tube. A bank of monitors recorded his vital signs. As I walked into the room, his cloudy brown eyes flickered open, but they did not see. He was drifting in and out of consciousness, swept away by an exhaustion that emanated from deep inside him.

My cousin Kaveh stood up from a chair near the bedside. His rounded shoulders carried the full weight of worry. He was forty-two, but in that moment, he looked sixty. Seven weeks earlier, my father had asked for his help. Kaveh had put his own life in California on hold and become my father's constant companion, doing whatever he could to keep my father comfortable. He was doing what should have been my job, and he was doing it with a lot of love.

"Shireen *jan*. I'm so glad you are here," said Kaveh. "Look, *Da-eejan*, Uncle, Shireen is here." His eyes sparkled as he wrapped me in a warm hug and kissed me once on each cheek. When he saw Charlie, his olive skin flushed slightly pink. He smiled broadly and said, "Look, Uncle Atta, Charlie is such a beautiful boy."

My father opened his eyes. He moved his head forward. I bent down to kiss him, first on one cheek and then on the other. Charlie's carrier swung gently under my father's nose, but somehow the tiny baby and his barely conscious grandfather couldn't quite see each other.

I didn't fully understand this yet, but the way in which Kaveh had repeatedly called my dad's name was a gentle attempt to draw him back into the present moment. Suddenly he spoke clearly and said, "Darling, I'm so glad you have come. Let me see Charlie."

I unhooked the carrier and held Charlie in front of my father's face. But his effort at speech had been too great and his eyes looked once again without seeing.

The door opened slowly. My cousin Neena poked her head into the room. Casually dressed in a striped pullover, white slacks, and sandals, with a thick braid of dark brown hair hanging down her back, she glanced at the bundle asleep on my chest and her eyes lit up.

"Uncle Atta, do you see Charlie? He looks just like you," she crooned.

"Yes, Neena *jan*, I see him. He is a beautiful boy," my father said and then slipped back into sleep.

Neena and I had not spoken in many months, ever since we had argued about why I wouldn't leave my life and my home in Colorado to help care for my father. Unlike me, Neena had built her life around doing what she was supposed to do. Strangely, my father's dying body bridged the gulf between us. Our eyes met across his belly, swollen with the fluid left behind by his failing kidneys, his failing heart. She reached for my hand and said, "Charlie is a beautiful boy."

The next two days blurred into endless hours at the hospital. A dozen cousins trooped in and out. My father was the uncle who always remembered birthdays and celebrated graduations. He consistently offered encouragement and praise. For some he offered advice on marriage or career. Most of my cousins were doctors, and each had an opinion about whether or not their uncle was dying or about how he should die.

I watched them clustering silently in that hallway outside my father's room. Pale faces. Damp eyes. It didn't matter if they had grown up in Manhattan or Tehran, when my father lost me after my parents' divorce, he embraced my cousins. I had often imagined that each of them had been so much easier to love.

I was the only one whose mother had been American. I was the only one whose parents had gotten divorced. I was the only one who had grown up in both countries. But it was really my mother's fear that had made me so difficult. So different. And yet no matter how hard I've tried, I've never really understood what frightened her. I've never understood what made her destroy our lives.

My parents married in 1954, and by 1961, they had moved to Short Hills, New Jersey. My mother, who had been a physical therapist and a fashion model prior to getting married, took care of me and worked to help my father build his medical practice. We spent our weekends with my uncle Mansoor and my cousins. Family often visited from Tehran. Together, my parents made yogurt every week. My mother often cooked *albaloo pollo*, rice with sour cherries. My father grilled shish kebabs on warm summer evenings. And my American grandmother worried about me eating too much caviar, pistachios, and baklava. I was tucked snugly inside my Iranian-American family until one morning, just a couple of weeks before my eighth birthday, my mother said, "You're not going to school today. We're going someplace safe. Your father wants to take you away to Iran."

Parental kidnapping was not yet part of our national vocabulary. She secretly took me to Saint Thomas, Virgin Islands. It was one of the few places to get a no-fault divorce in 1968. With the FBI's help, my father found us only seventeen days after our departure. It had been only two and a half weeks, but my entire world had changed.

I was falling asleep in my new bed in the concrete-block cottage on a hillside overlooking the Charlotte Amalie Harbor when his voice floated through the screened window.

"Shireen-*joonie. Aziz-am.* I'm here," he said softly.

My spine stiffened. My throat cracked. *I don't want to go to Iran.*

For the first eight years of my life, any sort of fear had driven me to my father's arms. On that night, I ran to my mother. Then I cautiously followed her back to the window, where we could see my father standing out in the shadows. I listened to him plead with her to come home. I heard him ask why she had taken me away.

I heard her say, "Shireen is mine now."

I don't think it's possible to ever really understand what goes wrong in a marriage. Eighteen months before I was born, my two-year-old brother had died of complications from severe Down syndrome. No doubt, Edward's life and death were part of their wound. My father, the pediatrician, hadn't been able to save their son. I can only imagine that grief combined with cultural disconnects compounded their unhappiness.

I've never found any evidence that my father wanted to abandon his life in America and take me away from my mother. And yet, he was a very powerful man. I can only think that when my mother learned that he *could* take me to Iran, where she would lose all her rights as a parent, she set something terrible in motion.

The court records show they didn't fight for money. They fought for control over me. They both wanted to win. There were investigations, lawsuits, threats. The court granted my father visitation, but each weekend visit ended badly. Within two years, my indefatigable father simply gave up. He retreated to Iran. Around the same time, my mother went from being the life of the party to becoming a woman who spent her days and nights sitting alone at a small dinette in our mobile home, typing variations of the same letter. She wrote about how my father had ruined her life. Her only companion was a glass of scotch. She never let it get empty.

By age ten, I was on my own. In different ways, both of my parents had abandoned me. I told myself that I didn't care. I told myself that I was fine by myself.

My father wrote me letters describing the new variety of apples he and my uncle planted in a mountain village called Jaboon. He wrote about the cherries that came from the family garden in Karaj. He told me he loved me and he often said, "You are my only hope." I didn't tell him that I used $30 out of every $100 check he sent me to buy my daily meals at Kentucky Fried Chicken. I didn't tell him that

I put the rest in a savings account to fund my escape. I didn't tell him that mostly I lived with my neighbors, a single mother named Jane and her youngest daughter, Tammie. I didn't tell him my mother was always drunk.

As bad as things were, I didn't trust him. I simply wrote him a thank you note.

By March of 1972, just before my twelfth birthday, Jane had begun to worry about me. One evening she called Tammie and me into her living room and asked us to sit with her.

"Shireen," she said. "I'm not one to get involved in other people's lives. Your mother has always seemed a bit strange, but very nice." She paused for a moment before saying, "It's just that you're only eleven and I'm wondering if there's someone else who could take care of you?"

"I don't know," I answered, looking down at my hands.

"Where is your father?" she asked.

"He lives in Iran."

"Don't you have anyone in the States who could help you?"

"I have an uncle in New York."

Jane wasted no time. She called Information. The operator gave her my uncle's phone number. She called him and arranged for me to visit. To everyone's surprise, my mother said I could go.

Two weeks later, when I arrived at LaGuardia Airport, Uncle Mansoor, Aunt Shekoufeh, and my father walked swiftly toward me. My father scooped me up in his arms. He kissed my head and my cheeks. I tried to step back, but he held me too tightly. I pulled loose. It had been almost two years since we had seen each other.

When I could finally speak, I said, "I thought you were in Iran."

"Uncle Mansoor said you were coming to visit, so I came right away."

"I'm just here for a few days. I'm not going to Iran," I warned him.

"Why did Mom let you come?" he asked.

"She's too drunk to care where I go," I said as I squared my shoulders.

My father stepped back. His face flushed red. He said nothing.

Being blunt with adults had become part of my survival strategy. I didn't care if I shocked people. My father didn't ask any more questions, but at the end of the week, he came back to Saint Thomas with me to see for himself.

Jane and Tammie were waiting for us at the airport.

So was my mother.

As soon as we entered the terminal, I saw her.

"Oh, no! There's Mom," I said. "She wasn't supposed to come."

"Where?" My father asked as he looked past the haggard blonde leaning on a cane. I realized I hadn't told him about the day she drove off a cliff.

"Right there," I said, pointing.

She was only forty-six years old. When my parents married, my father had adored her smooth ivory skin, her slender figure, and the wavy blonde hair that framed her almond-shaped green eyes. Now her swollen belly and spindly limbs reflected a body sickened by a constant infusion of alcohol. Her skin was a mosaic of pus-filled sores. Blonde hair hung limp. Dark sunglasses hid red eyes.

He raised his hand to his mouth and dashed to the men's room.

We spent the next two days with Jane. After much discussion, she convinced me that life in Iran had to be better than how I was living in Saint Thomas. Reluctantly, I agreed to go. I didn't tell my mother I was leaving. I just left her a note.

> Dear Mom,
> I can't stay with you. There's no food at home. The house is falling apart. It's filled with cockroaches. You're always drunk. I'm going to Iran, where my father will take care of me. I'm sorry.
> I love you.
>
> —Shireen

Jane gave it to her after I was already gone.

My father and I spent a couple of weeks in Manhattan before we boarded an Aeroflot jet for the ten-hour flight to Moscow. We used American passports at JFK and Iranian passports after that.

Technically, this was another case of parental kidnapping, but this time no one looked for me.

As we settled into our seats for the final four hours from Moscow to Tehran, I suddenly realized that I didn't know anything about where we were going.

"Where do you live?" I asked.

"With my family."

"But who is that?"

"Your uncle Noori, my sisters, and your cousins Neena, Nathan, and Nelson. They all love you very much." His deep brown eyes met mine as he spoke. He really wanted me to understand that I was loved, that they were waiting for me and had been waiting ever since I had disappeared into the Caribbean four years earlier.

I felt dizzy, my stomach swirled, but I reminded myself that I had made the decision to come to Iran—there was no turning back. I would have to adapt.

"Why do you live with all those people?" I asked.

"They are my family," he answered with a soft smile. "They are your family too."

He didn't understand that he was a stranger to me. He couldn't imagine the struggles I would face as I stumbled into the family diorama, and it would never have occurred to him to describe what lay ahead. He didn't realize that, unlike my cousins, I was used to making my own decisions. I couldn't fathom living in a house with all those people.

He took a deep breath and turned to face me. His body blocked the aisle. He looked deeply into my eyes. Then he said, "Darling, you must forget about your mother and Saint Thomas. You are starting a new life."

I shook my head. I wondered if my mother even knew I was gone. Saint Thomas was my home. I loved the sky, the sea, and the rocks. I loved Tammie and Jane. I loved the trade winds and the hibiscus. If I forgot everything bad, then I would lose everything I loved.

The plane began its descent. I looked out the window. The jagged peaks of the Alborz Mountains bordered Tehran to the north.

To the south was an expanse of desert. An endless swath of buildings flowed between the two. The sky was a brilliant blue. Iran was beautiful—not quite as beautiful as the Caribbean, but beautiful just the same, except that there were very few trees. A small flame of hope flickered inside my heart. *Maybe I'll be OK in this strange place.*

Mehrabad Airport was all shouting, hugging, kissing, and hundreds of people milling around, but our arrival didn't prepare me for the drive to Saba Street. Cars came in clusters. Pedestrians stepped blindly forward into the maelstrom at intersections, seeming to trust that they could safely cross. Motorcyclists looking for shortcuts rode up the sidewalks. There was even an occasional donkey competing with the traffic. As we maneuvered through the city streets, I wondered if anything would ever feel familiar again.

We pulled into the alley and walked up to the massive door made of opaque textured glass covered by an ornate brass grid. My father rang the bell. A short woman with a long, gray ponytail opened it and immediately ushered us inside. I didn't know she was my father's eldest sibling, his sister Gohar.

As I stepped into the large, empty hallway, she shut the door behind me, and I heard a strong tone of finality. My body stiffened. My eyes, always scanning for danger, narrowed against what I might find.

Gohar's bright brown eyes crinkled when she smiled, highlighting the many deep wrinkles in her dark olive skin. Her knobby arthritic hands trembled, and her voice shook as she reached for me and kissed me over and over.

She pulled back for a moment, and I saw tears running down her cheeks as she said, "*Man amejan.*" She placed her hand on her heart.

I held my breath. I braced against her tenderness. To be handled in such a familiar way by an elderly woman who spoke no English frightened me. Her touch was soft and loving, but it felt so foreign.

"Who is this?" I asked my father.

Smiling broadly, my father said, "This is my sister Gohar. *Gohar* means the oldest one. She raised us, my brothers and sisters and me. She is like my mother. She loves you like you are her daughter."

My chest hardened. I clenched my fists. *I don't want another mother.*

"*Cheshmehman roshaneh que amadi,*" she said, pointing at her eyes. "*Farsi, khoobeh. Farsi yad begere.*"

Suddenly, another of my father's sisters appeared in that giant hallway. She also grabbed me and hugged me and kissed me. I had met her once, when she visited New York, but she seemed different now. Foreign.

And I didn't know what anyone was saying. It had never occurred to me that I was going someplace where they didn't speak English. All my cousins in New York spoke English. I bit my lip, trying to hold back my tears.

I would eventually learn that the translation of *amejan* to "aunt" or "dear aunt" didn't do the word justice, especially when it was applied to Gohar. Having no children of her own, Gohar loved all of us with a ferocity and a selflessness that I have never experienced in another human being. She was just thirteen when her own mother died. Her love for the younger siblings she raised, and their children, is where she found her identity. She believed in simple pleasures. She couldn't read or write. She enjoyed TV, a delicious meal, the occasional cigarette, good health, and most importantly, she enjoyed family. Every day, she took me aside and said, "*Hameh khoobeh.*" Then she listed off the names of everyone, including my mother.

As I stood in the entryway to my new home, I didn't know that everything revolved around the family and the family would help you survive, but that in turn you were obligated to let your elders direct your life. I didn't know that a cousin made your clothes, a brother or sister helped raise your child. I didn't know that these were unquestioned facts in my Persian family. I didn't know that there was a sense of order, of duty without resentment. My father wouldn't have thought to tell me these things.

He didn't know that I had stopped thinking of myself as a child. He didn't know that I had become someone who questioned everything. He didn't know that my mother had schooled me in her philosophy: "Never trust your family."

Within a week, I joined my cousins at Tehran Community School, a college-preparatory international school. Classes were taught in English. The student body included a lot of Iranian kids but also many other children, whose parents worked for international companies. The shah was still in power. Tehran teemed with Americans, Brits, French, Germans, and Russians. Movie theaters played American movies. Very few women in central Tehran wore chadors.

My father joined a fancy country club with swimming pools, tennis courts, a bowling alley, and two restaurants. He took my cousins and me ice-skating at the Ice Palace. We ate at Ray's Pizza. He did his best to recreate the life we had lived in New Jersey before the divorce, but I wasn't adjusting. I wanted to hide in my dark room, listen to music, read, and eat.

Food became a means by which my father and Gohar tried to show me their world. It became a metaphor for many aspects of our lives.

"Come, have some fruit," said my father one day soon after my arrival.

Red grapes cascaded over apricots and a few unblemished bananas. Several small cucumbers graced the edges of the gigantic brass bowl that sat on the dining table in the large room with French doors.

"This fruit comes from Karaj. We have a garden there." He paused to smile proudly. "Apricots are in season and extremely delicious. Or you could have a banana from India."

In Saint Thomas we had wild mangoes, small native bananas, papayas, genips, and soursops. Sometimes a mealy apple or a shriveled orange survived the long journey by ship, but a bowl overflowing with fruit would have been unimaginable. When I reached for an apricot, he stretched his hand over mine and said, "Let me choose one for you. I want you to have the best." He gently grasped three or four before selecting a round globe that was the color of a Caribbean sunset.

"It's really beautiful," I said, smiling.

"Yes. The fruit grown in Iran is more delicious than anywhere else in the world."

The first bite filled my mouth with sweet, sharp juice.

Amejan walked in carrying a tray with cardamom-scented black tea and a bowl of sugar cubes, along with some warm flatbread and feta cheese soaking in water to mellow the flavor. I barely noticed her as I focused on my luscious apricot. I reached for a second just as she set down the tray.

"Shireen *jan, chai-to bokhor.*"

I looked greedily at the fruit. I wanted to eat those luscious pieces of Caribbean sunset until I could eat no more, but I knew better than to stuff myself in front of my father. He had already begun the habit of having me step on the scale to monitor my weight. He wanted everyone in the family, male and female, to be slender. I inhaled deeply. The tea smelled good. I picked up one sugar cube, dropped it into the china teacup, and watched it settle to the bottom. Then I gently stirred and slowly lifted the cup to my mouth for a sip of the hot, sweet liquid.

I looked at Amejan, who was still standing next to me. I smiled and said, "*Merci,*" which my father had told me means "thank you" in Farsi, a word borrowed from French.

She smiled, and her deep brown eyes became pools of joy.

My father's need to select the best fruit for me reflected his drive to make all my decisions. His demands were consistent with his culture.

"You will become a doctor."

"You must be thin. Then you will be beautiful."

"You must wear these clothes. Then you will look successful."

"You must, you must"/"I won't, I won't" formed a battleground between us.

During that first year in Tehran, I hid in my room. Unlike my cousins, I had my own TV. I watched *Marcus Welby, M.D.* and *Bonanza* in English. I read Edgar Allan Poe and Ian Fleming. And I ate. Then, in 1973, I learned that my mother had died alone in her mobile home. There was no definitive cause of death. Her body had begun to decompose in the summer heat before anyone thought to look for her.

I was thirteen years old. I knew she had drunk herself to death. I had left her and she had died. In my child's logic, I knew her death was my fault, and the feeling that I had failed her would haunt me for decades.

Unlike my cousins, I also had my own stereo. When despair overwhelmed me, I blasted Steppenwolf's "Born to be Wild" until it shook the glass in my windows. I gorged myself on pastries that were meant for the whole family. Unlike my cousins, I demanded sleepovers with my girlfriends. By age fourteen, I was dating a boy from school. And once, I got very drunk on vodka from our liquor cabinet and passed out in my bedroom. Unlike my cousins, when I didn't get to do what I wanted, I raged against my father and my uncle. I demanded explanations. I found my own way around the rules.

I thought I was making my own decisions. I thought I was a West Indian kid fighting against urban living. I thought I was an American kid fighting against Persian constraints. I thought I was my mother's daughter fighting against my father. I couldn't understand why my cousins obediently followed the rules.

I realize now that the losses I faced during my four years in Saint Thomas had made me different in ways that would take decades to untangle. I had become a wounded child. An angry child. My sense of self had been crushed. I didn't trust adults. I eventually came to understand that I would have had to fight this fight no matter where I lived. And yet, it was easy to think that living in Iran with my father was the problem. It wasn't until I was in my mid-forties, when my cousin Neena complained to me about how our fathers and Amejan always forgave my bad behavior, when she said that she couldn't understand how they kept loving me, no matter what I did, that I finally understood that their love, combined with all the structure that came with living in Iran, literally saved my life. As much as their love and their expectations felt suffocating, they gave me some ground to stand on until I could find my own way.

As I reentered my father's hospital room, I paused momentarily to kiss the top of my son's tiny head. I settled into a chair by my father's bed and marveled once again that so many times in his life, he had more than beaten the odds. And with his help, so had I.

He couldn't die now. Not yet. Not until both of my children had the chance to know him.

At the end of the third day, I finally spoke with the attending physician. He was a short man with brown hair and tortoise-shell glasses. He wore a white coat. It was the first time that I had spoken about my father's illness with a doctor who wasn't part of my family. I didn't believe him when he told me that my father wouldn't last more than a couple of days.

I went back into my father's room and stood beside him. I smoothed his forehead with my fingers. He shook his head and turned away.

"Dad," I said cautiously. "Dad, I can't stay with you. Chloe is home waiting for me."

I took his hand and the unbidden words tumbled from my mouth. "I've been away for three days. I need to go. She's only three and I've never left her before now."

He rested his hand in mine and looked into my eyes. "I am proud of you, my darling. You're a good mother—the best mother. You always put your children's needs first. I have my family here, my brothers, my sister, and your cousins. Go and be with your children. I love you, my darling. I love you. Go now."

I hugged him and kissed him goodbye. For the first time in my life, he didn't cling to me. As he drifted back to sleep, I could feel him slowly moving away. He had promoted me from child to parent, and in our final moments, the invisible cord that tied my father and me together unraveled and gently fell away. I knew I would never see him again.

Two days later, surrounded by his two brothers and one remaining sister, my father slipped away. I was home in Colorado, making a yogurt and rice for my daughter, when Neena called to say, "Uncle Atta has passed away. The funeral is in two days."

The finality of her words cut me. I gripped the kitchen counter and tried to feel something, anything, but my heart was tight, *delam tang shodeh*.

Then I heard Chloe saying to her baby brother, "When you get bigger, Charlie, Mama will make *maast* yogurt for you too."

And it was in that moment that I realized everything I had learned about how to really love a child had come from the Persian side of my heritage. Love in my Persian family was demanding, but also unwavering. It was an infusion of food and relationships, of guidance, demands, and expectations. It was also acceptance and hope. In that moment, I realized that I was now the parent and I would give my children the very best of what my father and his siblings had given me.

Walking with Zahra

Layla Maryam Razavi

She looked like an angel. Her small, wrinkled face was serene and expressionless, her eyes were shut, and it seemed that somehow she had shrunk in size. The nurses had placed a cool, white cloth around her, and it framed her face in a perfect halo. The machinery of the hospital buzzed quietly in the background of the small, windowed ICU room. Amir hung back in the doorway; he mumbled, "I can't be in here," and walked out of the room.

I stepped closer and grasped her hand. "Zahra, we're here." She let out a slight whimper, and I couldn't be sure if she knew we were in the room with her. My mother and my grandma came over and stood on the other side of her bed. Zahra kept letting out a quiet moaning sound.

I turned and looked back at the nurse, who had cornered me in the hallway earlier. "She's really suffering, and these machines are just making it worse," she had insisted. "She should be at peace."

"No, absolutely not," I had hissed back. "My aunts are flying down from the Bay Area. They want to see her. And we're not ready. Nothing is ready yet."

"OK," the nurse had responded with no hint of judgment.

She was hovering in the doorway now.

"OK, fine," I declared. "She's in pain, and there's no point in making it go on any longer. Go ahead. Do whatever you need to do, just make it stop."

"OK," the nurse said, again showing no signs of her opinion.

I turned and looked back at Zahra lying there. "Zahra, it's me.

Squeeze my hand if you can hear me." For a moment, I thought I felt her index finger move slightly. She continued moaning in pain.

"*Biya inja!*" Zahra screeched, cupping my face in her hands and pulling me toward her. I could see strands of chewed up *sabzi*, cilantro or parsley most likely, hanging out from in between her teeth, and her breath reeked of raw onion. "*Nemi-khaaaaaam*," I groaned, trying to pull away. She planted her wet saliva kiss on my cheek anyway, ignoring my protests. I was a little girl, in kindergarten, and we were making one of our regular visits from our house in San Diego to see my grandparents in Los Angeles. They were having some of their friends over for dinner, and my parents and I had arrived early to settle in and help my grandmother. I loved trips to see my grandparents, but I hated the drawn-out entrances and aggressive greetings of my relatives. All the old ladies with red lipstick on their teeth trying to kiss you were tedious enough, but I always especially tried to escape from Zahra's kisses. She had long, scratchy whiskers, there were always half-eaten clumps of food in her mouth, and strange kitchen smells—cardamom and turmeric—formed a halo around her at all times. I groaned and rubbed my cheek to erase the kiss stain.

My grandparents lived in a two-bedroom apartment in a three-story art deco building on a quiet street in Sherman Oaks, California—in "the Valley"—where a large portion of the Muslim Iranian population was concentrated. I loved exploring the neighborhood with my grandparents. They didn't have a car, so we would walk around Ventura Boulevard or take the bus. The stores had signs with Persian writing hanging in the windows, and the shops played Persian music and sold Persian food.

The apartment was crowded. My grandparents slept in the master bedroom, my uncle Amir in the second bedroom, and Zahra on the floor of the dining room. But to a little girl, the apartment provided ample space for the imagination to run wild. I would turn the small living room into a theater hall, where my relatives were forced to sit on plastic-covered furniture and watch me sing and dance. There was a small patio full of wicker furniture assembled on fake grass. Zahra would sit on the grass and spread mounds of *sabzi* out around her on Persian-language newspapers, separating all the freshly washed greens.

Zahra was an anomaly among the colorful cast of Iranian characters assembled in my childhood milieu in the Valley. The other elders, my grandparents and their friends, were sophisticated; they would go to Europe or Iran and come back with suitcases full of gifts and foods, they wore too much perfume or cologne, and they threw dinner parties where they played grown-up card games like rummy late into the evening. Aside from their overly zealous greetings, they were fun. They played games with me and teased me. But Zahra didn't socialize with anyone who came to visit. She sat in the corner, often on the floor, with one leg curled underneath and the other leg bent in front of her, with her knee functioning as a makeshift arm rest. She had a limited number of dresses—large, patterned housecoats in an assortment of navy blues and grays, which draped over her like a tent. She was the only person who wore a headscarf. She would tie it firmly beneath her chin every morning and keep it on until she got ready for bed. Her face was constantly scrunched up tightly. It was not a scowl so much as a permanent wince. It never occurred to me to question who she was or why she was there. She was just Zahra—our *naneh*— an odd fixture from my childhood who had always been there.

The other guests started to arrive. Zahra went and took her place in the kitchen. The small table in that cramped kitchen had room for only two chairs. Zahra's chair was easily identifiable because the wicker seat had sunken underneath her weight as she sat in the same spot each day for hours on end. Eventually we would have to replace the seat of the chair twice as the wicker strands began to fray and break. But that evening, the wicker seat remained intact, thinned and stretched down to the shape of Zahra's bottom. Outside the kitchen, the guests in the dining room were complimenting the food, and my grandmother began explaining which dishes she could take credit for and which ones were exclusively the result of Zahra's labor. As the meal wound down, Zahra brought out a tray of hot tea and my grandmother and my mom started stacking the dirty plates to carry into the kitchen. My grandma reemerged from the kitchen carrying a green felt cloth. The card game would begin soon. This was my cue to leave.

Already feeling bored, as the only child, I wandered into the kitchen. On these occasions, I didn't mind Zahra's strange smells. I walked up to her feeling listless, and without saying a word, I climbed up on her lap, her rolls of flesh shifting around to cushion me. "*Ghorboonet beram*," she said, a declaration of her willingness to die for me. "*Inshallah* you will have a husband, but he will be the best husband." She lightly tapped her finger against my pelvis from outside my pants. "We won't give this *nos-nos* to some nobody. He has to be a king. We will give our daughter to the king of kings." I smiled bashfully, and she laughed and pulled me into her. I buried my face in her large breasts as her entire body shook with laughter and her eyes brimmed with tears. Zahra didn't speak any English, so sometimes I didn't fully understand her meaning. But I knew I was special.

I heard the front door slam and the adults shouting happily. Amir was home. A few minutes later, he sauntered into the kitchen. My grandma was calling out to him from the dining room, insisting he eat some food. "*Chashm, chashm*," he assured her and walked up to me smiling and shaking his head. My uncle Amir, a teenager in high school, was the youngest of all my mom's siblings, and I looked up to him like a big brother who had already figured everything out. He plucked me out of Zahra's arms and hoisted me into the air. "Hi *goozoo*," he said, smiling at me and nuzzling his nose against mine. "I'm not a *gooz*," I stated matter-of-factly. "If I'm a fart, you're a fart." He laughed and ignored me.

"Zahra, what's wrong? Why are there tears in your eyes?" he asked.

Zahra looked up at Amir, shook her head, and held up her hands in surrender as tears streamed down her face. "What can I do?"

Amir put me down and bent down to Zahra's eye level. He scrunched up his face, mock crying, and said, "*Naneh jaan*, what can I do?" imitating Zahra's voice.

Zahra's face scrunched up even more, and she started silently laughing at Amir's impression of her.

Amir pushed ahead. He held up his hands and looked upward, imitating her. "God, please help me," he said in a high-pitched voice. "What am I to do? My poor children. My poor youngest daughter, she is still not married. Poor me, my terrible health, this diabetes, all these pains. God, help me. My poor Amir . . . well, not really Amir. He is handsome and brilliant. I really lucked out with him."

Zahra's entire body was shaking from laughter as tears continued streaming down her coarse and wrinkled cheeks. She had an uncanny ability to burst into tears and laughter simultaneously, and one could never tell if she was experiencing joy or sorrow. You got the impression that both emotions were always brimming beneath the surface. Zahra kept shaking silently and then said, "*Pedarsookhte*, you're making fun of me?" But her eyes gazed up at him in adoration.

Without missing a beat, Amir turned to me and said, "Hey, watch this. Zahra, say the four phrases you know." Zahra became perfectly still, and all her emotions seemed to escape her. She held out her hand to begin counting off the phrases on her fingers. "Shut-uph, fuhkyou, bowshiit, cosnaat." I gasped and put my hands over my mouth, shocked to hear the bad language but also amused by her terrible accent.

"Wait, I don't know the last one," I said.

"She's saying, 'Of course not,'" Amir explained.

"But that's not a bad word."

"I know. She hears them on TV and thinks they're all bad words."

I giggled and nodded my head approvingly.

My grandma entered the kitchen.

"Amir! Eh! Come eat food, *digeh*. What is this?"

"OK, OK. We're just asking Zahra to speak in English. She's so smart. Check this out. Zahra, who is the prime minister of England?"

We all turned and looked at Zahra.

"Marrh-geht Tatche."

"See?" Amir said proudly. "I bet you didn't even know that."

"Prime minister of England?" my grandma demanded. "*Deh*. I don't know any prime ministers. Your food is freezing cold now, and you're giving a lesson in politics? *Pssshhh*." She shook her head in disbelief and walked out of the kitchen.

"Come eat your food," she called out over her shoulder. "Everyone wants to see you."

Amir looked down at me. "Man, she's so smart. I'm telling you, if she had been born in any other country, she'd be the prime minister."

"What's a prime minister?"

Amir laughed. "It's called: stop being such a *gooz*." He grabbed a piece of lavash from the plate in front of Zahra, stuffing the bread into his mouth as he walked back into the dining room.

I turned and looked at Zahra. "I want ice cream," I announced. "But not the gross pistachio kind. Normal ice cream."

I skipped away.

We sat around Zahra's hospital bed making small talk. My mother came into the room. "Here, I brought you some pizza." I looked down at the cold, doughy individual-sized pizza on a paper plate and scrunched up my face in disgust. "It's all they had in the cafeteria," my mom explained. "You haven't eaten or slept in three days."

It was true. I had brought Zahra in to the doctor's office because she had been having trouble controlling her bladder and was complaining of stomach pain. The doctor, who was Iranian, took one look at her and ordered me to take her straight to the ER. There, two doctors, both white men, walked in and smiled, and I calmly interpreted the exchange between them and Zahra—a skill I had perfected as I had been doing much of her interpreting since I was a child, whenever my parents were at work or otherwise unavailable.

"Ask her how much pain she is in on a scale of 1 to 10," the older of the two doctors instructed me.

"Zahra," I turned to her. "How much pain are you in, from 1 to 10?"

Zahra squinted up at me as if I were speaking nonsense. She slowly raised her hands up to the sky and said, "*Naneh jaan*, what do I know? It's all in God's hands. When it's my time to go, I will go."

I didn't miss a beat. "Zahra," I continued, "that's fine. But these gentlemen are doctors. If you have pain, they can give you medicine. Do you have pain?"

I waited.

Zahra looked at me and shrugged her shoulders. "This is life. There is always pain."

"Zahra, don't tell me about life. Do you have any pain in your body? Right at this moment?"

"*Naneh*, I'm old. My whole body is always in pain. Sitting here hurts. Getting up hurts. Lying down hurts."

"OK, but where does it hurt the most right now?"

"There's a horrible pain in my stomach. It's unbearable. But I must learn to bear it."

"So, on a scale of 1 to 10, is it a 10?"

Zahra stared at me, not blinking, as if I were completely dense. "I wish it was 10. What is a 10? This pain is 100."

Satisfied, I turned back to the doctors.

"Yes, her stomach hurts. It's a 10."

The doctors looked at each other and back at me. "That's what she said?" the older doctor inquired.

"Yes."

"And you're sure you're interpreting her completely?"

"Yes."

We continued on like this for some time, with the doctors giving simple instructions, asking her to move her fingers or her toes or to describe her pain as they touched her abdomen, and Zahra and I having a mini-existential debate on fatalism, free will, faith in God, and modern medicine over each of their basic instructions. And each time, after much back and forth, I turned back to the doctors and gave brief replies.

Eventually, the older doctor spoke up. "I'm sure you're doing a fine job interpreting, but are you sure you're getting everything? It seems that you both say a lot more to each other than what you're telling us."

"Well . . ." I tried to think of an answer that would make me look competent and make Zahra seem like someone deserving of excellent medical care. "You have to understand—Persian is a very complicated language. So many of the words are compound words. For example, when you say, 'Move your toes,' I have to tell her, 'Move the fingers of your feet.' Did you know there is not even a word for 'toes' in Persian?"

"I see."

"Look, my grandmother is very old and religious." I always referred to Zahra as my grandmother around white people because that's essentially what she was to me—a third grandmother. Besides, it's too confusing to explain that after your family fled the Islamic Republic, they made sure to send for their servant to join them out of loyalty to her and her family. White people don't have servants anymore—well, they do, but they don't like to admit it, and they certainly wouldn't understand feeling love or obligation toward one. "She thinks her fate is in God's hands," I admitted. "So I have to ask her each question repeatedly and plead with her to get her to believe that you will help her."

The older doctor smiled with a look of amusement. "I see," he responded. "Thank you for doing a good job interpreting." I felt instinctively annoyed and protective toward Zahra.

The next seventy-two hours were a blur. The two doctors disappeared, more attendants came in and took tests, and then the younger doctor came back and showed me numbers indicating Zahra's white blood cell count. I was only nineteen years old, but I knew enough to know that it was bad. I called my parents, my grandparents, and Amir to explain that they were keeping Zahra in the hospital and that everyone needed to come as soon as possible.

She had pancreatic cancer, the elderly doctor explained to me. It's the worst form of cancer because it's usually undetectable until it's too late.

Zahra was checked into a hospital room. Her roommate was an elderly white woman. All our extended relatives, my mother's cousins and aunts and uncles, began filing in to visit Zahra. We crowded around her, laughing and talking loudly, with a single curtain separating us from the woman alone on the other side of the hospital room.

My family tends to do this in hospitals—we occupy an entire half of the room and shout and laugh loudly in a foreign language, while the other patient is forced to sit there pretending they're not in the same room as us. I always wonder about the patients who are there alone. I feel guilty that we're taking up so much space and sad that they don't have many visitors.

The following morning, I got to the hospital early. I had been there until late into the night and hadn't had much sleep, but I wanted to keep Zahra company until the others could arrive. Zahra was asleep, and her roommate was sitting up in bed. "Hi Susan," I smiled, trying to appear upbeat. "Good morning," Susan said, holding the hospital telephone in her hands. "Could you help me dial my son? He lives far away and he said he would call, but I haven't heard from him."

I dialed the number Susan gave me, but no one answered. "You know, he's probably at work," I offered. "Why don't we try him again tonight?"

Susan didn't respond and just looked down at the phone. I opened up the curtain separating the two beds, sensing that Susan didn't want to be alone. I pulled a chair up to Zahra and held her hands.

"Hi. How are you feeling today?"

"I hate that woman," Zahra said to me.

"Why?"

"I was moaning in pain all night. Because I'm dying from pain. And I heard her yell, 'Shut up.'"

Immediately, I understood. Despite all the morphine, Zahra had been keeping Susan awake all night. The poor woman, alone and exhausted, must have yelled at Zahra to let her sleep.

"It's OK," I assured her.

"What do you mean it's OK? I yelled back at her, 'Shut up *beh khodet*!' She thinks I don't understand what she's saying, so I added, 'Fuhkyou! Cosnaat!'"

I tried to keep from bursting into laughter.

Susan didn't have as much trouble sleeping that night as Zahra was moved into the ICU. She had woken up in the middle of the night in such pain that she struggled to get up. The nurses hadn't been able to subdue her and finally had had to cuff her to the bed, and then they moved her out of the room. I hated thinking how scared she must have felt with no one understanding what she was saying. When we got to the ICU, she said, "They're going to kill me here."

Eventually, we had her moved into a private room so she could spend her final hours in peace.

When Zahra took her last breath, it was so sudden that none of us noticed it at first. We were all sitting around her bed, talking as if nothing out of the ordinary were happening.

My cousin spoke up. "I think she stopped breathing."

Suddenly the room flew into a flurry of activity. My mom and grandma burst into tears. My mom's aunt started shouting instructions. "We need the doctor. Someone should get a nurse."

My grandmother started moaning at me. "You're so young. You shouldn't see this."

My grandfather jumped in to problem solve. "Layla, don't worry. Eat your pizza. It's getting cold."

I stared at him, stupefied.

The morning after my grandmother's dinner party, I entered the kitchen and Zahra was sitting in her chair. "*Biya inja*," she said and pointed to the chair across from her at the kitchen table. "I have your favorite breakfast ready for you." I smiled, ran up to table, and climbed onto the chair. Quince jam with butter on toasted pita bread. Zahra started slowly breaking the pita bread into small bites to feed me. I was more than old enough to feed myself, but I lapped up the extra attention each time I was at my grandparents'.

"OK, when you finish eating, we can go for a walk," Zahra offered.

I nodded in agreement.

I loved going on walks with Zahra through my grandparents' neighborhood. Unlike other grown-ups, who took charge and told me what to do, Zahra was always content to follow my lead and let me be.

My mom stopped us as we headed to the front door and tied a jacket around my waist. "Take this with you, just in case." I sighed, annoyed by the delay. Only my family made me wear a jacket when it was seventy degrees outside. "And make sure you stay close to Zahra and don't go out into the street." I nodded.

My grandparents' apartment building was on a broad, tree-lined avenue. To the left, we could see the intersection of Ventura

Boulevard and to the right, in the distance, the rolling green hills cordoning us off from the rest of LA. We turned toward the hills, leaving the traffic of Ventura behind us. We walked straight down the middle of the street, as there were no cars at this time of day and the neighborhood was quiet. The old trees on either side towered above us and reached toward each other, forming a canopy of shade. We approached a giant oak tree, and Zahra reached up and pulled down one of the lowest-hanging branches and handed me a perfect large green leaf. I twirled it around in my hand. When we got to a eucalyptus tree, Zahra stopped and lifted me up in the air. "Pick off as many leaves as you can," she instructed, and I grabbed and ripped off leaves by the fistful. "Good. I will show you how to boil these. They make a nice scent." She took the leaves from me and shoved them into the deep pockets of her housecoat. Boiling? Scents? I was excited at the prospect of a science experiment when we got back to the apartment. We neared a large house with a white picket fence and a porch with a huge American flag waving overhead. "Look at that orange tree!" Zahra exclaimed and rushed over to the fence. She stretched out her dress as though it were a large apron and began picking and placing oranges into the makeshift sack. Once she was satisfied that she had cleared off any ripe oranges within arm's reach, she returned to meet me in the middle of the street.

"Are you allowed to take things from people's yards?" I asked.

"*Naneh jaan*, there's no problem. They're not eating them."

I looked up toward the sky. The canopy of leaves cast shadows on my face as the clouds moved and the light shifted. I sensed Zahra, beside me, looking up too. I closed my eyes, squinting again, and waited as the color changed from dark to bright orange. I opened my eyes and straightened my head.

"I love going on walks here with you," I told Zahra.

"My favorite was going out in Tehran."

"Why?"

"Because Amir was a baby. I would tie him onto my back with a big cloth and go out into the bazaar to buy things for the house or for your grandmother's guests. I would go into the market and haggle with people and find the best produce, the best deals."

"But why did you like produce and deals?"

"Because no one told me what to do. There was no husband barking orders, just me and my boy. I was free."

She smiled at me. I smiled back.

"I get it. I hate it when my parents tell me what to do."

"No, you should obey your parents. Come on. Let's go back. My shows will be starting soon."

Zahra had two TV shows she watched religiously: *Animal Planet* and *Wheel of Fortune*. *Animal Planet* didn't require any knowledge of English—she just loved watching the slow-motion shots of lions and other majestic creatures running in the wild. *Wheel of Fortune* allowed her to practice the alphabet, and she would shout out the letters as they appeared up on the board.

We turned back toward Ventura Boulevard, and as we walked, Zahra continued speaking of Iran. Anyone who looked out at that wide avenue with high curbs and old streetlamps would have seen an odd sight: a strange figure swaying from side to side, her large housecoat swinging from left to right, right to left, at a slow and steady pace, with a little girl skipping beside her, twirling an oak leaf, moving along under the large canopy of branches, the trees having parted, making a clearing for them to pass through. Zahra, with her whiskers, headscarf, and rolled nylon stockings, and me, with my adjoining eyebrows and light smattering of upper-lip hair, wearing too many layers for the Valley heat. We strolled down past the 1920s streetlamps that Gene Kelly had twirled around in *Singin' in the Rain*, and we passed by 1960s stucco apartment buildings that eventually became the subject of many asbestos lawsuits. As the cars on Ventura Boulevard started to get louder, Zahra continued describing her memories of Iran. She painted a picture I could see clearly in front me. We may as well have been approaching the central bazaar in Tehran, with its merchant stalls, swarming shoppers, and packed alleyways. I could almost hear the throngs of people and passing motorists on the long avenue leading to Bazaar Tehran.

Halva

Nazanine Attaran

One sunny California afternoon, I walked into my granite-countered kitchen and was hit with the aroma of toasted flour and the pungent, sweet smell of rose water. My mother, visiting from Iran, was standing at the stove, stirring something in one of my stainless-steel All-Clad pots. Her face broke into a wrinkled smile behind her rimless glasses as she offered me a warm spoonful. I hadn't had any of the many different types of halva in a mind-boggling thirty-plus years, ever since I left Iran for what I thought would be only a few years of college in the United States. The Islamic Revolution in 1979, the ensuing devastating eight-year Iran-Iraq War, and political turmoil had abruptly closed that door.

That day, as I raised the spoon and put it in my mouth, I was once again twelve years old, walking through a long, beige-colored corridor cramped with bags of groceries. An intricately designed turquoise Persian runner cushioned my slippered feet. The clanking of pots, the gentle, intermittent murmur of voices, the rhythmic melody playing over the radio—all the sounds of a bustling kitchen floated in the air, growing louder and more distinct as I approached. The whole house smelled of baked sweets and toasted flour. I was excited. My older cousin had just returned to Shiraz from America—"Amreeka"—and Madar was throwing a party in her honor. I turned the corner past the blue-tiled bathroom to the oddly windowless yellow kitchen of my childhood.

Grandfather had designed the house himself. The rooms in the front of the house overlooking the walled garden, which was replete with climbing jasmine vines, orange blossoms, and roses, had huge windows that were usually flung open. The ones in the back of the building, the kitchen being one of them, overlooked the neighbors' homes and had no windows, or only tiny ones for ventilation. When Madar married into the family and moved in, she remodeled the kitchen and made up for the lack of natural light with bright yellow ceramic tiles and paint.

I stopped in the doorway and watched the three people in the kitchen for a moment. Habib, our cook of over thirty years, was hunched over a tray piled high with fresh herbs and was patiently separating the stems from the leaves. His eyes softened as he looked up with a half smile, revealing a sliver of his gold front tooth. His wife, Firoozeh, sleeves rolled up, stood at the sink. Since she was religious, she had a flowered gray chador wrapped and tucked in around her hip, ready to pull over her henna-dyed hair at the sight of an unfamiliar male. Not one to smile readily, she acknowledged my presence with a slight nod of the head without interrupting her work. Her chapped, darkened hands were holding one of my mother's tarnished silver candy dishes as she scrubbed the raised roses with a toothbrush dipped in some white powder. She was usually called in to help with the preparations and the serving at parties. Madar, her light brown hair in rollers, was standing by the mustard-colored gas stove. She didn't notice me until I walked over and stood beside her. As she gently touched my cheek, her face broke into the same smile lines that would become permanent years later. Her faded blue duster was stained with tiny smudges from the day's cooking. Even through the intense aroma of the toasted flour, I still caught her mom scent—Coty perfume and baked sweets. I watched her as she intently toasted the flour until it was just the perfect shade of pink—an extra minute over the flame and it could burn. I steadied a blackened iron pot with its broken handle as she quickly stirred the flour into the already-prepared mixture of water, rose water, and saffron. The sweet smell of the halva quickly dominated the air, masking that of her freshly baked famous lemon pie cooling on the tiled counter. As I looked on, Habib stepped closer and took over the endless stirring of the paste until it had the color and consistency of sweet potato puree. He poured it into a white porcelain serving platter and then allowed me to decorate this festive halva by making crescent shapes with the back of a spoon before sprinkling it with chopped pistachios. The silver now shiny and dry, Firoozeh moved to washing the herbs in an enormous metal colander as her ten-year-old daughter came in carrying freshly baked bread, *naan sangak*, wrapped in a thin cotton towel.

Habib had been with my family not only as long as I could remember but as long as even Aunt Mahin, the recounter of our family history, remembered. He lived in my grandfather's old house not far from ours with his wife, son, and three daughters and came to cook for us every day. It seemed as if he had always been there, aged and yet ageless, wearing neatly ironed gray pants and a white short-sleeved shirt. Years later, when I asked, nobody could tell me whether he had ever looked any different, if he had had more hair other than the ring of gray curly ones covering his temples, or had always been short and stocky, or had ever grown any facial hair for a change. There are a few details that I can no longer conjure up effortlessly, such as the shape of his eyebrows or the number of lines on his forehead, but I will never forget the exact shade of his skin. His skin was as brown as the halva he made for my grandfather's funeral when I was five years old. At the time, I remember thinking how he himself could be made of halva, like the gingerbread boy in the story Madar read to me. Standing on a stool by the stove, staring into the huge, hammered and dimpled copper pot, I had watched him stir the thickening chocolate-colored halva with increasing difficulty as the overpowering, sweet smell of rose water invaded my nostrils. His wife and older daughter had solemnly wrapped spoonfuls of it in lavash bread and piled them high on trays to take out to the street. I remember the huge round trays heaped with pyramid-like stacks of the halva wraps being passed out to passers-by, who would suddenly slow down, the look in their eyes softening as they obligingly picked one from the tray. *Halvayeh mordeh*—halva for the dead.

"Why are you giving the halva to these people?" I asked Habib. It was confusing to me, spending so much time making food only to give it away.

"So they send a *fateheh* for Babaji's soul," he answered.

Babaji died right before Ramadan, the fasting month. Every evening as daylight began to wane at the edges, the muezzin's melancholy call to prayer would rise in the air. I remember thinking this was for Babaji and what an important man he must have been to have prayers chanted all over town for him. Later, as I got older, I realized that this public call to prayer was being made because it was Ramadan, a month devoted to practicing self-control, self-reflection, and devotion to God through fasting from sunrise to sunset. Habib explained it to me during our twilight walks to the corner store to buy the special gelatinous halva that was only made during this time. This was my favorite halva, partly because it was only made during this month and partly because it was cut and shaped into alternating colored diamond shapes—white and yellow. I cherished these walks even as I got older. Habib was quite a gifted storyteller. His world was rich with all kinds of supernatural presences, including *jinns*, devilish little creatures that could trick anyone into creating mischief, and *paris*, the fairies that were constantly combating them. As a child, I remember my eyes being wide and my imagination running wild as I listened to stories from Habib's youth, when he once tricked a *jinn* and when he battled enormous serpents with his bare hands right there in our backyard.

Soon after the revolution of 1979, when I was already in the United States, I was heartbroken to learn that Habib had left our family. Perhaps it was a time for leaving: the shah left, entire families hastily packed up and migrated to various parts of the world, and even those who couldn't obtain passports chose to leave the country, hiking through dangerous mountain ranges into Turkey and Pakistan. The older members of my family, deeply rooted in the land, chose to stay.

Shortly after leaving, Habib and his family filed a complaint against ours, albeit in vain. They felt entitled to Babaji's old house, the one they had lived in rent free for so long. A few years later, Madar came across Habib selling cigarettes at a cigarette stand. When she attempted to ask after his family, he looked away, his eyelids heavy with sorrow, his glance laden with all that had been left unsaid. It wasn't long after that that I learned he had died of a stroke.

I didn't know what to think about the whole affair. I only knew that my heart felt heavy under the weight of a thousand *jinns* at the thought of how oblivious I had been to his discontent. And then I obsessed over who had made his *halvayeh mordeh*. Had it been made flawlessly? Had they toasted the flour just so, until it was the right shade of brown? Had they patiently stirred the paste until it reached that perfect consistency, not too wet and not too dry?

And sometimes even now, I like to pretend that he never left, that I could go back with my children and he would be there, telling them stories about *jinns* and *paris* in that yellow kitchen while getting ready for a party, a funeral, or just a family meal. And my children would smell the aroma of cooked rice, spices and herbs, baked sweets, and halva—all the aromas of a life I left behind.

I was still listening to Habib when my mother's voice, indiscernible at first but growing more distinct, emerged from a distance.

"How is the halva?" she was asking.

I opened my eyes slowly as innumerable images flowed together and then separated. It was daytime, and we were in California, and the sun was streaming in through my kitchen's big bay window. Madar was standing in front of me, her eyes laughing, a thin smile on her lips.

"Sweet," I replied. "Very sweet."

Her Orange-Blossom Tea

Maryam Atai

I take an aluminum box from the top of the fridge. I remove the lid and open the ziplock bag inside. With my fingers, I take a scoop of tea—proper Persian tea—and drop it into the tea maker. Then I open our spice cupboard and take out a humble plastic container. With reverence, I open the top and take a melancholic sniff. *Bahar naraenj*—dried orange blossoms. I take a pinch and add it to my tea.

This was my mother's and my shared passion: we loved *bahar naraenj* in our tea. The *bahar naraenj* in my teapot is from my mother, who gave it to me when I was moving to the United States, along with the cumin she had brought from Kerman. She insisted that I take these and a bundle of other Iranian spices with me. She packed them all carefully so that they would stay fresh and wouldn't get crushed in my suitcase. I had no idea what my life in the States would be like or whether orange blossoms and cumin would have any place in it. But I imagined that I at least could always come back and eat her delicious cumin-infused food or sip orange-blossom black tea on our terrace in Tehran. I didn't fully realize that she was giving me a piece of the familiar, a piece of home, to take with me into my new and unknown future life. I didn't understand that this was her way of coping with having her daughter move to the other side of the world. I didn't understand that in those carefully packed bags, she was sending a piece of herself with me. I didn't understand that, with the help of those spices and teas, she wanted to somehow protect and love and feed me in that faraway land.

This was the epitome of my mother's strength and her vulnerability.

After waiting a bit for the tea to steep, I pour a cup for myself. I breathe in the fragrance of the orange blossoms.

I never got another chance to have orange-blossom tea with my mother on our terrace. When I did see her again, it was when she was on her deathbed. Four months after I moved to the United States, they found a benign tumor in her brain. It was supposed to be removed in a relatively simple operation that would keep her in the hospital for only a week. But for two months, complication after complication ensued. I sat next to her in the hospital for her last two weeks. I repeatedly whispered in her ear that she would soon get better and we would sit on our terrace with the jasmine in full bloom, sipping our orange-blossom tea. But she never got to come home. And now what I have left of her is the cumin and orange blossoms she packed for me in this faraway land.

I take a sip of the orange-blossom tea, tear up, and smile through the tears. I understand it now—the cumin and the orange blossom of my mother's love.

The Iranians of Mercer Island

Siamak Vossoughi

The Iranians of Mercer Island were trying—that much I knew. They were trying in a language that was not their own. It made them look like they weren't even trying. I didn't think I was part of them because I felt like I was always trying. I knew that, technically, I *was* part of them. I was Majid and Nahid's son. My father sold houses, and my mother cut hair. But I felt like I was trying around them even when they looked like they weren't trying at all—at the end of the night, when they would sing songs from the old country.

We would see each other around town, and it would be like a discovery: "My God, here you are, too—an Iranian on Mercer Island!" And of course, "Hello, how are you?" But then: "What do you make of this place?" This last part was unspoken but present. One way to be was to act like Americans, which was to act like that was no kind of question to ask at all, because that place was bigger than you and your job was to fit into it. But I always thought, *All we're doing is asking. That can't be so wrong, can it?* It was nice sometimes to think of things that were bigger than you, but you might as well think really big if you were going to do that. The earth, the sky. Things that Iranians and Americans had in common.

Other times, the town would be a perfectly good size to fit into—at a high school basketball game or a summer fair—and we would think, *Who are these people we are fitting in with?* They are American. It is a matter of course that we know them better than they know us. What are we going to do with that knowledge?

That was what their nightly singing sounded like to me: This singing is all we *can* do. *OK, but what am I going to do*, I thought. Their singing was above everything. It was above Mercer Island and the limitations of Mercer Island. It was above the acquiescence we had to make to the limitations of time and space. I was glad that they felt that acquiescence acutely. They felt it acutely when there was something they wanted to say that they couldn't say because they could only say it in Farsi. I couldn't claim that. I almost wished I could. I almost wished I had a language barrier to claim as the reason why I couldn't say what I wanted to say. Then maybe I could feel as free as they looked when they sang at the end of the night.

It was wonderful, though, when we could build something that created a sense of community for everybody—the adults who remembered Iran and the children who didn't. We would all remember *something.* You didn't have to remember Iran to know that the people you felt the most comfortable around were the ones around whom you didn't have to think about how to *be.* There was always a part of me that felt like my successes were American and my failures were Iranian. But all of that fell aside when the Iranians of Mercer Island would gather at the community center. I was more than my successes or failures then. I was a part of something that was big enough to embrace both, because we could look in one another's faces and see that there was both joy and sorrow, and it was much more beautiful and human to see the world in those terms than in terms of success and failure. They were all too connected, anyway. A man could be happy about where he was and sad about where he was not at the same time.

Little by little, we began to see that the place we could have here was the place we could make for ourselves. It meant that who you were had to emerge. We owed it to one another. I owed it to the Iranians to try out for the basketball team even though I got cut every year, because if I *did* make the team, there would be an Iranian name on the back of one of the high school jerseys. Then nobody could say that we weren't a part of that place.

We had a chance to show them what Iranians were, but this meant that first we had to know ourselves. I didn't know how we were supposed to do that when even the air I breathed was American before it was mine. But I breathed it in deeply until I knew that that wasn't true—it was mine before it was American. It needed a boy to breathe it in, before anything else. It needed a boy the same way that the evening sky needed a boy to dream under it and the stars needed a boy to wonder at them. America needed me, I thought. It didn't always know it, but in its quiet moments, it did.

And it needed the Iranians to sing long into the night. It didn't know it needed that at all, but *we* did. I didn't know how we knew, but I would listen to the singing and tell myself to remember that there was a secret knowledge in the world. Something that wasn't seen in the rush of the day. But the next morning, I would wake up and it would seem like the only thing secret was wondering and asking again. I didn't know how to bring that secret part of myself together with the part that knew something for sure. If I had Iran the way they did, I thought, then I would know it. I would know what longing really was.

The singing always sounded very sad to me. It was the only time that I saw people making room for sadness together. In America, sadness seemed like an individual's road, and I tried to make the street behind our house that ran along the school and the fields my version of it. It was good to have a street like that. I'd walk up and down it, thinking of the American girl in my class and whether she could really help me love as much as it seemed like she could. I'd come home, and my mother and father would ask me what I was thinking about, but they wouldn't ask me what was wrong because the memory of the last time there had been singing in our house was still within them. They knew there was plenty that was wrong if you wanted to look at it that way. You were stuck in the business of living, and maybe that meant you were stuck living far from home or maybe it meant you were stuck living in a world that felt too small at some times and too big at others. But either way, there was a respect for sadness because we couldn't know ourselves without it.

So I listened and thought of all the things that wouldn't keep going here in America. There were a lot of them, and most of them I didn't even know yet. The Iranians knew it. They didn't expect us to carry on *everything*. The best we could do was to be quiet when they sang, which we were. Then we would joke with one another about their extended goodbyes, full of bows and ceremony, knowing somewhere inside of us that their goodbyes would last longer than our joking. They would still have the last word. We had to joke because it softened the edges of the two sides we sat upon. Those two sides were far apart most of the time, but they were close when we were all together. And those sides were close inside me when I walked along that street behind our house. I just didn't know how they could ever be close in a way that was meant for all the world to see—like the way it could be seen in the Iranian singers. Even an American could hear the sadness of their singing. I saw it firsthand the night that the singing got too loud and one of our neighbors called the police.

He was a lonely American cop who knocked on our door late at night. My father told him that we would sing more quietly, and then it felt too impolite to just send him off into the night, so my father invited him in to have some tea and listen to the singing. I was thrown for a loop because I thought that one way to be Iranian in America was to be against the "agents of state control." But my father, who knew much more about agents of state control, didn't care about all that and brought him in and gave him a place to sit. The Iranians of Mercer Island were very happy. It was a chance to show their lives, to show that whatever else the cop *thought* Mercer Island was made of, it also had this: Iranians singing in the night. It was a part of Mercer Island the Iranians had always known. They were introducing the cop to his own town—the quiet town he had been patrolling at night. I was going to have to find something more when it came to being Iranian in America than just being against the agents of state control.

"You see," my father told him, "the singing is sad because we miss our country."

"I can see that. It *is* sad."

"Yes." My father smiled and the Iranians smiled, as if to say, Tell us what you are sad about.

"Thank you," the cop said.

"I hope you can come again," my father said.

"Thank you," the cop said again. "Hopefully it won't be because you have been singing too loud for the neighbors."

My father smiled and shrugged. "Yes. You see," he said, "we forget. We forget when we sing."

The Iranians had something. To not only sing but then to invite in a cop called to stop the singing and have him listen to more—albeit quieter—singing. We were seeing something of their lives too. We were seeing how something hard could also have moments of being very easy.

They started saying their elaborate goodbyes again, but we didn't joke about them. We were only kids, but we were starting to pay attention to what lasted and what did not.

Acknowledgments

This book owes its existence to our meeting in Anita Amirrezvani and Persis Karim's outstanding writing workshop "Exploring Iranian Identity" in Berkeley, California. With their kind encouragement, generosity of spirit, and masterfully in-sync teaching techniques, Persis and Anita encouraged us to delve deeper into our writing—to approach it with honesty and vulnerability. We are forever indebted to the indefatigable Persis, who passed on to us the torch of anthologizing the nonfiction segment of the literary Iranian diaspora and then stayed by our side through every twist and turn along the way. We also thank all our fellow workshop participants, some of whom entrusted us with their work for this collection. Berkeley native Deedee Dyer generously provided us with a tranquil space in which to think and write. Caitlyn Dlouhy and Kate Moses gave us invaluable advice and encouragement and helped us navigate the uncharted waters of the publishing world. Thanks also to Jenny Sadre-Orafai, Kaveh Akbar, Sarah Farizan, and Rajiv Mohabir for their encouragement of this endeavor and for their writing, which provided more inspiration than they may ever know. A huge thank-you also goes to the Johns Hopkins MA in Writing Program for sending Leila to the 2018 Association of Writers and Writing Programs conference, where she had the opportunity to meet several of this collection's authors in person.

Thank you to my mother for your support and your ever-present ear. Undying gratitude to Leyla and Kian for giving me so much more than I could ever give you and for permitting me to weave your story into my own. And to Farhad, my beloved husband, who not only took me to Iran and laid bare this culture but also supported me through the many years it took to pull this book together, feeding and nurturing me as we pulled it across the finish line.—K.W.

Eternal thanks to my incredible mother for teaching me to find beauty in small moments and for giving me glimpses into Iranian culture while lovingly allowing me the freedom to explore it on my own terms. Thanks to my wonderful dad for his generosity of spirit and boundless capacity for empathy, which has informed how I see the world. And thanks to James, my love, for making our home a refuge and for making me laugh every day.—L.E.

We gratefully acknowledge permission to include previously published material in this collection. Salar Abdoh's essay "Gilad, My Enemy" originally appeared with the title "Gilad, My Enemy: Iran, Iraq, Gaza, Israel, Shia, Sunni, Muslim, Jew" in *Tablet* magazine at tabletmag.com (April 6, 2015). Jasmin Darznik's "The Summer I Disappeared" was originally published online at Shondaland.com (February 9, 2018). "The Color of the Bricks," by Farnaz Fatemi, first appeared in the *Tupelo Quarterly* (2, no. 7 [2015]). An earlier version of Persis Karim's essay "In Praise of Big Noses" was published in *Global Beauty, Local Bodies*, edited by Afshan Jafar and Erynn Masi de Casanova (New York: Palgrave MacMillan, 2013). Raha Namy's essay "Transmutations of/by Language" first appeared in *World Literature Today* (89, no. 2 [March 2015]). A version of Mehdi Tavana Okasi's "When We Were Lions" was originally published in *Catapult* under the title "What Will Become of My Iranian Generation?" at catapult.com (November 14, 2017). A version of Daniel Rafinejad's essay "Two Minutes to Midnight" first appeared on Medium.com (April 3, 2018). A version of Iraj Isaac Rahmim's essay "Sacrifices" was originally published in the *Antioch Review* (63, no. 2 [Spring 2005]). "The Name on My Coffee Cup," by Saïd Sayrafiezadeh, first appeared in the *New Yorker* (March 20, 2015). Roxanne Varzi's essay "Am I an Immigrant?" originally appeared online on the *London Review of Books'* LRB blog (February 21, 2017).

Contributors

Salar Abdoh lives in Tehran and New York City, where he teaches in the MFA program at the City University of New York, City College. He is the editor/translator of *Tehran Noir* and author of *Tehran at Twilight, Opium*, and *The Poet Game*.

Dena Afrasiabi's fiction has appeared in *Michigan Quarterly Review, Monkeybicycle,* and *The Toast*, among other publications. Her work has received fellowship support from the National Endowment for the Arts, the Helene Wurlitzer Foundation, and the Millay Colony. She works as an editor in Austin, Texas, where she's also at work on a novel about an Iranian theme park in Texas.

Maryam Atai has an MBA from Sharif University and is currently associate director of a nonprofit organization active in the education sector. Maryam was born in Iran and currently lives in San Francisco. Having spent her childhood and adulthood in both Iran and the States, she feels comfortable in both worlds. Iran is her motherland, San Francisco her home. She loves to read, write, take hikes in the Marin Headlands, and kayak on the San Francisco Bay.

Darius Atefat-Peckham is an Iranian-American poet and essayist. His work has appeared in *Texas Review, Nimrod, Brevity, Crab Orchard Review, Cimarron Review*, and elsewhere. In 2018, Atefat-Peckham was selected by the Library of Congress as a National Student Poet, the nation's highest honor presented to youth poets writing original work. Atefat-Peckham lives in Huntington, West Virginia, and attends Harvard College in Cambridge, Massachusetts.

Nazanine Attaran was born and raised in Shiraz, Iran, the beautiful city of nightingales and poetry. She left Iran after high school to come to the United States to study dentistry, never realizing that a revolution, a war, and life would prevent her from returning for close to twenty years. She received both her BS in biology and her DDS from Indiana University. She is married to another Shirazi, has two lovely daughters, and lives in Northern California.

A graduate of the Wharton School of the University of Pennsylvania, **Mandana Chaffa** is a former strategist and corporate counselor to executives of privately held and publicly traded companies in diverse industries. Her work has appeared in *Jacket2, Corium Magazine*, and elsewhere, and she was once a finalist for the American Short Fiction Prize. Born in Tehran, Mandana lives and writes in New York

City, where she conducts regular poetry discussion groups and occasionally serves as a dramaturge.

Cyrus M. Copeland is the author of *Off the Radar: A Father's Secret, a Mother's Heroism, and a Son's Quest* (Penguin/Blue Rider), which won the Chautauqua Prize for literature. Prior books include *Farewell, Godspeed: The Greatest Eulogies of Our Time* (Random House), *A Wonderful Life: 50 Eulogies to Lift the Spirit* (Algonquin Books), and *Passwords: 7 Steps to Writing a Memorable Eulogy*. Cyrus is a resident of New York City and is currently at work on his next book.

Jasmin Darznik's debut novel *Song of a Captive Bird* was selected as a *New York Times Book Review* Editors' Choice book and was a *Los Angeles Times* best seller. Jasmin is also the author of the *New York Times* best seller *The Good Daughter: A Memoir of My Mother's Hidden Life*. Her books have been published or are forthcoming in seventeen countries, and her essays have appeared in numerous periodicals, including the *New York Times*, the *Washington Post*, and the *Los Angeles Times*. Born in Tehran, Jasmin came to America when she was five years old. She holds an MFA in fiction from Bennington College and a PhD in English from Princeton University. She is a professor in the MFA program at California College of the Arts. Her next book, a historical novel set in 1920s San Francisco, is forthcoming from Ballantine.

Shireen Day is an Iranian-American who grew up in New Jersey, the US Virgin Islands, 1970s Iran, and Iowa. She earned a BA in sociology from Colorado College and an MS in social work from the University of Denver. Her essay "Unexpectedly White and Privileged" was published in the 2016 anthology *What Does It Mean to Be White in America? Breaking the White Code of Silence*. Her essay "Unexpected Strangers" was published in the 2017 anthology *The Kindness of Strangers*.

Babak Elahi holds a PhD in English from the University of Rochester. His work has appeared in *Iranian Studies, symplokē, Iran Namag, MELUS*, the *International Journal of Fashion Studies*, and *Cultural Studies*. His album of original music, *Error and Trial*, was released with his band, the Resonant Freqs, in 2018. He now serves as the Head of Liberal Studies at Kettering University in Flint, Michigan.

Leila Emery's work has appeared in the *Michigan Quarterly Review, Parentheses Journal, Matter*, and *Lines + Stars*. Her poem "How Do You Say That In Farsi?" was nominated for the 2019 *Best of the Net* anthology (Sundress Publications). Originally from New England and currently residing in the South, Leila received a BA in comparative literature from Smith College and an MA in creative writing from Johns Hopkins University.

Shideh Etaat is a writer and teacher. She received her MFA in creative writing from San Francisco State University. An excerpt from her novel appears in *Tremors: New Fiction by Iranian American Writers*, and she has published short stories in the

Delmarva Review, Amazon's online journal *Day One*, and *Foglifter*. She was a 2011 Bread Loaf Writers' Conference Work-Study Scholar and a 2015 James D. Phelan Award recipient. Her first novel, in progress, is about grief, Tupac Shakur, and an Iranian-American teenager exploring her love for girls in the 1990s.

Omid Fallahazad is a bilingual fiction writer. His recent novel in Farsi, *Gahvareye Div* (NaaKojaa, 2016), centers on house-burning riots against Baha'is in Shiraz on the eve of the 1979 revolution. His other works in Farsi include a collection of short stories, *Se Tir-baran Dar Se Dastan* (H&S Media, 2016), and a young-adult novella, *Razi* (Madreseh, 2001). Omid's English-language stories have appeared in publications such as *Glimmer Train, Paul Revere's Horse, World Literature Today*, and *Tremors: New Fiction by Iranian American Writers*. He and his wife, media artist Rashin Fahandej, live with their daughter near Boston.

Leyla Farzaneh was born in San Francisco to an Iranian father and an American mother. She recently graduated from the University of California, Los Angeles, where she took classes in Farsi and wrote for *FEM* magazine. She is currently working in the tech industry in San Francisco and trying to learn not to burn *tadig*.

Farnaz Fatemi's poetry and prose has appeared or is forthcoming in *Grist, Catamaran Literary Reader, Tahoma Literary Review, Crab Orchard Review, Tupelo Quarterly, Delaware Poetry Review*, the anthologies *Halal If You Hear Me* and *Let Me Tell You Where I've Been: New Writing by Women of the Iranian Diaspora* and elsewhere. She has been awarded residencies from Djerassi, PLAYA, Marble House Project, I-Park Foundation, and Vermont Studio Center and has been honored by the International Literary Awards (Center for Women Writers), Poets on the Verge (Litquake SF), Best of the Net Nonfiction, and Pushcart. She taught writing at the University of California, Santa Cruz, from 1997 to 2018. www.farnazfatemi.com.

Roia Ferrazares is half Persian, half Italian and was born in the United States. The year she spent in Iran, 1970–1971, provided her first memories, and she writes about it in her blog *persianchyld*. A prose and short-story writer, Roia has found that her connections through her Persian mother with Persian language, food, music, and poetry are the most profound and influential in her writing. Her writing grapples with Iranian-American identity formation in the diaspora.

Persis Karim is a poet, editor, and professor of comparative and world literature at San Francisco State University, where she also serves as the Neda Nobari Chair of the Center for Iranian Diaspora Studies. Her poetry and essays have appeared in a variety of publications, including *Callaloo*, the *New York Times*, the *Markaz*, and *Reed Magazine* and at poetsanddreamers.com. She was the coeditor with Anita Amirrezvani of *Tremors: New Fiction by Iranian American Writers*, the editor of *Let Me Tell You Where I've Been: New Writing by Women of the Iranian Diaspora*, and the coeditor with M. M. Khorrami of *A World Between: Poems, Short Stories, and Essays by Iranian-Americans*. For more: www.persiskarim.com.

Renata Khoshroo Louwers is a writer and the editor/cofounder of *Months To Years* (www.monthstoyears.org), a journal of nonfiction and poetry that explores death and dying. Her writing has been published in the *Philadelphia Inquirer*, in *STAT News*, and on Stanford Medicine's *Scope* blog. She holds a BS in journalism from Boston University.

Amy Malek is an assistant professor of international studies at the College of Charleston. She holds a PhD in anthropology from the University of California, Los Angeles and an MA in Near Eastern studies from New York University. Her work has been published in *Memory Studies, Anthropology of the Middle East, Comparative Studies of South Asia, Africa, and the Middle East, Iranian Studies*, and *Iran Nameh*. Her research examines the intersections of diaspora and transnationalism, citizenship, memory, and cultural production, with a focus on Iranian communities in North America and Europe.

Poupeh Missaghi is a writer, Persian<>English translator, and *Asymptote*'s editor-at-large for Iran. She holds a PhD in English–creative writing from the University of Denver, an MA in creative writing from Johns Hopkins University, and another MA in translation studies. She currently teaches in the Writing Department of the Pratt Institute, Brooklyn, as well as working as a writing consultant at Baruch College, City University of New York. Her nonfiction, fiction, and translations have been published in *Diagram, Catapult, Entropy*, the *Brooklyn Rail*, the *Feminist Wire, World Literature Today, Guernica, Copper Nickel*, the *Denver Quarterly*, and *Asymptote*, among others. Her first book, *trans(re)lating house one*, was published by Coffee House Press in February 2020.

Raha Namy is a writer and translator. Her work has appeared in *Guernica, World Literature Today*, the *Quarterly Conversation*, the *Barcelona Review, Short Fiction Magazine*, the *Baltimore Review*, and elsewhere.

Mehdi Tavana Okasi's work has appeared in *Guernica, Glimmer Train*, the *Los Angeles Review of Books*, and the *Iowa Review*, among others. He is the recipient of grants from the Massachusetts Cultural Council and the National Society of Arts and Letters, and he was named a 2016 National Endowment for the Arts Literature Fellow. He is currently completing a novel and teaches creative writing at the State University of New York at Purchase.

Daniel Rafinejad was born to Iranian parents in the San Francisco Bay Area. A graduate of Columbia University and the University of California, Los Angeles, he taught Persian language and literature at Harvard University before devoting himself to full-time writing and translating. He lives with his cat, Khāvar Khānom, in Manhattan, where he is at work on a collection of essays.

Iraj Isaac Rahmim's essays and fiction have appeared in the *Antioch Review, Commentary, Commonweal, Fugue, Guernica, Gulf Coast*, the *Houston Chronicle*, the

Missouri Review, Reason, Rosebud, and *Zócalo Public Square,* and have been broadcast by Pacifica Radio. He was selected as a Fellow of MacDowell Colony, Yaddo, Vermont Studio Center, Herzliya Artists' Residence, Virginia Center for the Creative Arts, and Texas Commission of the Arts; was a Bread Loaf Writers' Conference Scholar; and was twice winner of First Prize in Prose from *Fugue.* His writing has been selected six times as a Notable Essay by the Best American series, was nominated twice for and received a Special Mention from the Pushcart Prize, and was nominated by the Sewanee Writers' Conference for Best New American Voices. Winner of the San Miguel Writers' Conference Fiction Contest, Isaac holds a PhD in biochemical engineering from Columbia University.

Shokoofeh Rajabzadeh is a new mom and a writer, teacher, scholar, and activist. She is currently a PhD candidate in English language and literature at the University of California, Berkeley. Her research and academic publications focus on the racialization of Muslims and the history of Islamophobia in premodern England. As an activist, she is committed to antiracist pedagogy and increasing inclusivity in academic institutions. Her poetry has appeared in *Poetry Northwest* and *Modern Poetry in Translation.* She is currently working on a graphic memoir with her sister, Reyhaneh Rajabzadeh, titled *Always Not Quite* that tells the story of their experiences immigrating to the United States and growing up Muslim after 9/11. Small chapters appear in biweekly installments on their Medium website, @ alwaysnotquite1.

Layla Maryam Razavi is a civil rights advocate who specializes in promoting inclusion and equity for all immigrants and crafting legislation that upholds and strengthens due process, including the right to counsel for people in detention. She holds a JD from the University of California, Davis School of Law and previously served as advocacy and policy counsel at the American Civil Liberties Union (ACLU). She was born and raised in San Diego and resides in San Francisco. Her parents were studying abroad during the revolution.

Dena Rod is currently the assistant creative nonfiction editor for Homology Lit, and the former managing editor of *Argot Magazine,* a Webby-nominated queer nonprofit with a mission to highlight and sponsor LGBTQIAA+ perspectives and art across the globe. Dena works to illuminate their diasporic experiences of Iranian-American heritage and queer identity, combating negative stereotypes of their intersecting identities in the mainstream media. Their poetry and creative nonfiction essays have appeared in *Endangered Species, Enduring Values: An Anthology of San Francisco Area Writers and Artists of Color, Forum Literary Magazine, Beyond Bloodlines* (funded in part by the Yerba Buena Center for the Arts), *Argot Magazine,* and *Imagoes: A Queer Anthology.* They were selected for RADAR Productions' Show Us Your Spines Residency and for the Kearny Street Workshop Interdisciplinary Writers Lab. Dena received their MA in English literature from San Francisco State University and is currently residing in the San Francisco Bay Area with their wife and cat.

Saïd Sayrafiezadeh is the author of the short story collection *Brief Encounters with the Enemy* and the memoir *When Skateboards Will Be Free*. His stories and personal essays have appeared in the *New Yorker*, the *Paris Review*, the *New York Times*, and *Granta*, among other publications. He teaches creative writing at Columbia University, New York University, and Hunter College. He is the recipient of a Whiting Writers' Award for nonfiction.

Roger Sedarat, an Iranian-American poet, is the author of *Dear Regime: Letters to the Islamic Republic*, which won the Ohio University Press's 2007 Hollis Summers Poetry Prize, *Ghazal Games* (Ohio University Press, 2011), and *Haji as Puppet: An Orientalist Burlesque*, winner of Word Works' 2016 Tenth Gate Prize for a Mid-Career Poet. He is also the author of *Emerson in Iran: The American Appropriation of Persian Poetry* (State University of New York Press, 2019), the first full-length study of the seminal American writer's engagement with the verse of Iran. A recipient of the Willis Barnstone Prize in Literary Translation, he teaches in the MFA Program at Queens College, City University of New York.

Roxanne Varzi is a writer, artist, filmmaker, and anthropologist. She was the recipient of the first Fulbright fellowship to Iran after the revolution and the youngest Distinguished Senior Iranian Visiting Fellow at St. Antony's College, Oxford University, and is a professor at the University of California, Irvine. Her writing has been published in the *London Review of Books*, *Le Monde Diplomatique*, the *Detroit Free Press*, the *Annals of Political and Social Science*, the *Feminist Review*, *Public Culture*, *American Anthropologist*, and other venues. Her short stories have appeared in two anthologies of Iranian-American writing as well as in the *New York Press* and in *Anthropology and Humanism Quarterly*, for which she won a Short Story Award for Fiction. Her film, *Plastic Flowers Never Die*, distributed by DER, has been shown in festivals all around the world. She is the author of *Warring Souls: Youth, Media, and Martyrdom in Post-Revolution Iran* (Duke University Press, 2006) and the 2016 Independent Publisher Book Awards Gold Medal–winning novel *Last Scene Underground: An Ethnographic Novel of Iran* (Stanford University Press).

Siamak Vossoughi was born in Tehran and grew up in Seattle. His short stories have been published in *Glimmer Train*, the *Missouri Review*, the *Kenyon Review*, *Gulf Coast*, and other journals. His collection *Better than War* received a 2014 Flannery O'Connor Award and was shortlisted for the William Saroyan International Prize for Writing. He was a 2018 Bread Loaf Writers' Conference Fellow. He lives in San Francisco.

Katherine Whitney is a writer and museum consultant in Berkeley, California. She was drawn into the Iranian diaspora by marriage, and writing has helped her make sense of her place in it. Her essay "Iranian Revelation" was published in *Because I Said So: 33 Mothers Write about Children, Sex, Men, Aging, Faith, Race and Themselves* (Harper Perennial, 2005).